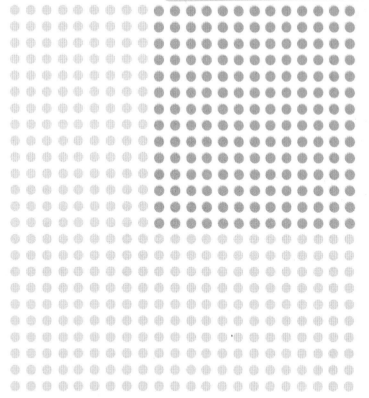

Spanish Cinema:
A Student's Guide

Barry Jordan and Mark Allinson

Hodder Arnold

A MEMBER OF THE HODDER HEADLINE GROUP

First published in Great Britain in 2005 by
Hodder Education, a member of the Hodder Headline Group,
338 Euston Road, London NW1 3BH

www.hoddereducation.com

Distributed in the United States of America by
Oxford University Press Inc.
198 Madison Avenue, New York, NY10016

© 2005 Barry Jordan and Mark Allinson

Hodder Headline's policy is to use papers that are natural, renewable and
recyclable products and made from wood grown in sustainable forests.
The logging and manufacturing processes are expected to conform to the
environmental regulations of the country of origin.

The advice and information in this book are believed to be true and
accurate at the date of going to press, but neither the authors nor the publisher
can accept any legal responsibility or liability for any errors or omissions.

British Library Cataloguing in Publication Data
A catalogue record for this book is available from the British Library

Library of Congress Cataloging-in-Publication Data
A catalog record for this book is available from the Library of Congress

ISBN-10: 0 340 80745 8
ISBN-13: 978 0 340 80745 3

1 2 3 4 5 6 7 8 9 10

Typeset in 9.5/13pt Baskerville Book by Servis Filmsetting Ltd, Manchester
Printed and bound in Malta by Gutenberg Press

What do you think about this book? Or any other Hodder
Education title? Please send your comments to the feedback
section on www.hoddereducation.com.

Contents

For Margaret and Ed

and for Rosa María

INTRODUCTION

The study of Spanish cinema in the English-speaking world has come a long way in a very short time. In the early 1980s it was a marginal area of study: in Hispanic Studies departments, a few Spanish films found their way onto the curriculum alongside the dominant literary academic culture; and in Film or Media Studies departments, Spanish film was virtually absent, a very long way behind French, Italian or German cinema. Today, Spanish cinema modules are taught in the vast majority of university Spanish departments, and in some cases they feature even more prominently than traditional literature courses. This is in part the result of the broadening of curricula and of the shift towards cultural studies, but also the increasing availability of Spanish films in Europe and the UK, (starting with Almodóvar after *Mujeres al borde de un ataque de nervios* and then Bigas Luna, Trueba, Medem, Amenábar, Aranda, Alex de la Iglesia, Icíar Bollaín and others). More and more Spanish films are finding their way onto general film programmes. The increasing interdisciplinarity of university programmes is likely to continue this trend towards diversification into previously marginal film cultures. And the current popularity of all things Spanish, plus the relatively healthy state of Spain's film industry, further contribute to this encouraging vitality within the field. These developments create corresponding challenges, however: how to respond to the needs of those who know more about Spanish culture than they do about Film Studies, while still addressing a Film Studies community who are interested in Spanish cinema.

Academic writing on Spanish cinema is growing constantly, largely from an original focus on single directors or single films, and on themes relating to national identities and, more recently, gender and sexuality. But clearly, there is much more to a national film culture than those areas. In this book, we want to address existing areas of study, and at the same time, set down some signposts for areas that are only recently coming into focus (such as stars and genres). We have based most of our chosen examples on the films most frequently studied in UK and US Spanish departments, after a useful, though unscientific, survey of what is being taught.

Acknowledging the existing work on the history of Spanish cinema, Chapter One is a summary of the chronological development of cinema in Spain from 1896 to 2003, thus bringing into one essay material that is currently only available in separate volumes. Chapter Two – Film Studies basics: technique, narrative and style – is a user's manual for

1

studying film, but unlike all the existing 'How to read a film' guides and readers, it takes its examples and case studies entirely from Spanish cinema. Chapter Three deals with the concept of Authorship, using three different directors as case studies, while Chapter Four focuses on Genre in Spain (both home-grown and imported varieties), also taking three case studies to illustrate the concept. Chapter Five takes approaches long established in relation to US (and even British and French) stars, and begins to apply them to Spanish cinema. And in Chapter Six, we look at how cinema both reflects and also shapes society, via case studies on representations of national identity and gender. Finally, Chapter Seven offers a tentative survey of Spain's own academic discourses on cinema – its indigenous 'film theory' – which we define in a fairly wide and eclectic way.

As a modest response to the slightly differing needs of Spanish and non-Spanish speakers, we have included a glossary of film terms in English and Spanish, and we have separated the bibliography into works in English and works in Spanish. Film titles are given in Spanish but we have translated all quotations from film dialogues and secondary sources.

A number of people have given us information, advice and general support in our writing for this book: Federico Bonaddio, Ann Davies, Peter Evans, Mayte Gómez, Helen Graham, Chris Perriam, Rob Stone, Sarah Wright. Particular thanks go to Carmen Rabalska, Agustín Rico-Albero, Antonio Sánchez and Katy Vernon who each read draft versions of certain chapters and made useful suggestions. For help with the transcription of the song 'Americanos' from *Bienvenido Míster Marshall*, *gracias* to Mari-Carmen and Mario. Thanks to Paz Sufrategui from El Deseo and Rosa García Merino from Sogecable for help with illustrations, and to Gejo Cánovas for the shots diagram. We also thank our editors present and past, Eva Martínez, Abigail Woodman and Lesley Riddle for their patience and support.

The authors and publishers would like to thank the following for permission to reproduce copyright illustrative material: SOGECINE for figures 2.1 and 6.3; SUEVIA FILMS for figure 2.3. Every effort has been made to obtain permission for the reproduction of copyright material. Owners of copyright material reproduced here who are not credited are invited to contact the publisher.

Chapter One

HISTORY

BEGINNINGS

Writing in the mid-1990s, Spanish film scholar Julio Pérez Perucha argued that the historiography of Spain's early cinema remained unreliable: 'Spanish cinema still needs to be researched, mapped, catalogued and described' (1995: 20). Over the next decade, this situation improved greatly, with the publication of far better informed and more seriously researched studies such as Pérez Perucha (1995) and García Fernández (2002).

We know, for example, that Edison's bulky *kinetoscope* (a kind of individual peepshow booth) was demonstrated in Madrid in mid-1895 (García Fernández, 2002: 21). We also know that, nearly a year later, Erwin Rousby demonstrated the *animatograph*, involving moving images projected onto a screen for collective viewing (Seguin, 1995: 7–8). Rousby may well be the inventor of cinema in Spain. But, it was the Lumière brothers' *cinématographe* (an all-in-one film camera, projector and printer, patented in February 1895) which would quickly come to dominate early Spanish film making and especially film exhibition. Bordwell and Thompson argue that even if the Lumières did not exactly invent cinema, they largely determined the specific form the new medium was to take (2001: 401). The first demonstrations of the new machine appear to have been carried out in May 1896 in Madrid's Hotel Rusia, firstly in a private showing on the 13th and then to paying audiences on the 14th and 15th, at one peseta for a 20-minute show. (García Fernández, 2002: 21). In the following 12 months or so, the *cinématographe* would be demonstrated in public in most of Spain's major cities, offering Spanish entrepreneurs (photographers as well as theatre and fairground owners) the opportunity to modernize their businesses and transform their public entertainments with the latest technology. Of course, from the very start, Spaniards would depend very heavily on imported films to fill up their programmes and, if shooting in Spain, on film stock and printing technology initially available only from France. This would lock Spanish film making into an inexorable cycle of technological dependency for decades to come.

PIONEERS

The founder of Spanish film making was arguably the inventive Catalan cabinetmaker and photographer Fructuoso Gelabert (1874–1955) who, in 1897, built his own, hand-crafted version of the Lumière *cinématographe* in order to film the visit of the Spanish royal family to the Catalan capital (García Fernández, 2002: 44). Following the fashion for documentary shorts established by the Lumières, Gelabert also shot numerous scenes of children coming out of school, workers leaving a factory (*Salida de los trabajadores de la España industrial*, 1897) and the visit of the English fleet in 1901, some of which he sold to the French studio Pathé. For this reason, he has been seen as representing a certain realist and observationalist tradition, broadly linked to the Lumières. This is a gross simplification of the Lumière story (see Powrie and Reader, 2002: 3–4), as well as of Gelabert's career since he is also credited with making the very first fiction film in Spain, the comedy *Riña en un café* (1897) in which two men quarrel over a young woman in a bar. The film follows the pattern established by the Lumières' comic short *L'arroseur arrosé* (1895) and it also bears a strong narrative resemblance to a Méliès short *Une altercation au café* (1897). Gelabert's outstanding technical expertise was also apparent in an early 'special effects' film *Choque de dos trasatlántico*s (1899) and quickly resulted in jobs fitting out early cinemas with projection equipment and lighting facilities. He also oversaw the shooting of numerous literary adaptations and melodramas (*Terra baixa*, 1907; *María Rosa*, 1908; *Guzmán el bueno*, 1909). However, despite several attempts in the 1910s, such as *Mala raza* (1912), he was never an accomplished film director, preferring to share responsibilites with the Valencian director Joan María Codina. His lack of entrepreneurial flair also resulted in major losses for his company Boreal Films, forcing him to sell his premises to Studio Films in 1918. His career went from bad to worse, and apart from the odd documentary made for Gaumont and his final fiction film *La puntaire/La encajera* (1928), he left the business, to return only briefly in 1952 with a sound remake of *Riña en un café* (Ramón Sala, in Borau, 1998: 405–6).

Often referred to as 'the Spanish Méliès', the other major pioneer was undoubtedly Segundo de Chomón (1871–1929). He was hired in 1899 by Georges Méliès to work in his colouring laboratory in Paris. Chomón learned quickly and even invented a new stencil or *pochoir* with which to speed up the tinting process. Returning to Barcelona in 1902 to open his own colouring lab, he also helped establish Spain's first film production company, with partners Alberto Marro and Luis Macaya. Using experience gained in France, he also began experimenting with early forms of special effects and superimpositions, which he used in *Choque de trenes* (1902) and the fairy tale, fantasy film *Gulliver en el país de los gigantes* (1903). However, fantasy films and primitive filmed *sainetes* (one-act comic playlets or sketches, based on lower class stereotypes) failed to attract audiences and the company began to fold in 1905. Taking refuge in Paris in the same year, he went back to Pathé as special effects adviser and following experiments with his *Eclipse de sol* (1905), he developed a new form of stop-motion photography, seen in the very costly, French-financed *El hotel eléctrico* (1908). Photographed one frame at a time by manipulating the camera's crank handle, the film recalls the trick photography techniques he had perfected at Méliès' Paris workshops and which he now paraded under the banner of a major competitor. On several other occasions, Chomón returned home to work as cameraman, film producer as well as Pathé's franchisee in Spain, hoping to develop the local industry but without success. Later, he was hired by Itala Films of Turin as a special effects supervisor, on such epics as *Cabiria* (Giovanni Pastrone, 1914) and by French auteur Abel Gance to work on the major silent epic *Napoléon* (1927). Following a final collaboration on Benito Perojo's *El negro que tenía el alma blanca* (1927) and a tragic working visit to Morocco where he fell ill, he died in Paris in 1929.

OBSTACLES TO DEVELOPMENT

The experiences of Gelabert and Chomón indicate that Spain was an enormously difficult market for the development of early cinema, let alone an incipient national film industry. Pérez Perucha offers a startling statistic: Between 1896 and 1905, and leaving aside the dozens of domestic actuality shorts being churned out, fiction film production in Spain totalled all of two comic scenes and four 'trick' films (1995: 29; see also Pérez Perucha, 1997: 13). In other words, through a lack of established companies able to diversify into film making or generate sufficient risk capital, the production of fiction films was simply too costly and risky. By contrast, a one-minute touristy short or newsreel about the war in Morocco needed no investment in infrastructure, studios or personnel and could be replayed ad infinitum by exhibitors. Some might even be sold to Pathé. However, only with great difficulty could these films generate the sort of profits which could be reinvested in fiction film making and in more costly projects. Hence the minimal presence of Spanish films on early Spanish screens, which were dominated by better made French and US imports. These were major hurdles, which the early Spanish industry would never manage to overcome. Moreover, as noted above in the case of Chomón, there was nowhere in Spain to do any basic training in film making and film technology. Spaniards had to go abroad since such instruction was only available within the developing French studio system of Pathé, Méliès/Gaumont and Éclair.

EARLY GENRES

In 1908 in France, the Film D'Art company (backed successively by Pathé and then Éclair) brought the high culture and respectability of the theatre into the domain of the cinema (Austin, 1996: 3; Powrie and Reader, 2002: 5), seeking to raise it from its fairground origins via film adaptations of great literary works. Catalan film makers, such as Gelabert, Narciso Cuyás, Ricardo de Baños and Adrià Gual (co-founder of Barcinógrafo, 1913) also sought to imitate their Gallic colleagues with their own art films, bringing Cervantes, Calderón and Ángel Guimerá to the screen. However, as the intended audience, the Catalan bourgeoisie was unimpressed and continued to snub the cinema, while popular audiences found such fare stuffy and lacking in entertainment value. Far more popular and profitable were the filmed serials, a sub-genre the French had borrowed from the Americans which were now increasingly seen in Barcelona and Valencia. The *Nick Carter* series of detective stories (Victorien Jasset, 1908–10) and Louis Feuillade's *Fantômas* mystery series (shot 1913–14) established models and formulae which were widely imitated across the world, including in Spain. It was Joan María Codina who developed the prototype of the Catalan serial for Condal Films with *El signo de la tribu* (1915), the first serial in Spain, dealing with bandits and gypsies. But it was Alberto Marro's *Los misterios de Barcelona* (1915) for Hispano Films, which captured the public interest. This was soon followed by a sequel *El testamento de Diego Rocafort* (1917).

WINDOW OF OPPORTUNITY

With the outbreak of the First World War, the French stranglehold on world cinema was severely set back. France's Eastern European and Russian markets were closed off and the threat from Germany halted film production domestically for more than a year (Austin 1996: 4). A gap in the European market opened up, from which Spain might have benefited, had it possessed a reasonable number of large and viable film companies, making decent films, with international appeal. According to Mérida de San Román, Spain produced in all some 250 films between 1914–18 (2002: 16). Yet, the prospect of Spain becoming a serious exporter of films to European markets never materialized. During wartime, Spanish film makers found it increasingly difficult to procure raw film stock, lacking any such manufacturing facilities at home. There was only one small, relatively solid and viable production base (Barcelona), and Catalan companies lacked the resources to produce the sort of volume and quality of attractive fiction films required for export (see Palmira González, in Pérez Perucha, 1997: 38).

NATIONAL GENRES: RECYCLING 'DEEP SPAIN'

By 1918, film making in Spain was so far behind that of Europe and America that it could not compete on any level. In the face of such difficulties, the few viable Spanish film producers in existence looked to native theatrical traditions to save the day. Filmed versions of popular theatrical forms, such as *zarzuela* (musical theatre or operetta) and *sainete* became Spain's cinematic life preserver. Set mainly in Andalusia, these comic/folkloric musical fantasies of lusty, macho bullfighters, devout lower-class songbirds and their dreams of social mobility in a rigidly hierarchical society were relatively cheap to produce, very popular and usually quite profitable. Known also as '*españoladas*' – stereotyped, clichéd, false and folksy versions of Spanish identity (Triana Toribio, 2003: 22) – they also provided a more sustained level of film making in Madrid in the early 1920s, and contributed to the gradual shift of production from Barcelona to the capital. The success of José Buchs' *La verbena de la paloma* (1921) opened the way to a flood of filmed *zarzuelas*, including Buchs' own *Carceleras* (1922). Seeking to cash in on this sucess were bullfighter films such as *Gloria que mata* (Rafael Salvador, 1922) and *Nobleza baturra* (Joaquin Dícenta and Juan Vilá Vilamala, 1925), the latter remade in 1935 by key figure Florián Rey. Pérez Perucha talks of 'the uncontrolled exploitation of filmed zarzuela' (1995: 90), causing their rapid exhaustion among audiences by 1925, leading to a more varied and diversified output by the late 1920s, including comedies, melodramas, historical films and adventure films.

SOUND CINEMA AND ITS DISCONTENTS

As Bordwell and Thompson have shown (2003: 210–11), the arrival of sound cinema created problems for all film-producing countries in the late 1920s. While silent films could circulate fairly easily and any language difficulties could be remedied by re-translating the intertitles into the appropriate language, films spoken in English, for example, created language barriers, which became obstacles to exports. The main problem was that dubbing a completely new soundtrack in another language was extremely expensive as well as potentially troublesome, with perfect lip synchronisation very difficult to achieve in repro-ducing dialogues. In order to preserve the foreign language market, the solution among the major American studios was to re-shoot additional, foreign language versions of the same film with different teams of actors speaking different languages in each. MGM set up its multilingual production operation in Hollywood, importing many actors from abroad, Paramount bought the studios at Joinville, near Paris and would churn out the same American film in up to 14 different languages. Laurel and Hardy even did their own Spanish version of *Night Owls* (1932), voicing their own soundtrack by speaking Spanish phonetically. However, such multilingual solutions were expensive, labour-intensive and on the whole unable to recoup costs. Moreover, audiences were not generally keen on seeing minor or unknown foreign actors playing roles made famous by stars such as Gary Cooper, James Cagney, Jean Harlow, Lon Chaney and Bela Lugosi (though Seguin [1995: 19–20] claims that a Hispanic version of *Dracula* (1931) was better than the original). However, by 1932, advances in dubbing and subtitling were beginning to allow the new talkies to overcome the language barrier.

The coming of sound in Spain coincided with the Great Depression, the end of the Primo de Rivera dictatorship in January 1930, a collapse in the value of the peseta, and a massive flight of capital (Torres, 1994/96: 13–14). On top of this, the arrival of a period of demo-cratic Republican government (April 1931–July 1936), which raised such huge expect-ations for reform initially, quickly brought political instability and disappointment and a polarization between classes and regions, leading eventually to civil war in 1936. This impacted massively on film production. Whilst 59 features were made in 1928 (Torres, 1994/96: 11) only five feature films were made between 1929 and 1931 and only six in 1932 (Seguin, 1995: 22).

The lack of the new sound technology in Spain was catastrophic, virtually wiping out Spanish film production between 1929 and 1932. The country lacked even the most rudi-mentary film production infrastructure, let alone decent equipment and studios which could be easily adapted to sound, giving rise to an 'unfortunate paralysis of film produc-tion' (García Fernández, 1985: 45). Film theatres were not equipped to project imported sound films, especially those coming from the USA. The conversion process and installa-tion of new compatible sound systems would also take far longer in Spain than elsewhere (five to six years rather than two or three). Thus, while cinema in the USA and the rest of Europe began to speak and attract new audiences, in Spain the silent era continued well into the 1930s, further prolonged by rivalries and patent disputes over synchronized sound systems and the reluctance of many exhibitors to invest in what they saw as a passing fad. Moreover, the impact of sound on jobs, in an industry only geared up for modest levels of silent film making, was immense, with many professionals put out of work and obliged to look abroad for job opportunities. Key Spanish personnel, including directors, actors, writers and technicians therefore emigrated to Europe or went to Hollywood. Edgar Neville, for example, on his return from working in Hollywood as dialogue consultant, struggled to make a short film in Spain about the problems involved in making sound cinema: *Yo quiero que me lleven a Hollywood* (1931); the soundtrack was finally added in Paris (Pérez Perucha, 1995: 126).

Only in 1932 did any appreciable signs of life in Spain's film industry begin to re-emerge. While José Buchs made a poor sound version of his silent musical hit *Carceleras* (1922/32), Buñuel shot his first Spanish film, the surrealist documentary *Tierra sin pan/Las Hurdes* (1932). Ostensibly an attack on rural poverty, the film was also a rather manipulative tract concerned with human (Spanish) degradation; so shocking was its imagery that the film was banned by the government in 1933 (Pérez Perucha, 1997: 89–91). In terms of new infrastructure, until CEA studios (Cinematografía Española Americana) and ECESA studios (Estudios Cinema Español, S.A.) began functioning in Madrid, at the end of 1933, Spain's only sound film studio was Orphea Studios, established in Barcelona in 1932 by director Francisco Elías.

1935–6: THE 'GOLDEN AGE' OF SPANISH FILM MAKING?

A number of scholars regard the period 1935–6 as one which witnessed serious signs of industrial development, ushering in something of a 'golden age' of Spanish film making, sadly cut short by the civil war (García Fernández, 1985: 65; Gubern, 1995: 156; Caparrós Lera, 1999: 57; Seguin, 1995: 22). In view of what happened in July 1936 and the terrible consequences the civil war had for Spanish film making, such a view is understandable, if perhaps wide of the mark. If we regard continuity of production as a key measurement and indicator of industrial potential then Spain remained seriously underdeveloped in terms of viable enterprises. Only two companies reached minimal levels of continuous film production: CIFESA (Compañía Industrial Film Española, S.A.) and Filmófono.

CIFESA became Spain's leading production company in the mid-1930s. Founded in March 1932, it was based in Valencia and originally owned by the Trénor family. However, after acquiring a controlling stake, it was taken over by local olive-oil magnate and right-wing republican Manuel Casanova and run by his son Vicente. CIFESA moved into film distribution in the summer of 1933 on behalf of Columbia Pictures, making healthy profits and doing well from the success in Spain of Frank Capra's comedies, such as *It Happened One Night* (1934) as well as local hits such as Eusebio Ardavín's *El agua en el suelo* (1934). CIFESA then moved into film production in 1934, but with no studios of its own, it rented CEA studios in Madrid, where many of its projects were made.

Conservative and populist in outlook, the CIFESA label or brand quickly gained public recognition as a guarantee of quality. The company was also able to attract big-name directors such as Florián Rey and Benito Perojo and major screen stars such as Imperio Argentina, Miguel Ligero, Ricardo Núñez and actor-turned-director Juan de Orduña. The key to CIFESA's success in the mid-1930s was arguably its policy of remaking successful genre pictures of the silent era, such as *La hermana San Sulpicio* (Florián Rey, 1934), a remake of the 1927 silent feature and the film which first introduced Argentinian-born star and songstress Imperio Argentina to Spanish audiences. On the strength of this success, CIFESA hired Benito Perojo to make a series of films in 1935, including the highly successful *La verbena de la paloma* (a remake of the 1921 silent musical comedy classic made by José Buchs). Over a two-year period between 1935–6, apart from some 20 documentaries and shorts (including films on historical figures, geography and regional customs), CIFESA would produce a dozen creditable and largely profitable commercial features. These films embraced traditional genres such as religious and bullfight films, musical comedies and rural melodramas: *Nobleza Baturra* (Florián Rey, 1935), *El Gato Montés* (Rosario Pi, 1935), *La Reina Mora* (Eusebio Fernández Ardavín, 1936), *Morena Clara* (Florián Rey, 1936), *La Señora de Trevélez* (Edgar Neville, 1936) and *Nuestra Natacha* (Benito Perojo, 1936), whose release was prevented by the outbreak of the civil war in July 1936. CIFESA's main rival was Filmófono, another family firm, based in Madrid.

Founded in August 1931, Filmófono was initially a distribution and exhibition outlet run by liberal Basque engineer-turned-entrepreneur Ricardo María Urgoiti Somovilla (also director of Unión Radio, shareholder in the Sagarra cinema chain and with wide interests in the Basque press). The Filmófono label derived largely from the name given to the synchronized sound system promoted and sold by Urgoiti to cinema exhibitors, based on disks, which sadly failed to prosper. The name was also that of the Madrid film club: Proa Filmófono, where Urgoiti screened non-commercial products and used Buñuel to promote foreign art films, such as works by Pabst, Stroheim, Eisenstein, Clair and his own *L'age d'or* in 1931. As time went on, the company aim was not only film distribution and allied sound services, but would also include film production.

Given his long association with Urgoiti, his reputation, and a 150,000-peseta investment in the company, Buñuel was brought in as executive producer to build a production team for the company. Alongside other duties, this entailed nurturing local creative talent among directors, actors and technicans, and overseeing the production of modestly budgeted social comedies and melodramas. In June 1935, production began with an adaptation of Arniches' stage play *Don Quintín el amargao* (Luis Marquina, 1935), which made money and allowed the production of *La hija de Juan Simón* (1935). This was a '*comedia flamenca*', co-written by a Catholic priest, and used as a vehicle for Andalusian singers Angelillo and Carmen Amaya. (Urgoiti also hoped to sell gramophone recordings of the dozen or so '*coplas*' contained in the film by his singers.) The film was begun by Nemesio M. Soldevila, but after two weeks he was sacked by Buñuel for shooting too slowly. Filming was completed by José Luis Sáenz de Heredia, a director who would be a key figure in the Franco regime's propagandist historical cinema of the 1940s.

Benefiting for a short while from Buñuel's creative and technical expertise, Filmófono only managed to complete four feature films before the outbreak of the civil war. The final two were a family comedy entitled *¿Quién me quiere a mí?* (José Luis Sáenz de Heredia, 1936), a vehicle for blonde child star Mari Tere. The other was a musical drama *¡Centinela alerta!* (1936), shot mostly by Frenchman Jean Grémillon, though Buñuel in fact finished the film off after Grémillon fell ill. Based on another *sainete* or comic social drama by Arniches, the film was very much in the mould of the earlier very successful *La hija de Juan Simón* (with an almost identical narrative). The film was concerned with abused and victimized women, abandoned by predatory upper class cads (*señoritos*), left holding illegitimate babies and saved by sentimental but supportive flamenco singers. In this vein, Filmófono offered a kindly if clichéd perspective on the struggles and woes of the popular classes, anxious for social mobility and success in a hard, hierarchical and unchanging social order (Gubern, 1995: 139).

THE CIVIL WAR

With the onset of war, not surprisingly, privately-financed, commercial feature film production fell drastically (Gubern, 1995: 164; Caparrós Lera, 1999: 63). With the division of the country into two zones (Nationalist and Republican), and the effects of the militarization of crews on each side, the shortages of film stock, electricity and other materials, the lure of exile, and especially the withdrawal of investors, any new projects were quickly shelved. Yet, at the same time, film theatres across Spain continued to do remarkably good business during the war, still screening popular American imports and local hits such as the *españolada Morena Clara* (Florián Rey, 1936).

On the Republican or 'loyalist' side, overall control of the main urban film-making centres allowed for the production of well over 200 films during the war. Administrative control over and the exploitation of film production infrastructure were unevenly split among the many competing political parties (Republican, Socialist, Communist, Anarchist), trades unions sections and government departments and agencies, all engaged in pursuing often conflicting and opposed agendas within the broad project of defending the legitimate Republican government. As Gubern has shown (1995: 166–79), these divisions were reflected in different views about film making and differently inflected forms of film output. For example, Anarchist film making took place mainly in the CNT-dominated (Confederación Nacional del Trabajo) stronghold of Barcelona, where various branches of the entertainment industry trade unions had collectivized the sector, while commandeering Orphea and Trilla studios, plus processing labs, as well as over a hundred cinemas. The CNT had its own production-distribution company: SIE Films (Sindicato de la Industria del Espectáculo-Films). Guided by the CNT slogan 'No victory without revolution', anarchist film production comprised newsreels, documentaries, agit-prop films (such as *Reportaje del movimiento revolucionario*, Mateo Santos, 1936), narrative fiction features and shorter 'filler' films, made to accompany features. Most of the newsreels focussed on military action at the various fronts, while dramatized documentaries recreated on screen successful collectivizations in rural communities and the anarchist 'social revolution' in the rearguard, as in *Castilla se liberta* (Adolfo Aznar, 1937) and *El frente y la retaguardia* (Joaquín Giner, 1937). The CNT–SIE's largely separatist and sectarian propaganda film production would be seriously eroded after May 1937, with the departure of the CNT from government and the halting and reversal of the collectivization process enforced by the Communist Party.

Rather problematic because of their complexity, higher costs and committee-driven preparation in a wartime context, the small number of Anarchist feature films were somewhat eclectic in genre and narrative, borrowing freely from commercial formats and including farcical comedies, musicals and literary adaptations though, initially, attempts at a form of social cinema were also made. In this vein, we find Pedro Puche's politically trite and sentimental *Barrios bajos* (1937), the tragic story of a kind-hearted dock worker linked to a denunciation of prostitution; there was also Fernando Mignoni's more explicitly 'libertarian' comedy *Nuestro culpable* (1937), shot in Madrid. But it was Antonio Sau Olite (not an Anarchist) who made the celebrated *Aurora de esperanza* (1937), a very sympathetic, though relatively anonymous, testimonial portrait of a pre-war Catalan proletariat. Originally entitled *La marcha del hambre*, Sau's debut feature dealt with the dire effects of unemployment and poverty on an ordinary, apolitical, working-class family. Following multiple humiliations, family head of household Juan organizes a protest march of his comrades to the city in search of 'bread and justice'. With the outbreak of civil war and the 'dawn of hope' of the film title, Juan then sets off to the battle front with his friends to join up with the anarchist militias (see Ramón Sala Noguer, in Pérez Perucha, 1997: 110–12). Arguably too solemn, sentimental and didactic, too reliant perhaps on the codes of poetic realism borrowed from French directors Marcel Carné and Julien Duvivier, overly concerned with the issue of consciousness-raising and the message of social revolution, the film failed to engage popular audiences. According to Sau himself, this perhaps reflected their unfamiliarity with the canons of social realism rather than with an aversion to the subject matter itself (Triana Toribio, 2003: 35).

War-time film-making activities under Communist organizations such as Spain's Communist Party (PCE), its Catalan counterpart (PSUC), its youth wing (JSU) and the Anti-Fascist Alliance of Intellectuals for the Defence of Culture were geared to one basic aim: the need for military unity as a key pre-condition for victory over fascism. This was part of the Popular Front policy orchestrated from Moscow and underpinned by the requirement for order, discipline and a single military command structure on the

Republican side. Central to this objective in terms of film making was the Communist production and distribution arm Film Popular, the party's commercially run, anti-fascist (and anti-CNT) film company, based in Barcelona, though under PSUC auspices. It was committed to denouncing the non-intervention pact (as seen in *Nuestros enemigos*) and anarchist sectarianism while promoting the official line of 'single command'. This it did, with films such as *La defensa de Madrid* (Ángel Villatoro, 1936, a co-production made with the International Red Cross, *Por la unidad hacia la victoria* (Fernando G. Mantilla, 1937) and *Mando único* (Antonio del Amo, 1937). This propaganda effort was reinforced by means of a weekly newsreel, *Espanya al dia*, developed by the legendary Joan Castanyer of Laia Films, and funded by the Catalan *Generalitat*. It was initially narrated in Catalan, but re-voiced into Castilian for the rest of Spain and even made in English and French versions. Film Popular also distributed a good deal of Soviet material (well over 20 films, such as Yefin Dzigan's *Sailors of Kronstad* (1935) and Vasiliev Chapaiev's *The Red Guerrilla* (1934). The company also made didactic films (e.g. on how to fire a machine gun) as well as modest fictional narratives involving peasants and their political 'consciousness raising' (as in *Frente a frente*, Mauro Azcona, 1936).

As regards official, Republican government film-making operations during the war, these comprised not only production and distribution activities organized from Madrid (and from January 1937, from Valencia) but also in the regions (especially by the *Generalitat*), as well as the work of the various military film units. Of these, the Republican Army of the Centre film unit, for example, made many useful didactic documentaries (on how to use Soviet weaponry purchased by the government) as well as propaganda features such as *Resistencia en Levante* (Rafael Gil, 1938). Official control of film making emanated from the Propaganda section of the Ministry of State, run by Basque film critic Manuel Villegas López. Responsible for a series of Soviet-style, agit-prop, montage-based shorts, Villegas López also coordinated relations with sympathetic governments and film makers abroad, including communist sympathizers Luis Buñuel and André Malraux. In the context of non-interventionism and the international blockade imposed on Spain, it was Buñuel who, from the Spanish embassy in Paris, commissioned French Communist director Jean-Paul Dreyfus to make *España 36/España leal en armas* (1937), a compilation documentary designed mainly for foreign distribution, whose aim was to emphasize the legitimacy of the Republican government and the treachery of Spain's leading insurgent generals, shamefully supported by German and Italian fascism. The Spanish government, via its embassy in Paris, also funded the sonorization (in English and French) and foreign distribution of Buñuel's documentary *Tierra sin pan/Las Hurdes* (1932), adding an anti-fascist propaganda voice over as a coda.

It is perhaps the filmed version of the final part of Malraux's 1937 novel *L'espoir*, known as *Sierra de Teruel* (1939), which is best remembered internationally, not only for its plea of solidarity for the Republican war effort but also its unlikely fate. Funded by the Spanish

government via its embassy in Paris, scripted by Malraux and Max Aub, the film was deliberately made for foreign (especially American) consumption and sought to emphasize the
importance of maintaining international, anti-fascist solidarity for the Republican cause,
while carefully playing down any religious issues or 'atrocity' stories. Completion of the film
was interrupted by the Nationalist capture of Barcelona in January 1939 and the 11 remaining sequences were finished off in Joinville, where the film was cut and dubbed.
Remarkably, *Sierra de Teruel* was screened only twice in closed sessions in July 1939 before
being banned by the French government and had to wait until 1945 for a commercial
screening with its new title *Espoir* (see Santos Zunzunegui, in Pérez Perucha, 1997: 125–8).

On the Nationalist side, it is generally assumed that, compared with production totals on
the Republican side, documentary and propaganda films were numerically far fewer and
played a far less important role as a tool of indoctrination and ideological control. In broad
terms, this seems to be the case, given the fact that up to 1937, unlike Republican Spain,
Nationalist Spain had but two political movements to contend with, Falange and the
Carlist *Requetés*. These groups were brought together forcibly by Franco in April 1937 into
one single unified grouping, or '*Movimiento Nacional*'. Before so-called 'unification', in film-
making terms, Falange operated partly through its Delegación de Prensa y Propaganda
in Salamanca, which put out early propaganda shorts such as *Arriba España, Madrid, La
reconquista de la patria* (all by Ricardo Gutiérrez, 1937). Also, Falange supported films ema-
nating from Spain's High Commission in Morocco, such as *La guerra por la paz* (1937) and
Victoria (1937), both by Joaquín Martínez Arboleya, which were finally edited in Berlin and
Buenos Aires (Caparrós Lera, 1999: 68).

After April 1938, the Nationalists' Departamento Nacional de Cinematografía, based in
Burgos and ultimately controlled by the Ministry of the Interior (run by Falange and
Franco's brother-in-law, Ramón Serrano Suñer) would centralize all activities and decision
making to do with the production, distribution, exhibition and control of all propaganda
shorts on the insurgent side. Apart from the nationalist newsreel *Noticiario Español* (of
which 23 editions were made), the new department also recruited directors such as Edgar
Neville and Manuel García Viñolas to produce propaganda shorts such as *Juventudes de
España* (Neville, 1938) and *Prisioneros de guerra* (García Viñolas, 1938). And from his base
in Berlin, where he oversaw all Nationalist film interests in Germany, Falangist Joaquín
Reig would put together the compilation documentary *España heroica/Helden in Spanien*
(1937), a memorable legitimation of the rebel rising. Of course we must not forget that
Francoist propaganda also found another useful vehicle in a number of fiction films,
mainly folkloric musicals, shot in Berlin and Rome.

Hispano Films Produktion was the joint Spanish-German co-production company
founded in late 1937 by ex-CIFESA employee Norberto Soliño and Johann Ther (Fanés,
1982: 73–4). The idea was to help sustain a commercial Spanish cinema made abroad for

home and foreign consumption, but also one allied to the racial ideology of the Nazi regime. Thus, several leading Spanish directors such as Benito Perojo and Florián Rey, and stars, including Imperio Argentina, Miguel Ligero and Estrellita Castro, made five musical films in all, which not only recycled traditional popular genres, such as the *zarzuela*, but also emphasized a folkloric Spanish nationalism, refracted through the exoticism of Andalusian and Moroccan stereotypes, including *El barbero de Sevilla, Suspiros de España* and *Mariquilla Terremoto* (all by Perojo, made in 1938). Florián Rey successfully adapted Merimée's *Carmen* in *Carmen la de Triana* (1938) while his *La canción de Aixa* (1939) was less well crafted. Both films were made following a rift occasioned by an alleged affair between Rey's wife, Imperio Argentina, and Adolf Hitler, which would lead to divorce. Nazi Germany appears to have had a commercial interest in testing out the Latin-American market with the delights and fantasies of deep Spain and the racial distinctiveness of '*Hispanidad*' (Triana Toribio 2003: 35). Fernando Trueba's *La niña de tus ojos* (1998), starring Penélope Cruz, is both a homage to and a satire of such film-making genres and styles in Nazi Germany in the late 1930s.

DEFEAT AND EXILE

Republican defeat in the civil war was already anticipated by early to mid-1938 and many people in the film industry began to arrange their departures, the majority being sympathizers of the Republican cause. Directors such as Buñuel, Carlos Velo, Luis Alcoriza (all of whom worked in Mexico); actors such as Alberto Closas, Margarita Xirgu, Rosita Díaz Gimeno, Carmen Amaya, Angelillo, José Baviera; a long list of technicians including José María Beltrán (camera operator) and José Cañizares (editor), Joan Castanyer and most of the team responsible for Malraux's *Sierra de Teruel*, finally left Spain. The main destinations were France, Mexico and Argentina, the latter countries where Spanish speakers might have a chance to continue their careers. Buñuel, perhaps the classic case of a director adapting tolerably well to a life of exile, established himself in Mexico in 1946, taking Mexican citizenship in 1949. Of course, in a rather different type of adaptation, many film makers who had begun their careers under the Republic and had supported the democratic government would nonetheless stay and work in Franco's 'new' Spain: Benito Perojo, Edgar Neville, Florián Rey, Eduardo García Maroto, José Luis Sáenz de Heredia, Rafael Gil, Juan de Orduña, Luis Lucia and Antonio del Amo.

EARLY FRANCOISM 1939–1952

The civil war in Spain ended officially on 1 April 1939, resulting in the military dictatorship under General Franco, which lasted until 1975. Before the rise of Francoism, Spanish governments had been reluctant to define any clear film policy or legislation, beyond matters of taxation, censorship, health and safety and the protection of minors. In the 1940s, Francoist film policy can perhaps best be characterized as a mixture of repressive and protectionist measures (Monterde, 1995: 188). In a context of severe postwar shortages, rationing and a thriving black market, official policy sought to control and manipulate the film industry by creating a culture of profound dependency on a complex network of overlapping state bodies, including the Ministries of the Interior, Commerce and Industry, the National Movement, the Vertical Syndicates and Education (Monterde, 1995: 189). Not surprisingly, such bureaucracy and multiple levels of decision-taking could only be success-fully navigated by the widespread use of favours, backhanders, fraud and clientelism ('*enchufe*'). Let us briefly consider the three main forms of official regulation which would dominate the film-making landscape in Spain during the 1940s and have profound effects long afterwards: film censorship, compulsory dubbing and official state newsreels.

Having been introduced in wartime in 1938, film censorship was rolled out nation-wide after July 1939. Within its remit were such tasks as the pre-censorship of all submitted film scripts, the approval of shooting scripts and exhibition licences for Spanish films, the impos-ition of cuts and changes to sound and image tracks in completed films, the authorization of subtitling or dubbing, plus film classification. Given the severity of the post-war repres-sion and the fact that active film makers were unlikely to make trouble, there was little need for draconian measures. The real problems with film censorship were its total arbit-rariness, lack of consistency in decision-making, as well as its inefficiency and frequent stupidity (Seguin, 1995: 31), manifest flaws which remained endemic until its total sup-pression in 1977. Moreover, it is arguable that censorship had far less impact on Spanish film making than another measure which distorted and virtually undermined the entire industry: compulsory dubbing.

Introduced in April 1941 by the Ministry of Industry and Commerce, the taxation and compulsory dubbing into Spanish of all foreign films imported into the country are usually seen as a conjunctural response to Axis successes in the Second World War and the Franco regime's continuing attempts to '*españolizar*' (hispanicize) Spanish culture (Gubern, 1981: 19–20; Torres, 1996: 21; Caparrós Lera, 1999: 78). Taking into account illiteracy rates of between 50 and 60 per cent and public ignorance of other languages, Spanish film audiences quickly adapted to a mode of film viewing in dubbed Spanish which required little or no effort. Distributors and exhibitors soon saw that they could make far more money from dubbed than from subtitled films and film censors could also manipulate image and soundtracks far more easily. However, compulsory dubbing was a massive 'own goal', economically and industrially, delivering a near fatal blow to national film pro-duction. It put foreign (i.e. predominantly American, but also Italian and German) films on a par with the home-made product, making them equally accessible to national audi-ences, thereby abandoning a crucial weapon (the Spanish language) in the struggle against foreign competition (Besas, 1985: 24). Moreover, the importation of foreign films for distribution and exhibition depended on the concession of import licences to Spanish producers making 'wholly national' films (Torres, 1996: 21–22). These permits were doled out by official classification committees to local film producers on the strength of the ideological conformity of their films, based on the classification achieved. Typically, the producer of one modest but morally upstanding Francoist film would qualify for three to five import licences, though there were cases of films such as *El escándalo* (José Luis Sáenz de Heredia, 1943) and *El clavo* (Rafael Gil, 1944) winning 15 permits each (Caparrós Lera, 1999: 78). These would then be sold on for very large sums, often via the black market, to mainly American distributors based in Spain, since Spanish audiences tended to avoid local output in favour of foreign films (always better made, with better production values). As a result, as Triana Toribio argues, the regime achieved the ideo-logically 'correct' films it wanted, producers made good profits from selling import licences and distributors and exhibitors made fortunes from showing foreign films (2003: 53). Even if the national industry was made subservient to the power of the distributors in the process, such arrangements suited all parties. As a result, for nearly a decade, Spanish films were made simply as a means of earning very profitable import licences.

A further hammer blow to the national industry was the introduction in December 1942 of compulsory official newsreels, usually referred to as NO-DO (*Noticiarios y Documentales Cinematográficos*), to be screened in all Spanish cinemas. (Vernon, 2002: 68–69; Vicente Sánchez Biosca in Borau 1997: 628–9). These official propaganda vehicles replaced the German and Italian newsreels in Spanish cinemas and were in force until 1976. Their aim was ostensibly to celebrate the regime's achievements in public works (such as building dams, roads and hospitals), to report on official ceremonies (Holy Week, Saints Days, the Day of the Race [Columbus Day], the 18 July) and showcase all manner of national trivia (in sports, bullfighting, fashion, folklore). In reality, rather than bringing 'el mundo entero al alcance de todos los españoles [the world within reach of all Spaniards]', as their famous tag line so pompously claimed, the NO-DO specialized in disinformation, escapism and spin. Unfortunately for the film industry, the compulsory inclusion of NO-DO newsreels in all film programmes across Spain effectively barred many younger Spanish film makers from exhibiting their work in public (e.g. in documentaries, shorts or animations) and, in effect, acted as a massive disincentive to train in these areas.

To mitigate the catastrophic effects of the above policy decisions, the regime introduced a whole series of protectionist measures for Spanish films, including revised classification schemes, screen quotas (initially one week of Spanish film for every six of a foreign film), '*créditos sindicales*' (official loans with which to finance up to 40 per cent of a film budget), '*premios sindicales*' (official prize monies, of 400,000 pesetas, to be shared among cast and crew) and the category of '*interés nacional*' (national interest awards) for meritorious films, a most valuable commodity, which carried with them handfuls of import licences. By the end of the decade, virtually all Spanish film production was totally dependent on state handouts of one sort or another.

Until roughly 1944/45, the Franco regime favoured certain film genres, particularly the so-called '*cine de cruzada*' or war-inspired films, which celebrated the nationalist victory in the civil war, demonized the losers and celebrated the militaristic, colonialist, religious and warrior values of the new rulers of Spain, as in *Harka* (Carlos Arévalo, 1941), *¡A mí la legión!* (Juan de Orduña, 1942), *Escuadrilla* (Antonio Román, 1941), *Boda en el infierno* (Antonio Román, 1942), *Los últimos de Filipinas* (Antonio Román, 1945) and, until it was suppressed by the Ministry of the Navy, *El crucero Baleares* (Enrique del Campo, 1941). In particular, *Raza* (José Luis Sáenz de Heredia, 1941) was arguably one of the key films of the genre, allegedly sketched out by Franco himself (see Chapter Six). By 1945, however, with the impending defeat of the Axis, the declining influence of Falange and Franco's ideological adoption of National Catholicism, the values of the '*cine de cruzada*' became transmuted into other 'nationalist' sub-genres. These included the period melodrama, the historical film, the religious/missionary film as well as the folkloric comedy. By far the most popular and profitable genres at the box office were comedies, particularly the work of Rafael Gil, Edgar Neville and José Luis Sáenz de Heredia, who churned out clichéd, interchangeable, folkloric musicals and bullfighting films or *españoladas*. Cheap and cheerful, of poor quality but made for easy viewing and audience participation, these were vehicles built around the great singing stars of the age, including Lola Flores, Juanita Reina, Carmen Sevilla, Paquita Rico, Conchita Piquer, Estrellita Castro, as in *La Dolores* (Florián Rey, 1941) and *Currito de la Cruz* (Luis Lucia, 1948), perhaps the culmination of 1940s bullfighting kitsch. Yet, in a period of growing international isolation and ostracism for its fascist sympathies, the regime encouraged its film makers to resurrect symbols of national greatness and resistance to foreign aggressors (the Anti-Spain) in a series of cumbersome biopics, celebrating 'illustrious Catholic heroines' of the past, as in *Reina Santa* (Rafael Gil, 1946*), Locura de amor* (Juan de Orduña, 1948), *Agustina de Aragón* (Juan de Orduña, 1950) and *La leona de Castilla* (Juan de Orduña, 1951). Aligned to this stiff, theatrical and overly pious historical cinema, we also find a defence of Spain as a bastion of Catholicism and benign missionary colonialism, as in *Misión blanca* (Juan de Orduña, 1946), *La mies es mucha* (José Luis Sáenz de Heredia, 1948) and, prototypes for the sentimental, religious dramas of the 1950s, such as *Balarrasa* (José Antonio Nieves Conde, 1950) (see Labanyi, 1997).

Interestingly, it was also the same Falangist, Nieves Conde, who made *Surcos* (1951), a *succès de scandale*, dealing with the tragic consequences of rural exodus and migration to the city. *Surcos* appeared to represent a break, aesthetically if not politically, with the regime's false, escapist, historical propaganda cinema (championed by CIFESA) by proposing a realist cinema, actually concerned with daily life, the here and now, the problems of the lower orders, and with pressing social issues that were totally absent from Spanish screens. *Surcos* also became the centre of an ideological struggle between traditionalist Catholicism and 'social Falangism' when Director General of Cinema, José María García Escudero refused to award a 'national interest' prize to *Alba de América* (1951) in preference to *Surcos*. After serious pressure behind the scenes, the Director General was dismissed and the award given to Orduña's historical epic instead. This was a sign of the regime's impatience with realism and with film makers who dared expose the less attractive, problematic aspects of social reality in Franco's Spain. Yet, film realism had quietly filtered back into Spain via the odd example of Italian neo-realism and Soviet cinema in the late 1940s, smuggled into film programmes at university film clubs. Such films found fertile territory among some disillusioned Falangist film makers in the regime's newly created, official film school, founded in 1947.

Initially, the regime allowed the creation of the Instituto de Investigaciones y Experiencias Cinematográficas (Institute for Film Research and Experiment) as a means of imposing controls on professional access to the industry. The IIEC, renamed more digestibly the Escuela Oficial de Cine (Official Film School) in 1962, modelled its three-year programme on the curriculum for the Italian Centro Sperimentale in Rome. Despite its flagrant lack of resources, the very variable quality of teaching (mainly from working directors, favoured by the regime), the IIEC attracted 109 pupils in its first year alone (Stone, 2002: 41; Caparrós Lera, 1999: 85). Paradoxically, perhaps, it became something of a Trojan horse, a focus for both theoretical and practical renewal in Spanish film making, as well as intellectual and political dissidence. Many of its graduates would play key roles in the film club movements of the 1950s, in film reviews, and in acts of cultural and political opposition to the regime.

NEO-REALISM, 'CINE CON NIÑO', INTERNATIONALIZATION AND BUÑUEL: 1952–61

Two IIEC students, Juan Antonio Bardem and Luis García Berlanga, both disillusioned Falangists, became key figures in the 1950s' attempts at renewal of Spanish cinema. Together, under the banner of their production company UNINCI, they made *Esa pareja feliz* (1951, released 1953), a gentle, Capra-esque skit on working-class dreams of economic improvement, spiced up with parodies of CIFESA's grandiloquent epic cinema as well as the escapism of Hollywood romantic comedies. Berlanga (with help from Bardem) continued in similar satirical vein in the renowned *Bienvenido Míster Marshall* (1952), a parodic '*españolada*' with a critical edge, which garnered strong international recognition, but official disapproval at home. Indeed, right up to his satire on the death penalty in *El verdugo* (1963), with its criticism softened by the film's comic/parodic tone, Berlanga's films always had problems with censorship and poor distribution. As for Bardem, member of the clandestine Communist Party and one of the key organizers of the 1955 Salamanca Film Conference, his film-making career in the 1950s and '60s was punctuated with periods in prison for political activities. After a modest solo effort in *Cómicos* (1954), an autobiographical portrait of a travelling theatre company, he had significant international success with *Muerte de un ciclista* (1955), winner of the FIPRESCI prize at the Cannes Film Festival, and *Calle Mayor* (1956), FIPRESCI prize at the Venice Festival. With echoes of Antonioni (*Cronaca di un amore*, 1951) and hints of Soviet montage editing (Stone, 2002: 49), *Muerte* explored middle-class angst, hypocrisy and personal responsibility on the winning side. *Calle Mayor*, a free adaptation of a play by Arniches (*La senora de Trevélez*) focused on the repressions of Spanish provincial life for a convent-educated spinster and the cruelties of infantilized men. On the strength of these two films, Bardem was lionized abroad, especially in France, as the leading oppositional film maker of the decade (Caparrós Lera, 1999: 87). Sadly, his later work such as *La venganza* (1957) and *Sonatas* (1959) failed to bear out such expectations.

Meanwhile, in the false and rarefied world of state-supported commercial cinema in the 1950s, business continued as usual, with tried and tested genres and themes being recycled with alarming regularity. We find clear traces of continuity in the comedy and the folkloric musical whilst the fashion for historical epics and large-scale literary adaptations of the 1940s waned considerably. Not suprisingly, after the early 1950s, costly super productions like *Alba de América* (which failed disastrously at the box office) became something of a rarity (Monterde, 1995: 269). It was perhaps the folkloric musical, aimed at lower class audiences, with its singing starlets and comic/melodramatic storylines which prospered most in the early and mid-1950s, e.g. *Morena Clara* (1952) and *Esa voz es una mina* (1955), both by Luis Lucia, as well as *La pícara molinera* (Leon Klimovsky, 1954). However, these were overtaken in popularity by the cycle of light song or '*cuplé*' films of the late 1950s and early 1960s, triggered by the enormous success of *El último cuplé* (Juan de Orduña, 1957), starring Sara Montiel, whose winning formula was recycled by countless imitators (Paquita Rico, Marujita Díaz, Mikaela) until the seam ran out in 1962/3.

In comedy, many dissident film makers and writers (including Rafael Azcona and Italian director Marco Ferreri) adopted the genre as an appropriate vehicle through which to express their satire of Spain's social realities and class divisions, though treatments were obliged to pull their punches due to censorship (see Riambau, in Borau, 1997: 355–6). The success of Berlanga's *Bienvenido Míster Marshall*, for example, gave rise to a form of vaguely imitative '*comedia rural*', such as *Todo es posible en Granada* (José Luis Sáenz de Heredia, 1954). At the same time, an urban comedy, based on literary and stage precedents, is visible in Sáenz de Heredia's very popular *Historias de la radio* (1955). These would soon give way in the late 1950s to more narratively episodic comedies, using parallel editing, often dealing with young couples, which would pick up on Spain's slowly changing economic landscape, known in the 1960s as '*desarrollismo*' (economic development), in films like *Las chicas de la cruz roja* (Rafael J. Salvia, 1958) and *Los tramposos* (Pedro Lazaga, 1959).

Apart from rural dramas, home-grown westerns, pirate films and one or two notable crime films (a genre most definitely not favoured by the regime) such as *Apartado de correos 1001* (Julio Salvador, 1950) and *Brigada Criminal* (Ignacio Iquino, 1950), perhaps the most commerically successful cinema of the 1950s was the so-called '*cine con niño*'. Inspired by the child protagonists of Italian neo-realism, this child cinema existed in Spain in various hybrid forms – in religious, folkloric, and musical formats – becoming well established in

Hungarian Ladislajo Vajda's enormously successful *Marcelino pan y vino* (1954) and Antonio del Amo's *El pequeño ruiseñor* (1956). These were remarkably potent vehicles for Pablito Calvo and Joselito, the new, male child superstars of the 1950s (alongside many unsuccessful imitators) and were followed by their female counterparts in the 1960s, Marisol, Rocío Durcal and Ana Belén.

By and large, the 1950s reveal a decade of continuity and renewed exploitation of genres from the previous decade. Also, under the impact of Italian neo-realism as a crucial example of film realism, we also see numerous signs of a realist aesthetic in national film making, culminating with Saura's *Los golfos* (1959), a testimonial essay on juvenile delinquency. At the same time, reflecting the consolidation of the regime and its re-integration into world politics, with American backing, there is a certain easing of repression and an influx into Spain of greater levels of foreign film-making activity, with Spain becoming a preferred location for Hollywood epics, such as Rossen's *Alexander the Great* (1956), Kubrick's *Spartacus* (1960) and Mann's *El Cid* (1962). Indeed, Spain was quickly becoming a huge film set for foreign sword and sandal epics, westerns and crime films. Spanish cinema itself was also gradually becoming known abroad via film festivals.

The decade closed with the scandal surrounding Buñuel's *Viridiana* (1960/61). This was another example perhaps of dissident film making managing to infiltrate official channels and create all sorts of trouble for the regime. After being awarded the Palme D'Or at Cannes in May 1961, the Vatican newspaper, the *Osservatore Romano*, condemned Buñuel's film for blasphemy. This led to the dismissal of the head of Spain's Dirección General de Cinematografía, José Muñoz Fontán, the prohibition of the film in Spain and the withdrawal of its Spanish nationality. In effect, the regime made *Viridiana* disappear, which prevented its exhibition in Spain and impeded its distribution abroad. However, its status as Spanish-Mexican co-production made it possible to release it as a Mexican film, but with severe delays in being shown in Europe (see Llinás, in Borau, 1997: 878). The suppression of *Viridiana* also had a catastrophic impact on UNINCI, Buñuel's producer/distributor in Spain and on the production plans of Bardem and Jordá. *Viridiana* was not screened in Spain until 1977. And the role of UNINCI, as a potential focus for development of an opposition cinema, virtually came to a halt.

'NEW WAVES' AND 'OLD GENRES': 1962–1975

From the late 1950s, after two decades of negative growth and virtual bankruptcy, the Franco regime was anxious to shift the country decisively towards economic modernization and consumerism, but without allowing any political change. Desperate to attract foreign business and the incipient mass tourism of the 1960s, the regime's publicists saw cinema as a useful tool in a process of ideological makeover, emphasizing Spain as a modern, civilized country rather than the oppressive, military dictatorship that in many respects it still was. In July 1962, García Escudero was re-appointed as Director General de Cinematografía, with the aim of raising quality levels at home and promoting a new type of modern cinema: socially engaged, modestly realist, problem-centred, formally innovative, aimed at international festivals. In short, an art cinema, a quality product, geared to improving Spain's image abroad and portraying the regime as more like its European neighbours. Hence, the birth of the 'Nuevo Cine Español'. Ironically, the same regime that had closed the door to this type of realist cinema in the 1950s was now anxious to encourage its development. Unfortunately for the regime, however, the young film auteurs of the future invited to make the new cinema were Film School graduates and, by and large, to be found in the ranks of the political opposition. Moreover, social realism was not an aesthetic the Spanish censors were likely to welcome.

In 1962 and 1963, García Escudero introduced a series of new measures designed to promote the new cinema: access for younger film makers to the national industry became a priority; the new category of '*interés especial*' was introduced to distinguish and reward films which were artistically and intellectually challenging; the regime's film school was revamped, under a new name, the *Escuela Oficial de Cine*; films which had competed at international festivals would qualify for a 15% automatic, extra subsidy. However, in the end, the Nuevo Cine Español proved neither very experimental nor radical. Torreiro talks of a very heterogenous movement of some 48 first-time directors appearing over a period of five years (1962–67), making films of highly variable quality and interest (1995: 309). The usual narrative template involved young, normally educated but rather introverted, middle-class male adolescents rebelling against suffocating family circumstances, located in provincial settings. Thematics included romance, sex, family and generational rebellion, conflicts between demands for independence and family responsibilities, often against a backcloth of civil war divisions and hatreds. Given the still intrusive and arbitrary nature of censorship (which regularly demanded cuts and changes), most of these films were forced to adopt an indirect, elliptical style, open to various interpretations, where meaning often had to be wrestled rather than read from the scene. Reflecting the generic variety of this new trend, among the highlights of the movement, we find: *Del rosa...al amarillo* and *Juguetes rotos* (Manuel Summers, 1963 and 66), *Young Sánchez* (Mario Camus, 1963), *La tía Tula* (Miguel Picazo, 1964), *La busca* (Angelino Fons, 1966), *Crimen de doble filo* (José Luis Borau, 1964) and perhaps the paradigm film of the trend: *Nueve Cartas a Berta* (Basilio Martín Patino, 1965) (Triana Toribio 2003: 92–95).

By García Escudero's own criteria, Spain's new cinema of the 1960s was hardly a success. Though by no means a crucial factor, it evoked little or no public interest at home: box office was minimal, despite the creation in 1967 of special art cinemas in which to see local films and foreign films in original versions ('*Cines de Arte y Ensayo*', copied from the French version of '*art et essai*'). As for projecting the regime's benevolent cultural image abroad at foreign festivals, very few films were in fact selected for screening at these events. In fact, it was not the youngsters but film makers like Carlos Saura (a teacher at the IIEC/EOC in the early 1960s) and his oblique and allegorical study of the civil war in *La caza* (1965), which took the Golden Bear at the Berlin Film Festival in the mid-1960s. Young film makers did win prizes but the vast majority were awarded at festivals in Spain, such as San Sebastián and Valladolid. In 1967, following a ministerial re-organisation, García Escudero was replaced by the conservative Carlos Robles Piquer, brother-in-law of the Minister of Information, Manuel Fraga Iribarne.

Coinciding with the above trend, a rather different sort of 'new cinema', arguably more responsive to foreign models, was being developed in Barcelona between 1965 and 1971. It emerged from a heterogeneous group of middle-class, anti-Francoist, film enthusiasts and included Vicente Aranda, Jacinto Esteva, Gonzalo Suárez, Jose María Nunes, Carles Durán, (who had studied film in Paris) as well as Joaquín Jordá (who had studied at the IIEC/EOC in Madrid). The group managed to develop a film aesthetic in opposition to the *nuevo cine español* and more in tune with French auteurs such as Godard. As a homage to the New York School, it was dubbed the 'escuela de Barcelona' by communist producer and critic Ricardo Muñoz Suay in 1967, though it had little group cohesion, nor did it seek in any way to represent Catalan realities or the Catalan nation and language. Accused of being elitist, over-intellectual, apolitical and highly pretentious, this new '*gauche divine*' also set up its own production company, Films Contacto. Sometimes self financing, but relying mainly on government subsidies, the group made largely non-narrative, experimental, often surrealist pieces. These included Aranda's *Fata Morgana* (1965), where fashion, style and the beautiful Teresa Gimpera win out over an apocalyptic narrative, or Esteva/Jordá's *Dante no es únicamente severo* (1967), a manifesto for a certain 'pop' film aesthetic, self-consciously dependent on fashion and advertising (see Heredero and Monterde, 2003: 441–4). Most of the group's films failed to achieve a commercial release and are remembered as deliberately provocative 'ripostes' not only to the pedestrian realism of the nuevo cine español but also to Catalan directors who had studied in Madrid such as Pere Balañá (Caparrós Lera, 1999: 134; Riambau, in Borau, 1997: 319–21).

Interestingly, as Torreiro notes regarding the Nuevo Cine Español (1995: 311), in the early days, young debutant directors tended to be produced by old, established production houses (Ifisa, Procusa, Agata), which were quite happy to pocket official state subsidies provided for new film makers. However, as soon as producers realised that there was little or no extra money to be made from this unmarketable 'festival cinema', they quickly went back to the old generic favourites. These included an incipient Spanish 'horror' sub-genre, based on recycled versions of traditional gothic stories, with werewolves and vampires, in imitation of 1930s Universal 'B' pictures and Hammer films (as in *El secreto del Dr Orloff* [1964] and *El conde Dracula* [1970] both by Jess Franco). And following the decline of the great American trend, we have the phenomenon of the 'spaghetti western', which boomed after the success of Sergio Leone's *A Fistful of Dollars* (1964). By 1966, 67 low-budget imitations of Leone's hit had been shot in Spain (Torreiro, 1995: 334). Also, in the early 1960s, there is something of a 'boom' in the child musical, overtaken later in the decade by the deeply reactionary, but very popular folkloric musicals of Manolo Escobar, such as ¿Pero...en qué país vivimos? (1967) (see Chapter Five).

In the 1960s, popular Spanish film was dominated by the comedy, in all its variety and sub-generic hybridity. Pedro Masó was the leading producer, with Mariano Ozores, Pedro Lazaga, Fernando Palacios and Ramón Fernández among the big-name directors. Nationally-acclaimed actors, with a background in theatre, such as Alfredo Landa, Paco Martínez Soria, José Luis López Váquez and Gracita Morales were in big demand. Out of dozens of cheaply made, low-brow, generic 'sub-productos', one or two, such as *La ciudad no es para mí* (Pedro Lazaga, 1965) starring Paco Martínez Soria, became the blockbusters of the decade. They attracted huge numbers of Spanish spectators into the cinemas and were responsible for market shares of up to 25 per cent in the 1960s. (Torreiro, 1995: 335; Jordan, 2003a: 168–9). Slightly later, other sub-generic trends included the conservative moral melodrama, which dealt with risky subject matter (premarital sex, abortion, prostitution). Such films promised titillating imagery of nubile young women while serving up highly reactionary, didactic narratives as in *Chicas de alquiler* (Ignacio Iquino, 1972) and the paradigmatic *Experiencia pre-matrimonial* (Pedro Masó, 1973). Most of all, in the early 1970s, we find the incredible 'boom' in the Spanish sexy comedy or '*landismo*' as it was also called after the comic actor Alfredo Landa who starred in a string of such successful hits (see also Chapter Five). This sub-trend was short-lived but illustrative of the wider struggle between the regime's ultraconservatism and resistance to change in moral matters and Spaniards' general desire for greater sexual and political freedoms (see Jordan, 2003a).

Paradoxically perhaps, Buñuel's suggestive adaptation of Galdós' novel *Tristana*, after much official wrangling over the script, gained an *interés especial* classification, a major sign of official approval. This prompted some ex-students of the EOC to denounce the great exiled auteur for receiving special treatment and indeed of having sold out to the regime (Torres, 1996: 39–40; Company, in Pérez Perucha, 1997: 674–6). Yet, the success of *Tristana* encouraged a number of adaptations of Spanish literary classics, including Clarín's *La regenta* (Gonzalo Suárez, 1974) and Galdós' *Tormento* (Pedro Olea, 1974). As D'Lugo notes, this trend was part of a wider strategy usually termed '*tercera vía*' or third way (1997: 22), where film producers tried to make films aimed at foreign as well as national audiences, generating a product midway between the intellectualism of the art film and the sleazy, low-brow cultural designs of the sub-generic, sexy comedy.

This *tercera vía* cinema was arguably aimed at a more discerning, educated, urban, progressive audience. Its champion and main producer was José Luis Dibildos, who promoted a number of social comedies. These did not prosper very much financially but amomg them were some creditable titles, including Jaime de Armiñán's *Mi querida señorita* (1971) as well as *Españolas en París* (1970) and *Vida conyugal sana* (1973), both by Roberto Bodegas.

The same repressive context gave rise to what most critics and scholars of Spanish cinema consider to be the most acclaimed film of the period, if not of the whole of modern Spanish film making: Víctor Erice's haunting *El espíritu de la colmena* (1973). Metaphorical, allusive, atmospheric, this tale of a family from the losing side traumatized by the civil war, in which two young sisters (Ana and Isabel) seek to comprehend the 'silent' reality of early Francoist Spain through the myths and fantasies of cinema (James Whale's *Frankenstein*, 1931) is the self-reflexive art film par excellence. With its slow pace, chiaroscuro lighting, evocative shots of barren, rural Spain and multi-accented symbolism, especially that of the hive and the Frankenstein monster, *Espíritu* masterfully intimates, through Ana's inquisitive, innocent gaze, the realities of daily life under the regime and the desire for freedom.

DEMOCRATIC TRANSITION AND REFORM: 1975–1982

Reform of the Spanish film industry in the late 1970s took place against an unstable background (economic recession, political uncertainty over Franco's succession, a political process managed from above by different factions of the old regime, some in favour of democracy, others firmly against). While political change moved quickly, with Spain's first democratic elections being held by June 1977, change in the film industry lagged well behind and was largely piecemeal and unplanned. Reform largely involved the dismantling of the regime's repressive apparatus, incompatible with democratic principles. Film censorship was ended in November 1977 and replaced by a Board of Film Classification. Military law was used, though, to ban Pilar Miró's controversial *El crimen de Cuenca* (1979) until 1981 for its alleged injurious depiction of the Civil Guard, shown engaged in torturing two innocent men (see Riambau, in Borau, 1997: 259–60). The vertical syndicate structure and official control of professional associations in the industry were removed. The official NO-DO newsreels were also suppressed (though this process was finally completed only in 1980 (see Sánchez Biosca, in Borau, 1998: 628–9). Much of the protection apparatus, including automatic subsidies for film production, was retained, except for distribution quotas, which removed at a stroke the obligation on Spanish distributors to handle domestic output (a counterproductive interim measure mercifully rescinded in 1978). Overall, given that there were no fewer than six ministers responsible for the General Cinema Board (Dirección General de Cine) over a five-year period, it is difficult to discern any coherent strategy from the government's servants. Despite demands from the industry, there was no general, overarching legal framework for reform nor was a 'film czar' appointed. Meanwhile, film production boomed, with 90 features in 1976, rising to a remarkable 142 in 1982 (Torreiro, 1995: 372). Such overproduction was swelled by the huge numbers of low-budget, potboiler, genre films (comedies, horror, spaghetti western co-pros and above all, soft porn comedies) all accessing official subsidies. Yet, the Spanish film industry was still weak, suffering declining audience numbers, much greater competition from television and displaying little or no export potential. Moreover, from 1976, even under the old censorship apparatus, still officially in place, Spain was flooded by a massive backlog of films (national and foreign) which had been banned by the Franco regime for years, only to re-emerge and swamp more recent releases (see Torres, 1996: 43–4). For the first time in 40 years, the domestic industry, albeit briefly, felt the full force of competition from home and abroad.

Following Franco's death in November 1975, and reflecting wider intellectual and cultural trends, there was a proliferation of historical film making. This was not surprising, since one of the key cultural projects of the post-Franco, transition period (in cinema as elsewhere) was historical recuperation and retrieval. Initially, we find a number of feature-length documentary productions in the mid and late 1970s, freed from the monopoly power of NO-DO and showing a strong commitment to the conventions of authenticity and documentary realism. In this vein, Basilio M. Patino's *Canciones para después de una guerra* (1971/76) was finally released, as was his *Caudillo* (1976), a sarcastic biographical portrait of Franco. Jaime Chávarri's *El Desencanto* (1976) revealed the inner workings of the family of dead Francoist poet Leopoldo Panero and in *Raza, el espíritu de Franco* (1977) Gonzalo Herralde deconstructed the myth of Franco via a selective use of interviews and extracts from the original 1941 Sáenz de Heredia film *Raza*.

This documentary revival was accompanied by a host of features where the dramatic possibilities of fictional narratives were used to reconstruct historical events and review major political figures from an oppositional perspective. (Jordan and Morgan-Tamosunas, 1998: 21). Bardem's *Siete días de enero* (1977), for example, in the form of a pseudo-documentary thriller, offered an account of the assassination in Madrid of five labour lawyers in January 1977. From the Basque country, we also find Imanol Uribe's *El proceso de Burgos* (1979) which dramatizes the infamous trial of ETA suspects in Burgos in 1970, while *La fuga de Segovia* (1981), adopting the adventure thriller format, reconstructs the prison escape of ETA militants in 1976. In similar mode, in Catalonia, Antoni Ribas stages a re-engagement with modern Catalan history in both *La ciutat cremada* (1976) and *Victoria* (1983).

Such films were often criticized for their lack of serious historical engagement, however. Monterde accused them of creating a comfortable, non-problematic, often pamphleteering cinema, which did little to aid historical understanding (1993: 23). Moreover, until Ken Loach's *Land and Freedom* (1995) and Aranda's *Libertarias* (1996), the civil war remained one of the great unexamined topics, especially regarding the political causes of the war and its outcome. This was arguably because most of these features preferred to access the past via the personal and private, the intimate, the domestic and the everyday. In short, history was delivered to the viewer as personal memory, as subjective, individual experience, as seen in Chávarri's *Las bicicletas son para el verano* (1984) set during 1936–39, and tales of the maquis, as in Mario Camus' *Los días del pasado* (1977) and Manuel Gutiérrez Aragón's *El corazón del bosque* (1978). Even iconic public figures of twentieth-century history such as Franco were given a similar personalist treatment, as in Camino's bio-pic *Dragon rapide* (1986), with its stress on the private, reclusive, unheroic figure of Franco the man. Other treatments soon extended the range of Franco representations, however, as history migrated into the comedy domain, as in Antonio Mercero's satirical portrait in *Espérame en el cielo* (1987) and Francisco Regueiro's bizarre, fantasy vision in *Madregilda* (1993). The overlap between history and comedy is seen even more starkly in Berlanga's successful *La vaquilla* (1985) set during the civil war, and Fernando Trueba's Oscar-winning *Belle époque* (1992), raising issues over the suitability of lightweight genres being used to deal with serious historical issues.

In other respects, and leaving aside the predominant concern with history, film production in the late 1970s and early 1980s was strongly concerned with questions of sexual freedom and identity and incipient gender politics. Jaime de Armiñán offered ground-breaking treatments of transvestism in *Mi querida señorita*; an adolescent's love for his female teacher, in *El amor del capitán Brando* (1974); and in *El nido* (1980), an older man's sexual infatuation for a much younger woman (played by Ana Torrent). Chávarri's *A un dios desconocido* (1976) provided a sensitive homage to Lorca, while Olea's *Un hombre llamado flor de otoño* (1978) is a period tale of a Catalan lawyer imprisoned in the 1920s for his secret transvestism. In the work of Eloy de la Iglesia, after 1975, gay themes also emerged strongly in an otherwise commercial, generic format, overlaid with political overtones and graphic violence, especially in *Los placeres ocultos* (1976) and *El diputado* (1977). In documentary mode, theatre director Ventura Pons made his first feature focusing on a famous Catalan transvestite and street artist of the 1970s in *Ocaña, retrato intermitente* (1978). In Aranda's *Cambio de sexo* (1976), transvestism also re-emerges as a metaphor for the political transition and gender struggles of the period (Stone 2002: 115). Here, Victoria Abril plays an adolescent José María who becomes María José via a sex-change operation.

Among the older auteurs, Saura's hard-hitting *La prima Angélica* (1973), and the more melancholy *Cría cuervos* (1975), exploited the Francoist family and its abuse of women and children as a (none too veiled) microcosm of the traumas and repressions suffered by Spaniards under Franco. Up until then, Saura was undoubtedly the most visible and recognisable opposition auteur Spain possessed. Yet, after 1975, he found it very difficult to escape his reputation as a creator of anti-Franco parables (Stone, 2002: 71–2), while striving to make rather different, more personal films, (Caparrós Lera, 1999: 174). He ended up creating an impenetrable, overly personal essay on identity formation as in *Elisa, vida mía* (1976), a meta-theatrical denunciation of torture in *Los ojos vendados* (1978), a re-run of *Ana y los lobos* (1972) in *Mamá cumple cien años* (1979) and another self-reflexive theatrical tale in *Dulces horas* (1981), concerning the reconstruction of childhood memory and Oedipal anxieties. While Saura appeared unable to escape the repressions of the past, new film makers like Trueba and Almodóvar simply ignored them.

During this period of democratic transition, a number of new and important directors appeared, whose impact on Spanish cinema in the 1980s and 1990s would be highly significant. Before her rise to national prominence as Director General of Cinema in 1982, Pilar Miró made *La petición* (1976) and *El crimen de Cuenca*, the latter a *succès de scandale* following its passage through the military courts. She also directed *Gary Cooper… que estás en los cielos* (1980), a serious meditation on women working in the Spanish media, a culture dominated by machismo and misogyny (see Chapter Six). Also, in the context of what came to be called the '*comedia madrileña*' (Madrid comedy) of the late 1970s, Fernando Colomo made *Tigres de papel* (1977), a low-budget, off-beat, pseudo-documentary satire of Spain's young, left-wing, oppositional progressives, starring a youthful Carmen Maura (see Chapter Five). In similar mode, Fernando Trueba (erstwhile film critic for *El País*) launched his feature film career with *Ópera prima* (1980) starring young hopefuls Oscar Ladoire and Antonio Resines. In 1980, Almodóvar finally got a release for his first feature, *Pepi, Luci, Bom y otras chicas del montón* (1980), cult forerunner of the Madrid '*movida*' on film, also starring Carmen Maura as Pepi. The period also witnessed the remarkable endurance of old Francoist comedy formats, suitably spiced up to reflect changing political circumstances, especially from the prolific Mariano Ozores. His 'nostalgic', pro-Francoist *¡Todos al suelo!* (1982) and *¡Que vienen los socialistas!* (1982) constitute a notable, if ultra right-wing, critique of the democratic transition while celebrating the values and virtues of military dictatorship.

SOCIALIST FILM POLICY: 1982–94

Following the scare of the attempted military coup of February 1981 and the disintegration of the governing UCD party over the following year or so, Spain's Socialist Party, the PSOE, won a landslide electoral victory in October 1982. Pilar Miró was appointed new Director General of Cinema, the first woman to hold the post and the first incumbent with any experience of the film industry. She was aware that Spanish film production was broadly of three types: 1) 'S' rated films (low budget, exploitation films with significant levels of sex and violence); 2) Co-productions (many in name only) with foreign companies (again low grade, '*sub-productos*', including sex films, westerns, horror flicks etc., most of which were fraudulent and made cheaply simply to secure dubbing licences); and 3) A small number of artistically more ambitious art films, made largely by ex-EOC, liberal-left auteurs, mainly for the international festival market and for enhancing Spain's profile abroad. In order to rationalize this production landscape, Miró had to do away with bogus co-pros, radically cut the proliferating numbers of 'S'-rated films and diminish American dominance in distribution and exhibition by raising, if possible, the screening quotas for Spanish films. Above all, in line with PSOE electoral commitments, she had to focus official subsidies on supporting a 'quality' cinema of far greater filmic and cultural value, but one which was also attractive to foreign distributors and spectators. In other words, a 'European' art cinema which could travel and confidently represent the country and the government's new enlightened cultural policies abroad. Miró would also seek to link film output, as far as possible, to co-pro arrangements with the state television provider TVE, as seen in similar agreements already made in 1979–80 (see Torres, 1996: 46; Gómez Bermúdez de Castro, 1987: 116–25).

Miró's 'quality' auteur cinema did not replace, nor seriously challenge, domestic commercial genre cinema or dominant American imports. Indeed, some critics have argued that Miró promoted a cinema of '*films bonitos*' (visually pleasing/pretty films), whose thematic and aesthetic limitations, in the name of a higher European standard of film making, made them uninteresting and un-Spanish (see Triana Toribio, 2003: 131–2). In other words, they lacked the stark, gritty realism usually ascribed by some critics to Spain's own post-war social or neo-realist film tradition, a tradition and a national style seen by her detractors as compromised by the Director General's funding policies (Hopewell, 1986: 227). Moroever, Miró set up a funding system which in reality proved far too costly, with subsidized films making little or no money back at the box office and thus not replenishing the Protection Fund (Monterde, 1993: 105–6). Alarmed at the prospect of a funding 'black hole', new Minister of Culture Jorge Semprún, appointed in 1988, set out to redress the weaknesses of the Miró system and by 1994, under a new Film Law supervised by minister Carmen Alborch, the mechanism of advance subisidies was ended (save for new directors) and replaced by one based on box office receipts. State subsidies would now track commercial success. This shift of policy put the onus on producers to take financial responsibility for film projects and to regard film making as a commercial venture, dependent not on the whims of government committees but far more on the market and the tastes of Spanish audiences (see Jordan, 2000b: 187–88).

An alternative to the official quality cinema of the 1980s was of course the edgy, countercultural hybrid cinema of Pedro Almodóvar. Almodóvar was and remains the emblematic figure of post-Franco Spain, champion of the '*movida*', the Madrid 'underground scene' in the early 1980s. His films continue to enjoy almost canonical status, their hedonism, fluid identities, female centredness, generic mixing and obsessions with sexual desire having become so many auterist trademarks (see Chapter Three). However, the sexualization of Spanish cinema was happening well before Almodóvar arrived on the scene. Bigas Luna for example, was already exploring sexual transgression, fetishisim and generic mixing in the 1970s in *Bilbao* (1978) and *Caniche* (1979).

ONLY ENTERTAINMENT? SPANISH CINEMA: 1994–2003

PSOE film policy had been predicated on two basic principles: state subsidized quality cinema and greater Europeanization. Unfortunately, very little of Spain's auteurist '*cine de calidad*' (quality cinema) was attractive enough to domestic or foreign audiences, nor was it financially viable over the longer term. However, the gradual reversal of Miró's policy between 1988 and 1994 was unable to prevent a dramatic fall in production totals in 1994 to 44 features, only 39 of which gained a release. Added to this was a loss of 1.5 million spectators in 1994 and a very low market share of 7.1 per cent (Gubern, 1995: 402). And despite a few exceptions (Almodóvar's *Tacones lejanos*, 1991, Enrique Uribizu's *Todo por la pasta*, 1991, Alex de la Iglesia's *Acción mutante* and Juanma Bajo Ulloa's second feature *La madre muerta*, 1993), on the whole, Spaniards continued to ignore Spanish films. If they saw films, they tended to watch the latest American releases at home, on domestic video or on new, pay-per-view television services, unwilling to pay rising prices to sit in old, mainly unrefurbished film theatres (Caparrós Lera, 1999: 181).

After the 1996 March elections, with a narrow victory for José María Aznar's Partido Popular, conservative film policy was set firmly on the path of deregulation and commercial viability, very much a continuation but also a hardening of PSOE policy. Yet, by the mid and late 1990s, film production totals were beginning to rise, domestic market share improved to 13–14 per cent, new mergers in media and film production companies took place and the infrastructure of film exhibition went through a phase of refurbishment and construction of new multiplexes nation-wide (Jordan 2000b: 189). Underpinning these developments were the effects of key, longer term changes in the Spanish media landscape, particularly the removal of the state monopoly in television of RTVE in 1983/4, giving rise to new services in the autonomous regions. Also of crucial importance was the emergence in 1990 of three new private television channels (Antena 3, Tele 5 and Canal Plus España, with its subscription film service), whose programmers required more domestic film output to help fill out their schedules. Privatization, greater competition for television audiences, increased demand for film output and new market opportunities triggered the growth of new media companies, such as Sogecable (owned by Canal Plus France, PRISA and several Spanish banks), whose film division Sogetel (now Sogecine) began investing heavily in domestic film production. Shortly afterwards, the 'digital wars' between Sogecable and Telefónica in the late 1990s also accelerated growth, not only in film and television imports from the USA but also in funding local film production for digitial transmission (see Maxwell, 2000: 173). Also important were new EU directives which obliged Spanish television companies to invest up to 5 per cent of their annual revenues in domestic films and their transmission (Peláez and Rueda, 2002: 222).

Against the otherwise gloomy background of the early and mid-1990s, another major development was the massive renewal of personnel in the Spanish film industry, which affected all disciplines, particularly directing. Here, countless new names emerged, female as well as male, such as Icíar Bollaín, Marta Balletbò Coll, Isabel Coixet, Chus Gutiérrez, Gracia Querejeta, Eva Lesmes, Ana Díez , Mireia Ros, María Miró as well as Alejandro Amenábar, Juanma Bajo Ulloa, Alex de la Iglesia, Daniel Calparsoro, Agustín Díaz Yanes, Manuel Gómez Pereira, Gerardo Vera, Benito Zambrano, Manuel Huerga, Fernando León de Aranoa, Julio Medem and many others. A number of these young entrants had been to film school (e.g. Amenábar, Gutiérrez, Díez, Balletbò Coll), while many others lacked any formal training (Heredero, 1999: 19–20). Such a major generational shake-up has had significant effects on the formation of new production companies, new forms of working (a much greater number of co-directed and 'team' directed films) and with advance subsidies focused largely on new directors, we find rapidly rising production totals by first-time film makers. Such changes have had a profound impact on the business and have seen the emergence of a broadly commercial, entertainment-driven, Spanish cinema, involving new sets of narrative, generic, thematic, stylistic, technical, and casting concerns and choices, which are proving more and more attractive to mainly younger Spanish audiences, a largely forgotten demographic category until the 1990s.

However, this does not mean that other more established figures and trends do not continue to operate and even do good business. The post Franco, *movida* generation of Almodóvar, Trueba, Colomo, Bigas Luna, Garci, Chávarri, Ricardo Franco, José Luis Cuerda, Uribe, Armendáriz, Pons etc. are now in their fifties and constitute the senior core of the industry. They are the directors who have achieved major success at national and international levels, though of these only Almodóvar, Medem and perhaps Bigas Luna have achieved the distinction of transnational auteurs.

By contrast, a number of 1960s 'new cinema' veterans (Borau, Camus, Saura, Fernán Gómez, Gonzalo Suárez, Aranda and others) continue working, though committed to a serious, mainly realist, quality art cinema. Yet they still carry substantial weight and credibility within the industry, the film establishment and among the main critics. And in many ways, it is their unfashionable notion of cinema as a means of examining and acting upon social consciousness which has generated official recognition for a 'new social realism' of the 1990s, developed by a number of younger directors. In its awards policy in the late 1990s, Spain's Film Academy (founded in 1986, with its 'Goya' awards beginning in March 1987) has been particularly supportive and generous to new film makers who have taken up in their films controversial and difficult social issues: not only drugs, alcoholism, family breakdown, unemployment and bad parenting, but also Aids and domestic violence. Fernando León de Aranoa won Goyas for best new director in 1997 for *Familia* and best director and best screenplay for *Barrio* (1998) a portrait of teenage boredom on the bleak housing estates around Madrid. In 2000, alongside a Best Director award for Almodóvar for *Todo sobre mi madre* (1999), Benito Zambrano won Goyas for best new director and best script for *Solas* (1999), a poignant exploration of family relationships between brutal father, long-suffering mother and alcoholic daughter, trapped by domestic violence. Similar concerns underpinned the prize-winning *El Bola* (2000) by Achero Mañas and Icíar Bollaín's highly regarded, prize-winning *Te doy mis ojos* (2003), concerned with domestic violence. In similar vein, winning best film at San Sebastián in 2002 and Goya for best film in 2003, over Almodóvar's *Hable con ella* (2002), was Fernando León de Aranoa's third outing *Los lunes al sol* (2002), starring Javier Bardem, a moving chronicle of unemployed shipworkers in the port of Vigo, whose slogan is: '*Divididos, estamos jodidos*' meaning 'Divided, we're screwed'.

The 1990s have also seen a 'mini-boom' in gay and lesbian-themed films, already visible in *Family Album* (Marta Balletbò Coll', 1994), and evident later in *Amor de hombre* (Yolanda García Serrano and Juan Luis Iborra 1997), *Segunda piel* (Gerardo Vera, 1999) and *Amic*

Amat (Ventura Pons, 1999), plus Eloy de la Iglesia's *Los novios búlgaros* (2003) and Almodóvar's *La mala educación* (2004).

As noted earlier, Pilar Miró detested the popular, sleazy, late Francoist sex comedies. Recently satirized by Pablo Berger in his retro comedy *Torremolinos 73* (2003), their *costumbrismo*, camp styles, overblown Spanish stereotypes and focus on sexual repression were recycled in the early and mid-1980s in Almodóvar's '*cutre*' (dirty/bad taste) politically incorrect, crazy comedies. However, what Triana Toribio calls the 'neo-vulgar Spanish cinema' (2003: 151) re-emerged with a vengeance in the 1990s in the work of a number of new directors, in a much more aggressive and excessive set of forms and styles. This 'return of the filmic repressed' responded to a series of factors: 1) the severe financial situation in the early 1990s, the non-payment of official subsidies, and a collapse in audiences and box office receipts (Jordan, 2000b: 184–88). Producers thus looked to the comedy as a lifeboat and means of survival in troubled times. 2) Renewed interest in Francoist genre cinema was arguably a reaction to the failure of Miró's '*cine de calidad*' to attract audiences and stem the loss of public interest in Spanish film. 3) A number of young film makers reacted negatively to the PSOE's commitment to the European art film as a benchmark for official funding. 4) The youngsters who entered the industry in the 1990s, unlike Miró and her contemporaries, had no Francoist political antecedents, no axes to grind or political scores to settle. These were the media generation, some of whom had been to film school, but most of whom received their film education watching film classics and modern blockbusters, such as *Jaws* (Stephen Speilberg, 1975) and *Star Wars* (George/Lucas, 1977), on television. They were Spain's movie brats, perfectly au fait with Hitchcock and Ford as well as Scorsese, Tarantino, Woo and Rodríguez. Largely apolitical, they regarded cinema not as a tool of social engineering and developing citizenship but as entertainment and pleasure. And, though not radical venture capitalists, they acknowledged that film making was a business which needed to make a profit. This outlook arguably underlay the come-back of the commercial, popular genre film in the 1990s, within which various forms of black, surreal and grotesque parodic humour came to the fore (Triana Toribio, 2003: 155). By far the most successful film cycle in this vein has been Santiago Segura's *Torrente: el brazo tonto de la ley* and *Torrente 2: Misión en Marbella* (1998/2001) (See also Chapter Four). A *Torrente 3* is in the planning stage. Made without any government subsidy, the first *Torrente* (1998) was Spain's biggest box office hit of the 1990s, grossing double its nearest rival. *Torrente*'s appeal was based on its hybridity, its attractive combination of classic American genre conventions with certain Spanish filmic traditions such as vicious black humour, surrealism, explicit violence and crude, grotesque, stereotypes. It also aggressively reaffirmed its deviation from and negation of Mirovian norms of quality cinema, presenting itself as an 'anti-establishment' film on the basis of its unashamed commercialism and celebration of 'trash' cinema.

It would be mistaken to see recent Spanish cinema as too rigidly divided between an exportable, Euro-friendly, quality, art cinema and a dumb, sensationalist, xenophobic genre cinema, à la *Torrente*. The boundaries between the artistic and the popular are not tightly drawn, but blurred and highly porous, though unusually perhaps within the art cinema domain, we do find quite a lot of recycling of tried and tested formulae. There is Saura's recent *Salomé* (2002), yet another filmic excursion into the field of Spanish dance, already seen in *Flamenco* and *Carmen*, this time via a filmed portrait of the staging of the ballet *Salomé*. Also, we have the disturbing art house/horror hybrid made by Agustí Villaronga: *Aro Tolbukhin, En la mente del asesino* (2002), a false documentary portrait of a killer obsessed by an incestuous love of his dead sister. Also notable for its generic mixing is *El caballero don Quijote* (2002), Manuel Gutiérrez Aragón's intriguing sequel to his television version of the original novel, including a drag queen and postmodern 'irony'. In allied art-house territory, that of the literary adaptation, and leaving aside the flawed though visually striking version of Marsé's tale of adolescent desire in *El embrujo de Shanghai* (Fernando Trueba, 2002), we find the mysteries and myths of the past being investigated in David Trueba's *Soldados de salamina* (2002), based on the novel by Javier Cercas, and Anton Reixa's *El lapiz del carpintero* (2002), adapted from the novel by Manuel Rivas. Also notable in recent Spanish film making is not only the continuing glut of work from young, first-time directors (to name but a few: Eduardo Cortés, Chiqui Carabante, Jaime Rosales, Alberto Rodríguez, Luis Marías, etc) but the reinvigoration of the genre film, particularly the thriller, seen in *X* (Luis Marías, 2002), *La Caja 507* (Enrique Urbizu, 2002), *Palabras encadenadas* (Laura Mañá, 2003), *Intacto* (Juan Carlos Fresnadillo, 2001) and, on the back of *Los otros* (Alejandro Amenábar, 2001), *Fausto 5.0* (Álex Ollé, 2001), *El espinazo del diablo* (Guillermo del Toro 2001) and *Darkness* (Jaume Balagueró, 2003) as well as the rise of Spain's very own indigenous 'teen horror' (*El arte de morir* (Álvaro Fernández Armero, 2000), *Tuno negro* (Pedro Barbero and Vicente Martín, 2001), *No debes estar aquí* (Jacobo Rispa, 2002) and *School Killer* (Carlos Gil, 2001).

Clearly, the impact of popular Hollywood genre cinema on Spanish film making has been immense over many decades and remains so, allowing native Spanish directors to re-figure, innovate and transcend local film traditions and styles in ways which increasingly satisfy the demands of local as well as external markets (Allinson, 2003: 144). In terms of their production values, *mise-en-scène* and general look, as well as their subject matter, plotting, editing, camerawork and sound, they have become far more sophisticated and technically adept. More money is available, because Spanish films are now attracting good audiences. Spanish film makers are up to speed with the latest technologies and special digital effects. Moreover, post-production and processing facilities are far better than they were in the 1990s and have contributed to the 'quality' look of Spanish film, which was not there before. Broadly speaking, there has been a growing convergence, a visible increase in the formal, cultural and commercial crossover from Hollywood standards into Spanish film making. Spanish film is now able to combine local traditions, local stories and content with Hollywood modes of shooting and editing. Spanish films are also adept at recycling and borrowing elements of style and technique from other, mainly

American films, the so-called 'Tarantino effect' as in Bajo Ulloa's *Airbag* and Amenábar's *Abre los ojos* (1997), thereby downplaying signs of Spanish identity. This has made certain sorts of Spanish film far more attractive to a much larger slice of its massive youth market at home and rather more consumable and commercially attractive abroad. Technically just as professional, competent and well made as Hollywood movies, Spanish films (including co-pros) appear to be reaching a point where, with the right support and marketing, they are able to compete in the commercial mainstream, internationally, and make good money. This process of 'cross over' in relation to commercial Hollywood movies became well established in the 1990s, with Spanish films increasingly able to film, cut and market local stories and narratives in line with international standards and quality and with international audiences in view. It is as if Spanish cinema were at last in a position to develop a film industry in a truly meaningful sense.

CONCLUSION

Following the success of Michael Moore's *Bowling for Columbine* (2000) and *Farenheit 9/11* (2003), full-length documentary features have become attractive to commercial audiences not only in the USA but across Europe and in Spain. Since 1996, Spain's Film Academy has rewarded documentary work, initially in the form of '*cortos*' (shorts) but since 2001 there has been a prize for best documentary feature, won that year by José Luis Guerín's *En construcción* (2000). This newly fashionable genre has even attracted the attention of major Spanish auteurs in the last few years, none more so than Julio Medem with his *La pelota vasca* (2003).

A seeming radical departure from the sunkissed sexual exploits of *Lucía y el sexo* (2002), this documentary on the everyday realities of terrorist violence and its effects in the Basque Country was dogged by post-production difficulties and political attacks from various quarters. The film comprises a montage of some 70 talking heads, plus inter-cut bits of historical information, archive footage, clips from Medem's own films and from the game of '*frontón*' (Basque version of squash). It is shot in a variety of mainly rural settings, which provide a misty backdrop for the dramatis personae: politicans (not including the then governing Partido Popular), ex-Etarras, victims, activists and intellectuals (though not including key figures such as Fernando Savater). They discuss ETA terrorist activities, the movement's objectives and aspirations, the effects of violence on its victims, as well as issues of bias and objectivity in documentary making and the limits of free speech. Paul Julian Smith noticed in the film a rather questionable moral equivalence being drawn between victims and perpetrators of terror, leading to his ambivalent judgement of Medem as courageous for having made the film, but naïve in his representation of the issues (2004: 44–5).

ETA terror has been put into a whole different context with the tragic bombings of 11 March 2004 in Madrid. In principle, and unlike Medem's film, most Spaniards said

'*No al terror*' (No to terror), condemning unreservedly all forms of terrorist action on innocent civilians, whatever the cause or ideological justification. Sadly, given the timing of the
Madrid bombings (three days before the national elections, on 14 March 2004), the situation in Spain was complicated by the way the government, fully anticipating electoral
victory but without completing a full investigation, sought to lay the blame directly on
ETA for the outrage in order to capitalize electorally on the tragedy. This was a grievous
mistake, as it turned out, which was mercilessly exploited by the centre-left, leading to
mass demonstrations and a sufficient shift in voting patterns to effect a change of government, ushering in a PSOE victory.

Already in production before the Madrid bombings, a collectively-made feature documentary, entitled *Hay motivo* (2004) meaning 'There is good reason', was released at the
end of March 2004. Comprising contributions from 32 Spanish film directors (including
Vicente Aranda, Fernando Colomo, Imanol Uribe, José Luis Cuerda, Isabel Coixet, Ana
Díez etc.), each one produced a three-minute short on a wide range of topics, generating
a 'state of the nation under PP' film montage. Many other directors such as Almodóvar,
Erice and Gutiérrez Aragón were unable to take part, but nonetheless appear to have supported the project. What we have here is a reaffirmation of group solidarity among left-
wing film professionals, anxious to articulate a far wider collective anger, cynicism and
disillusionment among a majority of Spaniards, who have been ignored by national state-
owned media (notably TVE and its director Carlos Urdacci). The film, released shortly
before Spanish troops returned from Iraq, also signals a return of cinema as conscience,
as a tool of social critique, indeed as a form of 'direct action' and political interventionism.
Given the charges of degradation of political life under Aznar's conservative administration and official manipulations of TVE, the appearance of campaigning documentary features such as *Hay motivo* perhaps indicates that we are entering a new era in Spain of
politicized film making.

Chapter Two

FILM STUDIES BASICS: TECHNIQUE, NARRATIVE AND STYLE

Until we know how a film is speaking to us, we cannot be sure what it is saying. (Lambert, 1952: 7)

Writing on Spanish cinema (as with many other 'national' cinemas) has perhaps too often decided on the outcome of its research even before setting out to identify the technical and stylistic features which enable the films to create their represented worlds. The focus on representations (of gender, national identity, regionalism, etc. – see Chapter Six) has frequently relegated the study of *how* films work to a level of secondary importance. There are at least two reasons why this needs to change: the first, following Lambert, is simply that films are textual constructions, whose workings can and should be understood to allow for a deeper investigation of their meanings; and the second is that the analysis of film technique, narrative and style reveals just how much Spanish cinema has in common with most other cinemas. At a time when Spanish film makers are acutely aware of the increasingly globalized world of mass media entertainment, the critical apparatus working on Spanish cinema is still intent on explicating its difference from other cinemas, rather than addressing those elements which it shares with world film culture as a whole. The examples mentioned in the following chapter, though all from Spanish film, are used to illustrate features which are common to almost every film culture in the world. And they are features which are as commonplace in Film Studies courses as they are rare in work on Spanish film.

A basic knowledge of *mise-en-scène*, for example, provides a means of finding concrete examples to illustrate sometimes more abstract ideas (Gibbs, 2002: 98); and familiarity with cinematography reveals to us how the camera affects our perceptions of the characters and the ideas they represent. For example, the moving camera can be used either to follow the subject or to change it. Bazin points out that these are ethical questions, as they determine human relationships between artist, subject and observer (Monaco, 1981: 168). Similarly, an awareness of how film makers manipulate the stories of their films through different narrative structures allows us to avoid falling into the trap of discussing those stories as if they were real events, with real people. *Mise-en-scène*, cinematography, sound and editing can all be analysed as discrete systems. Together they constitute film style.

When used in a fiction film they also generate a narrative. The following sections will look at each of these systems in turn before concluding with two case studies of very different film styles.

MISE-EN-SCÈNE

The term '*mise-en-scène*' means 'putting on stage' or 'putting into the scene'. In cinema, *mise-en-scène* is usually taken to describe everything that is arranged in front of the camera in order to be recorded so that it appears in the frame. Thus, *mise-en-scène* encompasses framing, setting, décor, props, costume, make-up, figure, expression, movement and lighting, as well as the ways in which these elements are combined in the frame (composition). Given that each one of these elements operating in the frame is shared with at least one other of the visual arts (painting, sculpture, ballet, theatre, photography), *mise-en-scène* provides a rich matrix across which to analyse visual style in the cinema.

Setting and props indicate place and historical period. The director, often following the requirements of the screenplay, decides whether to film on location (this can be either indoors or exteriors) or in a studio. Unlike in classical Hollywood movies, Spanish cinema has tended to prefer location shooting, partly because it is cheaper than studio filming, and partly because films like *El espíritu de la colmena* (Víctor Erice, 1973), *Los santos inocentes* (Mario Camus, 1984) or *Vacas* (Julio Medem, 1992) require specific rural settings. Urban location shooting works best for films set in a period contemporary to their filming, as in the case of 1940s Italian neo-realism and the remarkable Spanish equivalent *Surcos* (José Antonio Nieves Conde, 1951) set in the Madrid of 1950. Period films can represent a problem for on-location shooting: films like *Amantes* (Vicente Aranda, 1991) or *Tu nombre envenena mis sueños* (Pilar Miró, 1996) set in 1950s Madrid require parts of the city that have not lost their late 1940s look. But historical recreation is not the only purpose served by setting and props. They can indicate social status, as in the starkly differentiated worlds of the upper middle classes and the poor in *Muerte de un ciclista* (Juan Antonio Bardem, 1955). And they also set up expectations with regard to themes and genres. A hospital or a theatrical setting will set up expectations of melodrama, as in Almodóvar's *Todo sobre mi madre* (1999); a gambling den will suggest crime narratives, as in *Nadie hablará de nosotras cuando hayamos muerto* (Agustín Díaz Yanes, 1995); a church will indicate a moral drama, as in *Viridiana* (1961), though Buñuel, of course, sets up an expectation of morality only to shock with its opposite. Props can be there to make the setting more convincing or can have an active role (Abrams, Bell and Udris 2001: 94). The heroin-filled syringes and Civil Guard three-cornered hats of *El pico* (Eloy de la Iglesia, 1983) both figure in the story, but also represent two very different communities and sets of values. Props also form part of the iconography of genres. Weapons abound in crime narratives: guns in *Carne trémula* (Pedro Almodóvar, 1997), all manner of weapons in *Tesis* (Alejandro Amenábar, 1996), *La madre muerta* (Juanma Bajo Ulloa, 1993) and *El día de la bestia* (Alex de la Iglesia, 1995). Telephones tend to feature highly in comedies and romantic comedies such as *Mujeres al borde de un ataque de nervios* (Pedro Almodóvar, 1988). Apart from and as well as all these functions, setting and props can be used for purely aesthetic purposes, as in the beautiful aerial view of Barcelona towards the beginning of *Todo sobre mi madre*, or the camera roaming through the undergrowth in *La ardilla roja* (Julio Medem, 1993).

Closely linked to setting are costume and make-up. Costumes are part of the set and contribute to the establishing of place and time, class and character traits. Where costume in contemporary settings often goes unnoticed, in period or heritage films, costume is a primary signifying device. Films such as *¡Ay, Carmela!* (Carlos Saura, 1990) or *El crimen de Cuenca* (Pilar Miró, 1979) depend to a large extent on costume to anchor them in historical time. Often the costumes provide as much for visual pleasure as for verisimilitude, a good example being a film such as *El perro del hortelano* (Pilar Miró, 1996) the sumptuousness of its costume being a principal element in its appeal. Costume can indicate changes in circumstances or attitudes (Roberts and Wallis, 2001: 7). For example, in Almodóvar's *Carne trémula*, Elena is dressed in leather jacket and trousers in the early 1990s during her rebel, drug-taking phase, and in stylish, well-made suits in the mid-1990s when she has become more respectable. Sometimes exaggerated costumes are used to create larger-than-life characters: the dresses for the grotesque, media-machine presenter Andrea Caracortada in *Kika* (Pedro Almodóvar, 1993) designed by Jean-Paul Gaultier, provide a good example. Make-up is, of course, essential to all actors but most frequently is designed to go unnoticed. Where we do notice make-up it is because a specific look is required: the heavy but quite usual make-up of a performer (Marisa Paredes in *Todo sobre mi madre*); or the grotesque, mutilated faces in *Acción mutante* (Alex de la Iglesia, 1992).

Figure, expression and movement are all literally embodied in the actors. Actors communicate verbally and through their facial expressions and body language, but they also produce meaning through the star system. While their acting abilities and their star personae are categories we will analyse in Chapter Five, actors are also part of the *mise-en-scène* under the guidance of the director. An immobile actor, perhaps an extra in a crowd scene, represents little more than a prop, but any movement in a human form within the frame draws attention to itself. Having more than one character in the frame will immediately bring proxemics into question: how much space is there between the characters? Which way do the characters look vis-à-vis the camera (Giannetti, 1990: 72)? According to conventions established first in the theatre and then over a hundred years of film, an actor in the foreground is more important than one in the background. A clear and entertaining example of this appears in Fernando León de Aranoa's 1998 film *Barrio*: teenagers Javi, Manu and Rai appear on a local TV jobsearch advert, but it is Javi who is left to sell their very limited abilities, and he appears in the foreground while his two friends try to hide behind.

Once the director has arranged all of the above in front of the cameras (and probably rehearsed whichever sequences are about to be filmed), this hopefully coherent *mise-en-scène* must be lit if it is to be picked up by the cameras. Lighting is at least as important as all the other elements (and photography is, after all, 'writing in light'). From the earliest times, film makers realised that lighting could do much more than merely make the actors and set visible to the camera. Indeed, before sound, cinema learned to mobilize many expressive properties of light, partly in compensation for the lack of sound effects and dialogue. Lighting indicates who or what is important in the frame, as well as time, place and mood. Light can be motivated, increased to indicate daytime, for example, and in some cases the source is natural (i.e. the sun itself provides the sunlight) or artificial (with lamps). But while Hollywood and much mainstream cinema has always preferred lighting to reflect natural light and attempted to make the process of artificial lighting invisible to audiences, some film makers have preferred to emphasize design over verisimilitude (Monaco, 1981: 158). A good contemporary example is *Alas de mariposa* (Juanma Bajo Ulloa, 1991). Colour can be an important expressive code in lighting, and features prominently in Almodóvar's *Matador* (1985) and *Todo sobre mi madre* (1999).

Intensity is another factor in lighting. Much cinema uses lighting to represent everyday situations. 'High-key' lighting attempts a neutral balance by using filler lights above to obliterate shadows, and a key light (usually at a 45° angle) to provide the main light for the subject. Typical in musicals and comedies, this is not realistic at all, as we seldom see things in such bright, balanced light (Monaco 1981: 166). 'Low-key' lighting, on the other hand, hides details and creates lots of shadows so is ideal for films which exploit fear. The use of only key and back lights creates a chiaroscuro effect (sharply contrasting shadows and light) which is notable in *La madre muerta*. Light can be hard or soft. Hard lighting creates clearly defined shadows, harsh textures and crisp edges, while soft lighting blurs and softens (Roberts and Wallis 2001: 10). While hard lighting prevails in a film like *La comunidad* (Alex de la Iglesia, 2000), soft lighting is used to good effect in *Belle Époque* (Fernando Trueba, 1992).

The direction of lighting is a final factor worth considering. Hollywood has traditionally preferred what is known as a three-point lighting system comprising a key light (diagonally from the front), a back light (which counters 'unnatural' front lighting), and a fill light (which helps to soften the shadows produced by the key, coming from near the camera) (Roberts and Wallis, 2001: 11). Some studio-filmed Spanish films adopt this system when their objectives are similar to those of the US entertainment industry. The star vehicle films of Sara Montiel in the 1950s are often shot this way. But many Spanish films, with different objectives, prioritize more obtrusive, expressive lighting set-ups, a fine example being *Los otros* (Alejandro Amenábar, 2001).

We turn now to framing. Frames attract attention. An empty frame in an art gallery will provoke curiosity and anyone who walks across an empty stage and looks towards the empty seats of the theatre will feel strangely performative. Likewise, the frame in cinema is pre-invested with meaning: the bottom is more important than the top, left comes before right, the bottom is stable, the top unstable (Monaco 1981: 155). And, according to the conventions which film viewers unthinkingly adopt, the frame can either be self-sufficient, a 'closed' form in which the visual elements are carefully arranged and held in balance, much like in a theatre's proscenium arch (Giannetti, 1990: 72), or it can lead the viewer to assume that the world of the film continues outside the frame ('open' framing). This, in turn, allows for the convention of off-screen space: a character may look off-screen and we willingly construct another space for the fiction to continue outside our view. Classic Hollywood is characterized by largely closed form because its studios lent themselves to an 'on-stage' filming set up. Spanish cinema only rarely ventures into this type of framing, and when it does, the films are more likely to have something in common with Hollywood movies. Almodóvar's cinema between *¿Qué he hecho yo para merecer esto?* in 1984 and *Kika* in 1993 demonstrates a preference for this type of closed form, which suits the sometimes claustrophobic interior scenes of melodrama and bourgeois comedy. Much more common is the open form. A related quality in framing is whether it is tight or loose. Quite logically, tight framing conveys a sense of confinement, as in a film such as Saura's *La noche oscura* (1988). Loose framing can suggest freedom, but also, sometimes, isolation as in the beautiful extreme long shot of the tiny figure of Azarías silhouetted against the sunset and trees in *Los santos inocentes*.

Composition is defined by Abrams, Bell and Udris as the 'arrangement of elements within a shot' (2001: 96) In much the same way as we could analyse a painting, we can ask of any frame, where is our eye attracted first and where does our eye travel after taking in the dominant? (Giannetti, 1990: 72). Looking at the frame we can then ask, is it symmetrical or asymmetrical, balanced or unbalanced? Monaco affirms that an 'oblique composition stresses psychological space, while symmetrical composition stresses design' (154–5). In the famous last supper parody in Buñuel's *Viridiana*, there is a moment when Enedina pretends she is going to take a photograph of the assembled beggars. They all look at the camera, posing in what becomes a perfectly formed, framed picture, the composition recalling Da Vinci's famous painting, *The Last Supper*.

MISE-EN-SCÈNE IN *CARMEN*

Carlos Saura's 1983 film is self-consciously an 'art film', based on the Bizet opera and deliberately highlighting the parallels between art and reality. The titles appear over engravings of the Carmen story, testifying to the ancient pedigree of the original work. *Mise-en-scène* is to the fore, with no attempt to hide its workings. The dance studio location signals a performative world for the characters. This is contrasted with only two other locations in the film. The sequence in the *tablao flamenco* with the gaudy colours of its mock-Arab stage and black and red polka dot dresses, corresponds with tourist conceptions of flamenco, and is contrasted by the bare simplicity of the dance studio where neither décor nor costume competes with the movement of the dancers themselves.

The outside world is indicated only briefly, when Carmen goes to visit her husband in Carabanchel prison and we see a long shot of the corridor: she in foreground, he only just visible in the distance (the shot recalls the prison at the end of Berlanga's 1963 classic *El verdugo*).

The *mise-en-scène* exploits the difference between open and closed forms. When Carmen or Antonio are dancing, the camera follows them, keeping them centre-frame (every movement is important). This form is suitable for theatrical sections but when Carmen and Antonio are not performing an open form is used as this is the 'real world'. A theatrical *mise-en-scène* dominates the dance routines. When Carmen has knifed her adversary in the tobacco factory, the two groups separate, motionless (in stark contrast to the animated dance prior) and then the rhythmic military steps of the police erupt slowly and ominously from the left. This is filmed in a static long shot, framing the dancers as if in a theatre's proscenium arch. Framing is also used in a figurative way: when Cristina goes into Antonio's office to discuss Carmen, the latter moves to the one-way window/mirror and stares into it, becoming part of the scene between and behind Cristina and Antonio, incorporating all three in the frame at once, and suggesting that Carmen could come between these two professionals.

The lighting is far from the 'invisible' or 'natural' effect many mainstream films aspire to. Even when its source is natural (the enormous floor-to-ceiling windows), the effect is striking. But for much of the film, the lighting is non-naturalistic: strong overhead lighting catches the hair of the dancers and, in sequences such as the *habanera* routine, very strong artificial light creates a spotlight effect on props and scenery in a highly theatrical way. Lighting in the factory scene is in clearly differentiated strips and, as the two opposing factions move left and right across the horizontal plane, they come in and out of these strong light corridors, an effect which is far from invisible or 'natural'. And when Antonio plays out a dance/duel with Carmen's husband, strong front lighting casts ominous, heavy shadows on the walls behind and low-angle shots enhance the stature of the two sparring males; at one point they both leave the frame altogether, an absence which is curiously captivating.

Costume, make-up and props are also highly stylized. The colours of the flamenco dancers' costumes (reds, purples, pinks and blacks) refer to the vibrant culture of Andalusia but they are also the source of aesthetic pleasure. Carmen's black lace and *mantilla* complete with *peineta* recall Goya's famous portrait of the Duchess of Alba. As most of the performances we see are rehearsals, make-up and props are kept to a minimum. They feature more strikingly, however, in the sequence where the group are fooling around. Carmen appears dressed in a comically hyperbolic flamenco costume and with lots of hastily applied heavy make-up; in the absence of a red capote, a black headscarf is used, and a walking stick instead of a sword.

The final section of the film amply demonstrates how Saura has made visible the mechanics of his *mise-en-scène*. The dimly lit rehearsal room where a dancer is helped into his bullfighter's outfit in absolute silence is transformed dramatically into the bustle of the arrival of the rest of the dancers. The noise level rises, the curtains part to reveal the bright open space and hordes enter from the foreground. They form pairs and begin to dance a raucous *pasodoble*. There is another stark change of mood and *mise-en-scène* when Antonio angrily snatches Carmen from the bullfighter's arms first to silence as the men stare each other out, then to a raw *sevillana* about '*celos*' (jealousy) serving as a background to an altercation between Carmen and Antonio which we see but cannot hear. Close-ups alternate with shots of the whole group, who try to absorb and dilute the triangular aggression into their song and dance. When Antonio grabs Carmen again the knives come out and we return to medium and full shots of the male characters who dance their aggression; the next confrontation, between Carmen and Antonio, leads to him knifing her to death.

MISE-EN-SCÈNE IN *EL DÍA DE LA BESTIA*

While *Carmen*, in many ways, sums up a distinctly European type of film making, which prioritizes intellectual, not to say elitist, conceptualisations of cinema via minimalist spectacle (and minimal budget), *El día de la bestia* is an expensive film in which entertainment and spectacle are paramount. Alex de la Iglesia's remarkable second film has a long list of credits which reflects the extent to which the tools of *mise-en-scène* and technology are mobilized for spectacular effects. Real locations and studio filming are mixed in a seamless way which (as in Hollywood) is virtually invisible to the audience. Madrid becomes hell on earth and its beggars, ambulances, police, burns victims, and propped up buildings are contextualized by frequent shots of recognizable Madrid views, including the real statue of the *Ángel Caído* (Fallen Angel) in the Retiro which ends the film. In a climactic scene, the three protagonists climb out onto a neon sign on top of the Capitol building in Callao. Only the establishing shots of the building were filmed on location, along with the point-of-view shot of Cavan's fall, and a few shots with stuntmen. But the actors in close-up shots were filmed with a full-size replica created in the film studio. Similarly, the gunfight at the *Reyes Magos* (Three Kings) stage was split between crowd scenes filmed on location and close-ups and gunshot wounds achieved in a studio. The predominance of studio filming allows for a significant use of technology and the special effects by the team, led by Reyes Abades.

Much of the action takes place at night, so that a studio setting can permit the use of lighting for special effects, such as the sidelighting which hits the priests' faces as if through the windows of the church, or in Cavan's flat (while he is tied up): here the lighting accentuating the grotesqueness of Cavan's injuries. Special effects like lighting are easily added in the digital editing suite, outsourced here (just as it is in most mainstream US film) to a specialized company, Daiquiri. Digital postproduction also enables the use of models for the beast itself in the final sequence on the roof of the Kio Towers. Costume ranges from the simply denotative, such as priest's cassock, police uniform, heavy metal scruffiness of

Figure 2.1 Ángel (Alex Angulo) in *El día de la bestia*

José-Mari, or eroticized dress of Cavan's Italian girlfriend, to the specially-designed pros-
thetics of the beast itself. The make-up, by José Antonio Sánchez and José Quetglas, is
both spectacular and conventional. That is, very pronounced and specific make-up is
required for bleeding, swelling and even deep wounds (Ángel's ear is blown off), but these
effects are meant to convince the audience, to 'look realistic'. Similarly, choices about
framing and composition are made on the grounds of spectacle: when the landlady
smashes Ángel's head through the window, he is framed from above in close-up in a very
brief shot which we accept, not because we think there would be anybody watching the
space outside an upper-floor window, but rather because this type of shot is often included
in action spectaculars. The composition within the frame is also designed to be both
believable and impressive at the same time. When Cavan reveals the significance of the
Kio Towers as the Devil's temple, we see a shot of the building framed as if in a picture
with the comic, almost surreal touch of a Christmas decoration star in between them. But
these inclining towers also feature elsewhere in the film as a symbol of evil, providing a
visual coherence synchronically as well as diachronically.

Composition is, as Gibbs (2002, 40) puts it, 'the relationship between the parts and the
whole' which he calls 'organicism'. In isolation, each of the elements within the *mise-en-scène*

provides a powerful expressive component for an extremely flexible and manipulated medium. But the next three film-making processes to which they are subjected – cinematography, editing and sound recording – are even more versatile and manipulable.

CINEMATOGRAPHY

If *mise-en-scène* comprises *what* is to be filmed, then cinematography refers to *how* it is filmed. It is, therefore, the process by which the elements of the *mise-en-scène* are recorded within the shot. The shot can be defined as 'a single, continuously exposed piece of film – however long or short – without any edits or cuts'. 'Shot' is the term used in referring to the completed film; the term used while filming is 'take' (Roberts and Wallis, 2001: 24). A shot can last anything from a fraction of a second to 10 minutes. There are many variables in the operation of the camera that affect the final film. Varying the speed of the camera (while the projector speed remains constant) produces slow motion, fast motion and time-lapse (extreme fast motion) (Monaco, 1981: 76). And the choice of film stock can, among other things, suggest period, as for example in Pilar Miró's retro-thriller *Beltenebros* (1991). Overexposure (using a wide aperture to allow in more light) can be a problem when filming under the Spanish sun, but this effect is used to advantage in a film like Saura's *La caza* (1965) where the relentless scorching sun is a major presence in the film. Underexposure creates darkness. Perhaps more than any other aspect of film making, cinematography has evolved over more than a century of moving pictures in relation to technological developments. In cinema's earliest days, films were shot with static cameras, though by the 1940s zoom lenses and deep focus photography were being developed (allowing a sharp image in both the foreground and the background). By the 1950s, with smaller, hand-held cameras, camera movement became more pronounced, especially under the influence of the French *nouvelle vague*. The 1970s saw the introduction of the steadicam to be followed more recently by digital cameras.

Probably the most obvious variable in cinematography is camera position. Where the camera is stationed affects whose point of view it reflects and the degree of engagement or detachment with the subject. Camera angle is also important. Most cinema wants us to perceive its images as closely as possible to the way in which we see things in everyday life. Therefore, an eye-level camera position is normal. We tend to notice when camera angles are unusually low (a camera pointing up often suggests size or power), or unusually high (a camera pointing down emphasizes smallness) (Roberts and Wallis, 2001: 22). According to where the camera is positioned in relation to its subject, the shot produced ranges from an establishing shot (an extreme long-shot which shows us the whole setting for a sequence), through full-shots, mid-shots, close-ups, to extreme close-ups (which centre on a detail of a person or object). (See Figure 2.2 on page 44) A film shot in close-ups deprives us of setting and can be disorientating and claustrophobic, while a film with mainly long shots emphasizes context over drama and dialectic over personality (Monaco, 1981: 162).

LONG SHOT

MEDIUM CLOSE-UP

MEDIUM LONG SHOT

CLOSE-UP

MID-SHOT

EXTREME CLOSE-UP

Figure 2.2 Shot sizes

Camera movement adds a further range of expressive possibilities. The camera can move without being repositioned on either its horizontal axis (a pan) or its vertical axis (a tilt). A sideways pan can be used to follow a subject or to direct attention to a different one. A tilt upwards from ground level can reveal the height of a tall building, for example. Then the camera can also move itself from one point to another, which is called a tracking shot (where the camera is mounted on tracks), travelling shot or dolly (if the camera is mounted on a rubber-tyred dolly). Two further options are hand-held cameras and the Steadicam, which is strapped to a cameraman (Monaco, 1981: 79). Moving the camera offers a director the privilege of literally directing the viewer's perspective (unlike in the theatre, for example, where audience members can look wherever they want) (Monaco, 1981: 77). Point of view – which has implications for audience identification, representation, ideology and the star system – is tied to camera movement. At one extreme, a static camera, deep-focus photography (see below) and long shots will provide a very objective point of view where the audience does not see the action from the point of view of any characters. At the other end of this spectrum, a moving camera, shallow focus and close-ups encourages us to see things from a particular subject position (Monaco, 1981: 170). Convention is hugely important here: the shot of one character from the second character's point of view is usually called a reverse-angle shot, and plays a uniquely prominent role in cinema. Together, the range of camera shots in any film is called the 'shot scale'.

Another variable concerns the operation of the camera lens. Focal length for 35mm film is between 35 and 50mm, mimicking human vision most closely. Wide-angle lenses allow for a width of view greater than the human eye, while the telephoto, or long lens, acts like a telescope to magnify distant objects (Monaco, 1981: 60). Adjusting focal length while filming is by zoom lens (from establishing shot to detail or vice-versa) (Roberts and Wallis, 2001: 26). As well as width, the lens controls depth of field. A wide-angle lens has more depth of field so that elements in the foreground, middle ground and background will all be in focus. This means the viewer can choose where to focus attention within the whole field, so deep-focus photography is often associated with theories of realism. Shallow-focus photography (with characters in sharp focus and the background blurred) 'welcomes the limitations of depth of field as a useful artistic tool, [and] is more often used by expressionist film makers, as it offers still another technique that can be used to direct the viewer's attention' (Monaco, 1981: 70). A useful example occurs in *Hable con ella* (Pedro Almodóvar, 2001) where a shift in focus is used to convey the thought process: a shallow focus shot with Marco in sharp focus in the foreground and the comatose Lydia blurred in the background is adjusted, when his thoughts turn to her, blurring him and putting Lydia into sharp focus. Finally, nuanced differences in focus bring their own associations: soft focus is associated with romantic moods, sharp focus with verisimilitude (Monaco, 1981: 162).

CINEMATOGRAPHY IN *LOS SANTOS INOCENTES*

Mario Camus' 1982 film is an adaptation of Miguel Delibes' novel portraying the still feudal society of 1960s rural Spain. The cinematography in the film serves a broadly social realist ethos, pursuing verisimilitude above stylization. One of the few more formalist devices in the film is its splitting into four chapters, each corresponding to and given the title of one of the characters in Paco's family. To mark these formal divisions, Camus uses a repeated visual motif: a long shot of Quirce – then later Nieves, then Paco el bajo, and finally Azarías – dissolves into a medium shot and then a close-up as the attention homes in on each character. But elsewhere close-ups are rare: this is not a psychological drama. The predominance of long and medium shots emphasizes societal relationships. Simple but stark contrasts are reinforced by camerawork. A very long-distance establishing shot of Paco's shack indicates its extreme isolation before a dissolve shows it close-up, so that we can see figures emerge. A little while later, a parallel sequence reveals the Señorito's home in another establishing shot, showing its splendid isolation (gleaming white amid lush green countryside), before a closer shot reveals the hunting party.

Camera angles also underline social relationships such as that between the rich marchioness and her lowly tenants (see Figure 2.3). When Paco pleads for Azarías' former master to take

Figure 2.3 Camera angles and social relations in *Los santos inocentes*

him back, the camera adopts a high angle, looking down on Paco as if from the Señorito's point of view. Paco's reverse angle shots are from a correspondingly low angle. Mobile shots serve a similar purpose. The camera tracks to follow the hunting party, then slows down as they leave the frame to show Azarías, always behind, carrying their catch. The camera subtly comments on the social mores of the upper class as they sit in silence at their long table. Eschewing any subjective or point-of-view shots, the camera tracks around them, keeping outside its circle. But on the other hand, the camera encourages us to share in Azarías' delighted pursuit of his pet bird, a hand-held camera following him through the forest. Just as framing and *mise-en-scène* vary from the restricted spaces of Paco's shack to wide terrain outdoors, so too the contrast varies from very low in Paco and Régula's unlit shack, to high in open-air shots. The filmstock is low in colour contrast, in keeping with the uninspired terrain and bleakness of life around the *cortijo* and filming took place in the Castilian winter.

CINEMATOGRAPHY IN *LA ARDILLA ROJA*

Medem's 1993 film combines action sequences which would not be out of place in contemporary Hollywood with the arthouse values of metaphor, enigmatic characters and experiment in technique. The visuals of the opening sequence are stunning: the camera begins its movement from a shot of the black night sky, then slowly tilts down to discover Jota facing away towards the sea; then the camera rises above him (a crane shot) showing him on the edge of a high sea wall with the waves crashing violently below; this is then cut to an equally dramatic reverse shot from the sea looking up at the tiny figure of Jota who now looks down into the abyss and contemplates jumping; frustrated by his lack of resolve, Jota breaks the bars of the sea wall and this is interrupted by the arrival of a motorbike which crashes into the same bars further along. The connection between this non-jumper and the accidental faller is made by the startling camera movement, rapidly along the bars as if by some kind of telephonic communication. Then we get a dramatic point of view shot of the rider as she flies over the edge. When Jota goes to rescue her, a shaky hand-held shot, now from his point of view, confirms he is limping after kicking the railings. Their first conversation strangely subverts the traditional shot/reverse shot pattern because he looks at her eyes (the only thing visible) upside down. The visuals amount to more than stylistic exuberance: Medem has visually told us how two desperate strangers have escaped death closely together, one by falling, the other by not falling, and how their subjective point of view has been altered by this meeting.

But this is only the beginning. This film exhibits a technique which includes slow motion, as Jota relates how he was able to catch one helmet while he still had the other in his hands, fast motion as mad driver Félix approaches the campsite, and a spectacular car accident as Félix drives his car over a cliff. A fluid camera is allowed to roam into the rarest of territories: underwater, it adopts the point of view of someone or something unexplained; from inside a juke box, it appears to look out at Elisa. It even manages an impossible extreme close-up inside Elisa's pants. But the sequence which introduces the film's parallel protagonists, the squirrels, is perhaps the one that best encapsulates Medem's technique. Beginning on a television image of the red squirrel documentary in its 'lush and enigmatic wood', the camera tracks back and pans to Jota asleep in bed, a picture on the bedside table of him with his girlfriend; this then fades into a dream sequence: as the voice-over of the documentary relates the mating habits of squirrels – the aggression of the males and cunning of the females – we see images of Jota with his girlfriend, with Elisa; but then, the hand-held camera takes up the point of view of the squirrel inside the undergrowth as it scurries up a tree to a vantage point from which to observe the lovers, a delightful twist on the nature documentary where humans normally watch animals. Jota's dream, taking its cue from the soundtrack of the TV documentary, condenses his preoccupations: his masculine insecurity in the face of other males and the manipulation of the females, his confused perspective, and his fear about being discovered in this mating game.

SOUND

Sound is frequently ignored by film critics, just as audiences tend to take it for granted. But remove it and viewers will notice immediately the powerful effect of silence. For sound is perhaps the most instantaneous medium for getting the audience's attention, and helping to bring together and focus our perceptions of image and sound as one. How we perceive any image projected on the screen is strongly determined by the accompanying sound. It is the omnipresence of sound, coming from multiple sources and multiple directions, that leads humans in everyday life to filter out irrelevant material. The task of cinema is to replicate that process, offering us many and varied sounds at any given moment, but cueing us to identify certain sounds and give them special attention, as we do with the unexplained, unseen sound effects, the 'bumps in the night' that contribute to the suspense in Amenábar's *Los otros*. Of the three types of sound – speech, music and noise – dialogue is normally prioritized, since it often drives the narrative. Therefore dialogue tends to be reproduced to achieve maximum sonic clarity. Dialogue sequences are usually accompanied by a corresponding drop in the level of music and/or sound effects. In *Bienvenido Míster Marshall* (Luis G. Berlanga, 1952), the background noise of the enthusiastic crowd is alternately lowered for the words of the Mayor in his balcony speech and raised for the crowd's reaction shots. But background noise would be missed if absent (Bordwell and Thompson, 2001: 296). A good example of this requirement are the conversations between Isabel and Juan in *Calle Mayor* (Juan Antonio Bardem, 1956). The first time they stroll along the main street chatting, they are constantly interrupted by the greetings of acquaintances, and the soundtrack layers their conversation over the background noise of a busy street. The second time they walk together, we hear only their speech, and the 'emptiness' behind, recorded in a studio without added noise, is strangely jarring for the viewer. Sound technology in Spanish cinema lagged behind other countries from the beginning, and right up to the 1980s, this quality deficit is noticeable. Films which are dubbed later (post synchronization) often have dialogue which sounds as if it has been recorded in a sound studio, while those attempts at direct sound (recording while filming) have not always proved altogether successful. Many contemporary directors in Spain still prefer to use non-Spanish sound engineers.

As with the photographic image, film sound can be manipulated to create an enormous range of effects. But sound has two features which distinguish it from the visual image: whereas the eye has to take in details sequentially, the ear is 'able to absorb a number of distinct sound sources simultaneously' (Nelmes, 1996: 110). This allows the mixing of up to 16 tracks of sound, each independently controllable (Monaco, 1981: 106). Sound recorded on the set at the same time as shooting the picture ('direct sound'), may not be usable, and a bad take of sound can be much more easily repaired or replaced than a bad shot. Alternatively, in post-dubbing or looping, a few seconds of film are formed into a loop that is projected in a sound studio and repeated many times, so that the actors can catch the rhythm of the scene and then mouth their dialogue in synchronization with the image. On-location recording and direct sound have now become the rule rather than the exception (Monaco, 1981: 105). The advantages of multiple soundtracks are counter-balanced by a limitation, which stems from the second difference between sound and image: unlike film images which can be recorded discretely, sound must be recorded continuously, and the speed of sound cannot be changed without altering its quality (Monaco, 1981: 98). Consequently, rapid cutting between different soundtracks does not work in the way that it can in montage images, nor can altering the speed of filming or projection usually benefit sound.

Sound is not an isolated element of a finished film. Rather it relates to other film elements, giving it dimensions in rhythm, fidelity, space and time. Rhythm is based on the fact that sound has a duration. Most of the time, the rhythms of the images on the screen (the result of editing, see next section), will match the rhythm of the sound, whether it be dialogue, noise or music. In Carlos Saura's films based on dance performances, the music clearly directs the editing of the images. But a film maker may also wish, at times, to play on the disjunctures between the rhythms of editing and music, as in the case of Basilio Martín Patino's cleverly assembled documentary, *Canciones para después de una guerra* (1971, released 1976), a montage of newsreel footage, words and songs from the 1940s and 1950s. Fidelity refers to faithfulness of the sound to the source as we know it. If a film shows us a bull snorting, we expect the sound to conform to our idea of how that sounds in real life. But if we hear a different sound, then there is a disjuncture or lack of fidelity, usually for a specific effect. The use of unfaithful sounds abounds in comedies, a famous example being the 'baaing' of sheep superimposed on the hunting party in Berlanga's *La escopeta nacional* (1977).

Sound is emitted from a source and thus has a spatial dimension. As spectators, our conventional understanding of where sounds come from has a major impact on how we 'read' and understand the sound and hence the film. Most specialists differentiate between diegetic and non-diegetic sound. Diegetic sound has its source in the 'story', normally in the framed image. Characters speaking, a radio playing, a car braking or the sounds of a city street are all sounds that can be produced or reproduced on a soundtrack in synchronization with images of those objects. Thus, sound can help to create a locale. But diegetic sound can also be off-screen (Bordwell and Thompson, 1993: 306). *El sur* (Víctor Erice, 1983) starts with off-screen, diegetic sound (a dog barking) accompanying virtual darkness apart from a faint light from a window, and continues with the young Estrella hearing her mother go up and down the stairs frantically looking for her husband, who is missing. Finally, we have internal diegetic sound, the voice or thoughts inside the character's head (Bordwell and Thompson, 2001: 307).

Non-diegetic sound is any sound which is not perceived to be coming from the world of the film story. This could be in the form of a narrator, such as the voice of Fernando Rey in *Bienvenido Míster Marshall*, which is non-diegetic because this narrator is not a character in the story, but an omniscient commentator on it. But by far the most important non-diegetic sound throughout the history of the cinema has been music. Although music can be diegetic as, for example, in the stage performances of films like Jaime Chávarri's *Las cosas del querer* (1989) or Saura's *Bodas de sangre* (1981), *Carmen, Sevillanas* (1992) and *Flamenco* (1995), most often music represents non-diegetic, added-on sound. And despite the fact that it is not realistic to have an orchestra playing constantly in the fictional world of a film, music is one area in which we willingly suspend disbelief (Roberts and Wallis, 2001: 66), accepting that this musical score, though not motivated in the story, can be justified for its emotional effects. Since the beginnings of cinema, when piano, organ or even orchestral performances in film theatres accompanied the silent images, audiences have accepted the convention that a musical score enhances a film in a way that, alas, it never does in real life. But just how does music enhance cinema? Claudia Gorbman presents the ways in which music is used in films:

> Areas of concern are the ways in which music inflects scenes with emotional and dramatic resonance, suggests character, setting, and mood, influences perceptions of narrative time and space, creates formal unity and a sense of continuity, interacts with human speech and other sounds, and compensates for the loss of 'liveness' and spatial depth that characterize the cinema's elder sibling, the theatre. (1998: 44)

The huge range of possibilities offered by film music reflects the fact that music is non-representational: unlike photographic images, which irremediably reflect objects, music is much more open to subjective, emotional interpretation. Sometimes, the musical score of a film may be what remains with the viewer most once they have left the cinema, hence the huge market in CD recordings of film music. Research into just how music works on the film viewer is ongoing, but theorists such as Claudia Gorbman have identified 'two potential displeasures' which threaten the spectator's experience and which music can counter. Music can elicit certain responses from the viewer where there might otherwise be ambiguity: Bernardo Bonezzi's score for *Mujeres al borde de un ataque de nervios* tells us the car chase is to be read as comedy rather than violent thriller. And by its continuous nature, music can efface the discontinuities of the visual images caused by editing, special effects, etc. (Gorbman, 1998: 47). Not all music is used in this way, however. The use of popular songs works against classic Hollywood's conception of film music as an 'inaudible' accompaniment. Any song chosen by a director for the soundtrack of a film will bring its own cultural codes, which may or may not chime with the accompanying images. In *Bienvenido Míster Marshall*, Carmen Vargas, 'the greatest star of Andalusian song', makes an exception to her usual style in the Mayor's Western dream sequence, appearing on the saloon stage singing 'Though I'm from Arizona, I will sing flamenco style'.

Sound, both diegetic and non-diegetic, often works in conjunction with editing in the cinema. In its simplest form, sound can direct the attention of the viewer. A noise which sounds like a creaking door will encourage us to look for a door in the image or anticipate one in the next image (Bordwell and Thompson, 2001: 292). Another common usage is the dialogue overlap, where, instead of holding the shot on the speaker until they have finished talking, a cut is made for the listener's response as soon as a 'telling word or question has been uttered' (Bordwell and Thompson, 2001: 298). And where images are broken up, sound can reinforce continuity of action, either by a sound bridge (where diegetic sound continues from one shot to the next) or by the continuation of music from one shot or sequence to the next. In contemporary cinema, sound bridges tend to 'celebrate' transitions rather than disguising them in the traditional style of continuity editing (Nelmes, 1996: 110). Where montage or rapid cutting is used, the rhythm of these cuts can be matched to the sonic rhythms of the music or other sounds (Bordwell and Thompson, 2001: 302). The Latin rhythms of *Barrio* often form the soundtrack to rapid montage sequences, frequently bridging between shots.

SOUND IN *CARNE TRÉMULA*

Bernardo Menz's sound for Pedro Almodóvar's film *Carne trémula* (1997) provides a good example of the potential of sound in film. At key moments, sound takes precedence over image. The first event of the film is depicted by off-screen diegetic sound: Isabel's hysterical scream misdirects the viewer to think, perhaps, that some violence is being done to her, and only later do we discover that she is in labour. The radio announcement of the 1970 declaration of a state of exception (a suspension of civil liberties by the panicked and shaky Franco regime in its dying years), continues throughout the sequence in the background, demonstrating how, despite the actions of the state, the drama of everyday life goes on. In the next scene, Almodóvar circumvents the messy problem of visually depicting a birth on screen, replacing it with an aural version which is also a stroke of comic genius. As landlady Doña Centro rolls up her sleeves to deliver Isabel's baby on the public bus, her commands 'Keep going, keep going...' continue on the soundtrack even when the shot moves outside to a long shot of the exterior of the bus, upon which the vehicle itself seems to obey her instructions pushing forward with difficulty. The remainder of the birth, including the cutting of the umbilical cord (with the landlady's teeth) is depicted visually at a long distance. A crane shot gradually homes in on the bus, but we follow the action via the dialogue, Centro's instructions to the new mother and the sounds of the baby's cries. This is not verisimilitude (we could not possibly hear so well from high above the bus) but it is very effective, capturing the drama, edging it slightly towards the comic, and avoiding the blood. This aural intimacy, compensating for visual distance, is paralleled at the end with the birth of Víctor's own child in a car: mother Elena's screams from the contractions echo Isabel's, and here too, we hear them from the perspective of a long crane shot above the car. Background noise also helps to establish a contrast between these two very different historical periods. In the 1970s sequence, the outdoor birth is punctuated by a grim silence (there is a curfew in operation), but in the 1996 sequence, Víctor's words and his partner's screams compete with the noise of a busy Madrid street.

Elsewhere, and as in most films, the majority of the sound is synchronous and diegetic. Much of the soundtrack is used in a straightforward manner to depict a locale: the echo in Isabel's room, in the stairwell of Elena's apartment, or in David's massive loft apartment where he practises basketball. And after the claustrophobic, intimate sound of Víctor's prison cell, the busy street is suggested as much by its outdoor, multifarious sounds as by the visual shot. Simple sound effects are also used, such as the various gunshots, but these are often amplified and given an echo, the sound manipulation paralleling the way in which Almodóvar plays with the camera and editing. And sound is used as a simple cueing device: we hear Clara's phone ring and expect to see it; sure enough, the next shot shows Clara's phone as she picks up the receiver. Another example of this off-screen diegetic sound occurs while we watch David folding away his wheelchair ready to leave Víctor's house: we hear a voice (Clara's) saying 'I've brought you something', which cues us to a cut showing her taking a futon out of the boot of her car. Sound can also be used to punctuate rapid cutting, as when the click of David's camera shutter is matched to a sequence of shots which zoom out from a close-up of Víctor and Clara through their windows to the revelation of David spying on them and photographing them. Sonic/visual matching is also used for the action sequence of the basketball practice: the rhythm of the music (the Afro Celt Sound System group) accompanies rapid cutting to convey speed.

Diegetic sound can be used in highly imaginative ways. The narrator of the NO-DO (official Spanish newsreel), imitating the typical voice of the cinema newsreels, accompanies the black and white images of Isabel in hospital with her new arrival; a narrator would usually break the audience's perception of the fictional world of the film, but here one is diegetically justified as part of this 'film within the film'. There are also several examples of internal diegetic sound in the shape of the common device of using a voice-over to relate a letter (Isabel's to her son and his response). Later, we have a voice-over of Clara's goodbye letter to Víctor which is recorded over intercut images of her writing as well as Víctor himself and the other protagonists of the story as they converge for the climactic conflict scene. Much earlier, there is a good example of how sound can contrast physical and mental spaces. Elena's preoccupation with Víctor is marked by sound: when she is bathing her husband David, she recalls Víctor's words to her '*Te sono molto vicino*' (which we hear 'inside her head') and her internal diegetic voice contrasts with the external diegetic voice (the 'here and now') of her husband David, who is talking beneath the water, his voice literally drowned out.

Sound bridges account for more than half the scene changes in this film, functioning perhaps as reinforcing connectors in a film which could easily become too dispersed (there are five main protagonists). They can also help to ease abrupt changes in tempo, tone or mood. At the end of the film, Elena's screams at the sound of gunshot are replaced on soundtrack by David's voice-over letter of guilt, while we still see images of her still screaming. His calm explanation then flows 'smoothly' into the images of Víctor and Elena's new life together. Another good example is the sound bridge that connects the 1970 sequence with the next, 20 years later: 'a life on wheels' is the newsreel narrator's conclusion about Víctor's lifetime bus pass, and it forms a bridge, along with the opening bars of '*Mi perro*', to the main narrative section of the film. Music and sound have together provided a continuity to an opening 10 minutes of film which spans 20 years. The same theme tune is also used at the very end to provide a further degree of formal coherence.

Unlike Almodóvar's earlier films which often contain performances, *Carne trémula*'s music is entirely non-diegetic. Much of the excellent score by Alberto Iglesias functions in a very conventional way, guiding the emotional responses of the viewer with regard to characters, setting and mood. In common with much genre film, the score exploits the potential of music to build tension, for example in the shooting scene during which the music is virtually constant. In fact, Iglesia's scored music is present in much of the film without actually distracting the viewer. In this aspect *Carne trémula* is consistent with most genre films. But there are some moments when the use of music is self-consciously, almost parodically inscribed. During an early sequence when policeman David persuades Víctor to hand over his impromptu hostage Elena, she passes David, mesmerized by the policeman's composure, and this is punctuated by a slow-motion shot and melodramatic string music suggesting almost love at first sight between them.

Elsewhere, popular songs are used where music, lyrics and associated cultural references also come into play. Early on, the song 'Mi perro' is used to multiple effect. First of all, it helps to sustain what would otherwise be an over-lengthy tracking shot of Madrid low life. On one level, the lyrics of the song provide an ironic contrast: the loyal, noble canine friends contrasting with the drug-dealers and pimps. Viewers cannot help but wonder if our lowly hero Víctor is also to be treated like a dog. But beyond the literal significance of its lyrics, the song, by La Niña de Antequera, conveys a sense of longing for a rural existence long departed in 1990s Spain, and thus provides a poignant sound bridge from the 1970 to the 1990 sequence. Later, when Víctor sees TV pictures of a successful David from the prison cafeteria, his bitter reaction is depicted by the suspension of the diegetic sound around him (the noises of the other inmates) and its replacement by the all-consuming soundtrack of Albert Pla's song '*Sufre como yo*' (Suffer like me) which speaks his feeling much more eloquently than any dialogue or action.

EDITING

Editing is the process by which shots are selected, ordered and spliced together from the 'takes' of recorded film so that the finished film can produce certain effects in the audience in respect of space, time, narrative structure, rhythm and visual impact. The mechanics of editing are described by Monaco:

> The shot is the basic unit of film construction; it is defined, physically, as a single piece of film, without breaks in the continuity of the action. It may last around 10 minutes (since most cameras hold only 10 minutes of film); it may be as short as 1/24 second (one frame) [Each shot] must be physically spliced with cement or tape to the shots which precede and follow it. The craft of editing consists of choosing between two or more takes of the same shot, deciding how long each shot should last and how it should be punctuated, and matching the soundtrack carefully with the edited images (or vice versa if the soundtrack is edited first) (1981: 104–5).

Even more than in other components of film making, the aspiration to be invisible has characterized much editing. Encouraging the audience to 'enter the world of the film' (its diegesis) is dependent on *not* reminding us that we are watching a film (Abrams, Bell and Udris, 2001: 104). Avoiding anything which disrupts the viewing experience is known as continuity editing, a set of conventions that even by the 1920s had become the norm for dominant Hollywood cinema. Much of the time it is concerned with what we might call simple logic: if a character leaves the screen to the right through a doorway, followed by a cut to his appearance on the other side of the door, we expect him to enter the next shot from the left. If he enters from the right it will disrupt our sense of space. Similarly, if one shot shows a man in a taxi, we might logically expect a subsequent shot to reveal where he is going; if, on the other hand, the next shot shows him getting out of bed, this will disrupt our sense of time.

Continuity editing is designed to give maximum support to the viewer's attempt to 'construct' a story, in space and time, from the visual and aural information given. This narrative function in editing takes the form of questions and answers as the viewer looks for connections between shots. *Bienvenido Mister Marshall* has many examples of sequences connected by the last word in one scene forming the first word in the next, or a question asked in one sequence and then, quite literally, answered in the next. As Katz states, 'the simplest question and answer pattern requires only two shots – a shot of a person looking off-screen, followed by a shot of the object the person is observing' (1991: 147). Making connections between two shots (editing) thus corresponds to making connections between events (narrative). Editing necessarily selects which spaces to show the viewer, and which moments. More often than not, both the spaces shown and the time depicted are less than the diegesis – the space and time covered by the story. In such cases, editing can help the viewer to construct a coherent space and time frame for the diegesis. A typical exposition of spatial relationships will begin with an establishing shot of a general location, for example, a cityscape, and might be followed by a shot of a street or building, before moving to an interior shot of an apartment. Even though the building shown might not be really located in the city in the previous shot, and the interior might be filmed in a studio, the audience will accept and assume these three shots are different views of the same overall space. Even where no establishing shot appears, any series of shots of different spaces prompts the spectator to infer a spatial whole on the basis of seeing only portions of that space, and this is known as the 'Kuleshov effect' (Bordwell and Thompson, 2001: 259). Other conventions work to a similar objective: if a character looks off-screen at something, the next shot shows what they are looking at, and this is called an 'eye-line match'; and after a shot of one character speaking to another, the camera often takes a 'reverse angle' to film the second character's response. This does not correspond to the human eye, as no single person can jump from one character's point of view to that of another. But through frequent use in a century of cinema, this device has become an accepted convention.

Equally, editing allows the film maker to either compress or extend time. Of the two, extending time is much rarer, and is normally reserved for action scenes or moments of great drama where slowing down the image allows us to fully appreciate the detail of the action. A two-hour film can cover a story lasting up to centuries. Ellipsis is the omission of periods of time deemed surplus to the requirements of the story. Humans eat, sleep and use the bathroom, but these time-consuming activities are frequently left out of filming. A simple cut does not in itself imply the passage of time. Katz refers to the cut as 'a present tense segue' (1991: 321). But in fact, a cut is the most frequent device used to compress time and eliminate unnecessary activity. A woman is in bed when she hears the doorbell. Rather than follow her with the camera to the door, down the stairs and out onto the doorstep, a shot of her getting up will then cut to another of her on the stairs and then, a third from the point of view of her postman as he waits for her to open the door. Unless the *way in which* she crosses the room and descends the stairs is important, this process can be compressed with no disbenefits to the diegesis. Cuts like these must perform this ellipsis unobtrusively, normally by cutting away to another element of the scene (e.g. the waiting postman) or by changing the camera angle sufficiently so that the second shot is clearly from a different position. For such ellipses to function, each sequential shot needs to follow chronological time clearly (except for flashbacks, which require special cueing – see below).

Cutting can also enable the film maker to depict two events in the story occurring at the same time: a typical example might show one character searching for something, and another who, simultaneously, has already discovered it. Cross cutting in this way can be particularly useful in creating and maintaining suspense. A good example comes towards the end of Almodóvar's *Carne trémula* when all five main characters converge on Víctor's home in what will turn out to be the film's final confrontation. The rhythm of a film is affected by editing. The length of each shot determines the pace of action (Roberts and Wallis, 2001: 38). A rapid succession of shots has the effect of speeding up the action, as happens during the fight scene between the landlady and Ángel in *El día de la bestia*.

Apart from the straight cut, a shift from one image to the next, which involves connecting one strip of film to another (end to end), there are various transition edits which overlap one piece of film with another. In a dissolve, one image is superimposed onto another. It normally implies a change of space or time, and can be one cue for a flashback (another is where the 'present' image goes out of focus and dissolves into the flashback image, which gradually comes into focus). A fade from black or to black has the effect of setting off episodes from one another like chapter headings (Katz, 1991: 324). And a wipe, though extremely rare since the 1940s, is usually a cross-frame movement of a new shot over an old one, resembling a curtain being drawn (though wipes can be vertical, horizontal, diagonal, circular, square or spiral-shaped) (Katz, 1991: 323). These transitions, which are achieved in the editing suite, form part of what is known as opticals. Opticals also include multiple images (split-screen), freeze frame and masking. The laboratory also adjusts the image to correspond with what the director had in mind while shooting, and can alter the colour, light and size of the images (Monaco, 1981: 110).

The majority of the devices explained above serve traditional continuity editing. By no means all films follow the principles of continuity editing entirely. Discontinuity, whether graphic, rhythmic, spatial or temporal discontinuity, have all been used to create somewhat different effects (Bordwell and Thompson, 2001: 278). Godard used the jump cut – an abrupt, discontinuous edit – as part of his playful counter-cinema in films like *À bout de souffle* (1959). A systematic alternative to continuity is dialectical montage, championed by Soviet film makers and especially Sergei Eisenstein. Where editing in the US refers to the cutting away of unwanted material, the European-style 'montage' refers more to the dialectical process that creates a third meaning out of the original two meanings of the adjacent shots (Monaco, 1981: 183). Soviet film theorist Pudovkin identified five types of montage: contrast, parallelism, symbolism, simultaneity, and leit motif (1960). In these cases, rather than suggesting logical spatial and temporal connections, the juxtaposition of shots can be conflicting, or have a metaphorical or purely aesthetic function. Some of these tendencies of discontinuity are found in Buñuel and Dalí's celebrated *Un chien andalou* (1929) while Bardem's *Calle Mayor* (1956) is a clear example of continuity style supporting a classic narrative structure.

EDITING IN *CALLE MAYOR*

This film follows the conventions of continuity editing with every choice about where and how to cut made on the basis of spatial, temporal and logical continuity. As the narrative follows an entirely chronological path with no flashbacks, the temporal aspect of the editing concerns only ellipsis. The action transpires over the course of many days, but is condensed here into a film of 97 minutes. Although the dissolve to indicate the passage of time is also used, straight cuts are the most frequent, as most events occur shortly after previous ones in the diegesis. Especially accomplished are a few examples of cuts which correspond literally to the question and answer pattern outlined above. In one example, Isabel worries that something might go wrong in her new relationship with Juan, and her maid asks her 'What could go wrong?' This then cuts abruptly to Juan's friends shouting 'Nothing!' in answer to his question about what can be done to solve the problem of their cruel joke.

The way the editing enables the viewer to construct a coherent space for the action is also entirely conventional. The film begins with an establishing shot of the provincial town before a fade to the Calle Mayor (High Street) itself. The film is shot in various locations (under the orders of the Spanish censors who did not want the film to identify a particular geographical location), but they coalesce in the finished film as one town. Similarly, the various interiors filmed on different sets at the Charmartín studios north of Madrid are made to suggest a town and all its interiors. For example, when the group of young men mockingly refer to Juan's friend Federico '*el intelectual*' they bang on the floor with a billiard cue, suggesting he is on the floor below; a cut to the library reveals Federico talking to the writer, and they look up in response to the banging sound. In reality, both sets would be at ground level but editing (including sound) can suggest otherwise.

Elsewhere, editing is put to dramatic effect. Shots of Juan in his room wrestling with his conscience over the terrible trick he is playing on Isabel are intercut four times with shots of Isabel on her bed thinking about Juan and saying his name in different tones of voice. The music is also dramatically edited: sombre and tense for Juan; light and romantic for Isabel. And when Juan falsely proposes to Isabel during the procession, long shots of the soldiers marching are intercut with Juan talking to Isabel. We cannot hear their dialogue over the din of the brass band but suddenly there is a lull and we hear Juan say 'and I love you' as all eyes turn on him: there are then rapid cuts to close-ups of the almost grotesque faces of old, ugly women looking disapprovingly on.

EDITING IN *UN CHIEN ANDALOU*

It is hard to imagine now the impact Buñuel and Dalí's surrealist classic had at the time of its release in 1929, and three-quarters of a century of writing has not produced a definitive reading of this deliberately confusing film. This anti-narrative, anti-causality film has been interpreted as an attempt to mimic the free association of dreams as a 'truer' or superior sort of reality, and to reflect the liberating force of unconscious, unrestrained sexual desires.

Leaving aside the controversy over the film makers' intention, a closer look at the film's editing reveals some surprises. While a standard fiction film of 1½ to 2 hours can comprise 500 to 1000 separate shots (Monaco, 1981: 104), *Un chien andalou* lasts only 15 minutes but nevertheless comprises some 298 shots, making the average shot length only three seconds. Even discounting the 'content' of the images themselves, the very pace of this film and the number of images in quick succession would be unsettling for an audience that only a decade earlier was used to cinema as static, a filmed tableau. But looking at how these shots are edited is perhaps even more surprising. Of the 298 shots, only 30 break with continuity editing. Given the surrealist aim of automatic writing, this attempt to reconstruct the anarchic and opaque world of dreams relies upon (highly conventional) standard continuity editing for 90 per cent of its cuts. Of the remaining 30 edits which break continuity, only three involve a complete temporal, spatial, logical break, and they all come together: a close-up of the man's hand crawling with ants fades to the underarm hair of a woman, then to a sea urchin and finally to an aerial shot of a girl in the street with a severed hand. These edits offer no links in time, place or logical explanation to the audience. On three occasions, only spatial continuity is broken: the man is first on one side of a door with his hand trapped, then, without explanation or any break in the action, he is lying on a bed in the contiguous room. The second man (is it the first man's alter ego?) is killed indoors but falls to the ground in a park. And the woman exits an interior door in the middle of a city and appears on the other side outside on a beach. Temporality is abandoned without explanation in four edits where titles tell us of a change in time frame, but not in a way that allows us to reconstruct a story. Of the remaining 20 breaks, some could be accepted by audiences as representing the interior or fantasy world of the protagonist, for example, as he feels the woman's breasts through her dress but imagines them first as naked, then as having turned into her buttocks. Most of these illogical connections, however, remain a mystery to the audience, famous examples being the dead horse, the priests dragged along behind pianos, or the infamous eye-slitting.

This tells us two things about editing: first, it reveals just how firmly established the conventions of continuity editing already were in the 1920s and how hard they had become to resist, even in this most rebellious of filmic adventures; and second, given the film's stubborn resistance to interpretation, or to the construction of a coherent diegesis, it tells us how few (10 per cent) anti-continuity editing choices are necessary to throw the audience completely off the trail of a story. Having looked at editing and how it often serves narrative, in the next section we will look in more detail at film narrative.

NARRATIVE

Narrative concerns the stories told by films and the ways in which the viewer constructs these stories from the filmed material provided in the finished movie. Telling or re-telling stories became cinema's main objective very early in its history. A photographic image asks questions of us, making us want to know the stories behind the images; and once technology permitted moving images, their very nature – showing transformations from one state to another – inferred narrative. Merely by joining pieces of film together, a film maker encourages a viewer to look for connections. As Bordwell and Thompson put it, 'Given an incident, we tend to hypothesize what might have caused it, or what it might in turn cause' (2001: 63). Add to this the fact that film copied the respectable arts of the theatre and the novel, both of which told stories (Aumont, Bergala, Marie and Vernet, 1992: 68), and it is clear how naturally cinema turned to storytelling.

We will see how narrative works in favour of both 'realism' (because it follows a logic much like real life), and 'entertainment' (because it complies with conventions from which we derive pleasure) (Ellis, 1982: 63). Critical to the film maker is the assumption that the viewers will be able to construct a story (*the* story) from the sound and images. First the scriptwriter and then the editor choose which elements of a story to present to us on film in the plot. Then we put them all together and make the story as best we can. We have seen how, on one level, editing choices are governed by a simple question-and-answer principle: in terms of the narrative, too, 'we work actively at making sense of the individual scenes and particularly at predicting the story'(Nelmes, 1996: 88).

Narrative can be restricted (where we know only as much as the characters) and unrestricted or omniscient (where we know more than any of the characters). Not all narratives have a narrator. The idea of a voice-over indicating a guiding narrator is much rarer in cinema than in the novel. The type of narrator who is not a character, but who sounds like a voice of reason interpreting the images and sound for us, is associated with documentary film making. This is the effect sought by the narrators at the start of *Bienvenido Míster Marshall* and *Calle Mayor*. Where a narrator is a character, as is the case in films like *El diputado* (Eloy de la Iglesia, 1978), the result is a highly subjective narrative, following one character's point of view on events. In both these cases, having a non-screen voice commentary draws attention to the artifice of film. Many films have preferred to avoid anything which reminds the viewer that the film is constructed. Narrative film's overriding priority is verisimilitude: every element from *mise-en-scène*, cinematography, sound, editing and structure is designed to draw the viewer into the world of the film. This mode of film production is so established that critic Noel Burch referred to it as the Institutional Mode of Representation. More commonly, it is simply referred to as classic narrative cinema or 'classical Hollywood narrative' because the tradition dominated Hollywood from 1930s to 1960s. But its conventions have become those of narrative cinema everywhere and the overwhelming majority of Spanish films studied today are to a considerable degree within the same tradition.

Classic narrative cinema comprises a series of conventions that can be seen operating in almost every film. Their structure takes the form 'order/disorder/new order restored' (Roberts and Wallis, 2001: 54). As Todorov explained it, an opening equilibrium is disrupted, requiring action which leads to a resolution and the establishing, at the end, of a new equilibrium (Abrams, Bell and Udris, 2001: 136). The narrative is linear, meaning that time runs forward chronologically. Any digressions or flashbacks must be identified as such (see Editing, above). The action of the narrative is governed by the norms of cause and effect: we need to be able to see why things happen, what causes something else to happen, and these causal relations always concern the characters. Normally, only one or two characters provide the focus, and it is their motivations and resulting actions which drive the narrative. In Hollywood, the hero is often male, and this masculine agency, coupled with frequently passive female characters, has made for fascinating reading by those interested in gender representations on film (see Chapter Six). Finally, these films have a high degree of closure: all mysteries are resolved, characters settle into a stable existence and no loose ends are left dangling. These conventions may seem a constraint, but in fact, many extremely varied stories and scenarios can be made to fit them. Quite apart from their orientation towards verisimilitude, which aids audience involvement and identification, it is clear that audiences actually derive pleasure from the conventions them-selves. A certain satisfaction comes from being able to predict outcomes and having your expectations fulfilled (or sometimes not).

Given the high degree of formal conventionality in this type of cinema, it is not surprising that many different styles of film making have developed in reaction against it. One of the most famous of these alternative practices is Soviet montage cinema which privileges discontinuity, juxtaposition of images and the clash of ideas over a 'story' (Roberts and Wallis, 2001: 57). Alternative practices in narrative can function on any number of the conventions described above: the film may eschew storytelling altogether; it may have multiple narrative strands rather than a single diegesis. In some cases the narrative is foregrounded, that is, the fictionality or 'constructedness' of the film is emphasized by breaking the illusion of reality. It may stress the contingency of real life (open endings) rather than the closure of fiction. Many European films pull back from the wholesale rejec-tion of classic narrative cinema, and a more common alternative practice is to 'rebel' in only some of the categories. This is the case with our second narrative case study, Saura's *Cría cuervos*. But first let us briefly examine a classic narrative text in operation.

NARRATIVE IN *AMANTES*

Vicente Aranda's *Amantes* is an example of classic narrative cinema. It comprises a linear narrative with no flashbacks or other disruptions in time, and temporal editing concerns only ellipsis (cutting out unimportant details to forward the narrative). *Mise-en-scène*, cine-matography and editing serve verisimilitude, and the omniscient narration, with no narra-tor, furthers transparency (never drawing attention to the fact that this is a film). Human agency clearly pushes forward the plot, the motivations of the three main characters each driving the action. The male protagonist, Paco, leaves the army, ready to start a life with girlfriend Trini. This equilibrium is broken by his landlady, the experienced, overtly sexual

Luisa. The disorder she represents is, moreover, a prototype from classic Hollywood films, the *femme fatale* whose presence corrupts the upright male. The action of the film is clearly presented as a chain of events governed by cause and effect relationships:

Paco needs a room > meets landlady Luisa > falls in love with Luisa > girlfriend Trini resolves to win him back by offering him her virginity, turning herself into a *femme fatale* to match her rival > Paco decides to marry Trini but can't stop thinking about Luisa. Luisa needs money to pay off her criminal associates > Paco decides to get the money from Trini's savings so invents the purchase of a bar to get hold of the money > when Trini discovers this betrayal she begs Paco to kill her and he does.

After the murder and Paco's triumphant demonstration of his bloody hands to his lover Luisa, a closing title informs us that 'three days later police arrest Paco and Luisa'. As this film is based on a real story, the update adds to the impression of reality, which the film's adherence to verisimilitude has tried to maintain throughout. In stark contrast to this film, which ties up the loose ends of the story even beyond the limits of screen time, a film like *Cría cuervos* poses as many questions as it provides answers.

NARRATIVE IN *CRÍA CUERVOS*

Carlos Saura's 1975 film is a narrative film with a story to tell. But its diegetic structure is very different from classic narrative cinema, and its complexity makes difficult the task of unravelling the story for even the most careful and sophisticated analyst of narration. It tells the story of Ana, the nine-year-old second daughter of three in a middle-class Madrid family, from the death of her father and the arrival of their aunt Paulina as head of the household, to the girls' return to school at the end of the summer holidays. The sequences set in this 'present tense' are apparently presented chronologically, containing everyday events as well as more exceptional moments, such as their father's wake or confrontations with their new guardian Paulina. These events are episodic, i.e. they do not constitute a chain of cause-and-effect, but rather they reflect discrete episodes in recently orphaned Ana's world. But the film also flashes *back* to the time when Ana's mother was still alive (including her deathbed agony), and *forward* to the adult Ana recalling her childhood from the perspective of 20 years later. It would be possible to regard these adult recollections in the fictional future of 1995 as the present time of the film. They certainly provide the key to solving the 'puzzle' of how the various time frames fit together. A more conventional way of dealing with the multiple time frames would have been for the adult narrator to introduce the story and close it (a device which would have made the film much easier to understand). Between these narrated sections the main story could then have been narrated in a transparent way, following the norms of continuity editing, linear time, causality, human agency in propelling the action, and closure at the end. Closer examination of the text reveals how Saura has actively worked against transparency, drawing attention to the complex narrative structure of his film.

The film begins with the death of Ana's father and her careful washing of the empty glass by his bedside. Then she is joined by her mother, who asks why she is out of bed so late. Because these two events are depicted one after the other with no indication of any change in timeframe, we assume them to be chronological. Only later do we learn that Ana's mother had died *before* her father (and so could not be present at that moment), and that Ana had thought she herself was responsible for his death, having tried to poison him with bicarbonate of soda in his milk (hence the need to wash the glass and remove the evidence). Chronology is further confused when, on the morning of their father's funeral, Ana has her hair combed first by servant Rosa and then by her mother (already dead by this time). And when Rosa later tells Ana how her father used to chase after her (and any other woman within his sphere), Ana's concentrated look off-screen cues a cut to a flashback of him leering at Rosa, only to be discovered by his wife and daughter. This look off-screen suggests the flashbacks are Ana's childhood recollections of an earlier time, but Saura does not make the flashbacks obvious (via dissolves, for example). More tellingly, perhaps, Ana's childhood recollections are shown to be a confused mixture of real memories and fantasy memories. Unable to sleep, Ana goes downstairs and asks her mother to play the piano for her, thus firmly establishing the time as before her mother's death. When she finally agrees to go back to bed, Ana lingers and overhears an argument between her parents in which her mother cries 'I want to die.' Once in bed, she closes her eyes tightly, which appears to summon her mother, who promptly materializes and tells her a story. But then Ana realizes her mother is not there at all and calls out for her. Her new guardian comes instead, and Ana rejects Paulina, imitating her mother's 'I want to die'. The confusion of the two timeframes can thus be attributed to the child Ana rejecting the present and preferring a return to inhabit the past.

The flashbacks are not strongly motivated by means of voice-over ('I remembered my father leering at Rosa...') or opticals (a dissolve to indicate a memory). But transparency and verisimilitude are not abandoned completely. With some effort all these temporal transitions can be fathomed. Saura's technique for the 'flash-forwards' is more radical in its rejection of cinematic convention. Little Ana recovers a tin of what she thinks is poison from the cellar. Then, over the same shot, we hear the voice-over of the adult Ana (dubbed by Spanish actress Julieta Serrano) commenting on the action. As little Ana looks directly at the camera (a taboo in classic narrative and always an anti-cinematic gesture) a pan sideways reveals the adult Ana as if in the same space as her 20-years-younger self. This editing choice, where a dissolve would have safely indicated a change in timeframe, defies continuity editing and spatial/temporal logic (characters from different times appear in the same shot). As the adult Ana continues her recollections we do not – as we might expect – cut to a flashback introduced by her. Rather, her voice-over continues as we cut to the 'present tense' of Ana with her sisters and Paulina sitting at the table.

The action of this film – it is easy to forget that it contains two deaths, attempted poisoning, and adultery – is not arranged in terms of a classic narrative structure of the order/disorder/new order type. There is no closure: the end of screen time leaves Ana recently orphaned and still to come to terms with her childhood traumas; and the adult Ana in the 1995 sections seems no more certain of the inner motivations of her family. Where classic narrative cinema is clear about character motivation and its visible effects in propelling the action forward, here the child's perspective on the adult world of her parents is understandably innocent of the workings of adult motivation. Restricted narration in classic narrative cinema is used to create suspense, which is then relieved when the missing information is supplied in the dénouement of the plot. Here, restricted narration corresponds to a child's limited understanding which can never be fully enlightened as her parents do not live long enough to explain their motivations to her as an adult.

How might we account for Saura's rejection of linearity, character-motivated causality and closure in favour of complex temporal organization and ambiguity? The answer lies in his conception of film as representing reality in all its confusion, rather than as neatly structured fiction. *Cría cuervos* is not about a well-made fiction leading to satisfaction, but rather about the ambiguity of memory which can lead to dissatisfaction. The preference for an elusive and unsettling representation of an elusive and unsettling reality over a satisfyingly conventional fiction typifies a distinctly European attitude to film making. The differences between this European tradition and classic (Hollywood) narrative cinema are discussed in the next section.

STYLE

Analysing film style involves looking at all the details of *mise-en-scène*, cinematography, sound, editing and narrative outlined in earlier sections, identifying which techniques have been preferred and to what purposes. Often, directorial choices centre on dichotomies: location/studio, natural light/artificial light, open/closed framing, camera movement/ cutting, long shot/close-up, diegetic/non-diegetic sound, ambiguity/closure, and so on. And frequently these dichotomies reflect larger debates about purpose and style. The first of these oppositions is between realism and formalism. From the earliest days of cinema, film makers divided into those who saw it as a means of recording and reproducing real life, such as the inventors of cinema, the Lumière brothers, and those who saw film as a medium to turn images into fantasy, such as the magician turned film maker Georges Méliès. The realist cinema tradition prioritizes the faithful reproduction of reality with as little manipulation as possible, and is often more concerned with content and subject matter than with form. In formalism, on the other hand, the *how* rather than the *what* is paramount, and the very idea of a faithful reproduction of reality is questioned. These opposing tendencies in film making (and more particularly in film criticism and theory) found their champions in André Bazin and Sergei Eisenstein respectively.

Bazin argued for a cinema of transparency, which could imitate reality by means of the suppression of film's more manipulative devices in favour of others that he considered more objective. Deep focus photography keeps foreground, mid-ground and background all in sharp focus, thus allowing the viewer to decide where to look within the frame rather than directing attention. And the long-take, he argued, 'might create a kind of democracy of perception', unlike the manipulation of editing which he saw as the 'destruction of cinematic form' (Kolker, 2001: 14). Eisenstein took the opposite view. He championed montage, in which two shots together form a dialectical synthesis (the equivalent of Karl Marx's theory of dialectical materialism) and this was what created meaning (Kolker, 2001: 13). On shots, Eisenstein famously said, 'each taken separately corresponds to an object but their combination corresponds to a concept' (Buckland, 2003: 26). For the formalists, the manipulation of cinema's images according to the expressive inclinations of film makers was what made film an art. The question as to whether film is an art form or not is the basis of our second set of oppositions: between Hollywood conventions and the 'European' art film.

Stylistic differences between Hollywood movies and the European art film stem from the cultures which have produced them. Film emerged as a medium before it was an art. Initially, film's novelty value was exploited in fairground exhibits, thus ascribing to it a commercial objective, and setting forth along the path which leads to the globalized entertainment industry we know today. But, as Monaco points out, the neutrality of the film medium's use meant it could be used to record any of the existing arts, hence its close relationship to them (1981: 20). The film industry in Europe was based in the great cultural capitals of the old continent, and the artists and intellectuals of Paris, London, Rome (as well as Barcelona and Madrid) were keen to explore the potential of cinema. In the USA, the film industry chose to locate itself in the drier, brighter climate of California some three thousand miles away from the cultural capital of the nation, New York. The industry was led not by artists and intellectuals but by businessmen.

The Hollywood 'dream factory' was a production line for entertainment products. The awareness of film's economic potential, and the economies of scale provided by industrial production, quickly led to Hollywood's dominance of the world market in film. Its 'institutional mode of representation' (see Narrative, above) established itself as the norm against which all other types of film making would be judged. Soviet cinema from 1918–1948, German expressionism, Italian neo-realism, the French New Wave and contemporary movements such as Dogme '95 can all be best defined in opposition to Hollywood's mode of production and style. Spanish cinema provides a fascinating case study for the investigation of socio-cultural, political and economic attitudes to cinema. If the UK has been especially vulnerable to the appeal of Hollywood because of common language (and the failure of the state to support cinema), and if countries like Germany, Italy and especially France have boasted strong national film cultures, in Spain the film industry has been weak, despite a strong sense of national identity embodied in other arts and popular culture. Though Hollywood has always dominated the market, national cinema comprises, broadly speaking, two strands: a popular indigenous cinema tailored to Spanish

Table 1: **Stylistic differences between Hollywood conventions and European art film**

Hollywood convention	European art film
Production/Content	Production/Content
mass marketing	niche marketing
commodity	expression of an auteur
self-explanatory film	authorial insight required
pleasure aim	message aim
box office valued	critical reception valued
entertainment and commerce	self-consciousness as art
Mise-en-scène and cinematography	*Mise-en-scène* and cinematography
transparency	celebration of visual style
verisimilitude of fictional world	artistic integrity of fictional world
spectacle	understatement
'invisible' lighting	stylized lighting
Editing and sound	Editing and sound
makes itself invisible	self-conscious
serves narrative	not subservient to narrative
continuity editing (space & time)	plays with space & time
Narrative	Narrative
enigma and resolution	ambiguity
closure	open endings
linear (causality)	non-linear
human agency in narrative progression	not necessarily human agent for narrative progression

audiences and ideologically closer to Hollywood's conservative escapism; and a European tradition of formal experimentation, auteurism (see Chapter Three) and political engagement. From the 1980s and especially the 1990s, the Spanish film industry has gained considerable strength, to the point where it is now arguably one of the healthiest in Europe. Our two case studies in this section illustrate two variants of astonishing success: the first has been widely acclaimed by critics and is firmly in the style of the European art film; the second won mass audiences in Spain, a remake in Hollywood, and is remarkably close to Hollywood's preferred spectacular style. The details of the stylistic differences between the European art film and Hollywood conventions are set out schematically in Table 1, above. Many of them are exemplified in the stylistically worlds apart *El espíritu de la colmena* (Víctor Erice, 1973) and *Abre los ojos* (Alejandro Amenábar, 1997).

STYLE IN *EL ESPÍRITU DE LA COLMENA*

This is a very personal film by one of Spain's most admired auteurs, Víctor Erice. It is a perfect example of an understated, indirect style, in complete opposition to the spectacular entertainment film. Its pace is ponderous, its effects subtle and its message veiled. But time and place are specified, so it is not difficult to read 'between its frames' a political message about Franco's Spain. One of the devices Erice uses to distance the viewer from the world of the film is to cast it in the perspective of six-year-old Ana as she interrogates the world around her and some of its mysteries. The title sequence features drawings by the six-year-old actress Ana Torrent of elements from the film: a train, a mushroom, a house, a well, a cinema screen with a monster and a girl, girls jumping over a fire – all images which subsequently appear in the film. The opening title 'Once upon a time...' indicates that this is the story of a child, though not a children's story. The fairy-tale conception of the film is matched by the Frankenstein movie which foregrounds the film medium as a source of fantasy. The integrity of this fictional world is given priority over verisimilitude, especially in the late sequence where Frankenstein does appear to come to life for Ana, which is not explained in the film.

Mise-en-scène and cinematography work towards the celebration of a coherent visual style. The amber-coloured windows match the octagonal pattern of the beehives. Luis Cuadrado's cinematography uses the expressive potential of colour: a yellow filter for interiors which matches the amber windows and the metaphor of the bees; and then blue for Ana's fantasy world which links back to the cinema and dreams. Locations emphasize wide open spaces (Teresa on her bike, Fernando at his beehives, the girls on the hill overlooking the shack) and even the interiors seem empty, in tune with the lives of Fernando and Teresa. Framing is often symmetrical, as in the shots of the girls skipping through doors of the house, one after another; or in the final image (Ana framed in a window at night), a beautiful painterly tableau, with expressionist lighting creating a chiaroscuro effect. The *mise-en-scène* and lighting used for the girls' night-time conversation is also highly expressive: instead of showing us the girls themselves, we only hear their dialogue over images of shadow puppets through which the girls talk about Ana's visit to the hut; their dialogue continues over paintings in their room (a young girl held by the hand) until their father comes in, signalled by sound and their rapid extinguishing of a candle.

The use of sound and editing is also effective and often very economical in keeping with the understated technique of the film. The depiction of the fugitive's death is highly economical with the sound and flashes of a machine gun in the dark, far from the spectacular shoot-outs in mainstream fugitive films. And the scene featuring Fernando with his bees has the voice-over of his wife Teresa as she writes a letter to a former lover – this is finally cut to a shot of Teresa herself writing. The music is constant, binding the sequence together, as does the amber filter used in both. Later, Fernando can hear the dialogue from the Frankenstein film from his study and the echoing words seem appropriate for him, too. There is then a dissolve to the inside of the cinema, where we see first the audience, then their point of view on the screen images, then back to a close-up of Ana and Isabel enthralled, then back again to the monster with the little girl. The editing links Ana to the characters in the film and especially to the monster. The pursuit of Ana through the woods is like the original Frankenstein film (James Whale, 1931). Some opticals are used which serve to foreground the film medium (as opposed to the transparency of Hollywood convention). Time-lapse photography is used as a shorthand to show day turning into night, and again later to show Fernando has fallen asleep at his desk and now awakes at dawn. Repeated dissolves indicate the gradual arrival of children at school and later they are used again to show an ellipsis, as Isabel and Ana descend the huge field towards the hut. At one moment, editing is used figuratively to link Ana and the fugitive. A close-up of Ana asleep in bed is cut with a similar close-up of the fugitive in exactly the same position (a match-cut), but this shot then reveals Ana in the frame staring at the sleeping man, defying spatial continuity.

Without being excessively self-conscious, this film certainly foregrounds film as a medium. The presenter warns the villagers about the film 'don't take it very seriously' and this links to the next sequence, thus equating that statement with the rest of film. And Isabel tells Ana 'in cinema everything is a lie. It's all false'. In narrative terms this film favours enigma and ambiguity rather than enigma followed by resolution. There is little closure at the end of the film, and not everything that happens can be explained by the actions of the characters. We have shared some moments of mystery with little Ana, but we have not reached any clear answers.

STYLE IN *ABRE LOS OJOS*

Alejandro Amenábar's second commercial feature could not be more different from Erice's film. Action, multiple plot twists and revelations and editing give it a pace much more in line with Hollywood action films. This film makes no apologies for its prioritization of entertainment over any didactic, social or political comment (though it is not completely devoid of thought-provoking questions). Its *mise-en-scène* is consistent with mainstream entertainment cinema, favouring ultra-modern, non-culturally specific locations which serve to universalize the action (as opposed to the culturally and geographically specific of Erice and much of the European art cinema tradition). The world of skyscrapers, where the offices of the futuristic company Life Extension are located is a world away from the *castizo* Madrid we have come to expect in Spanish films. The climactic scene on the rooftop of this building (actually the Torre Picasso) features in the background the hyper-modern diagonally-inclining Torres Kio, which have come to feature in other films of futuristic or apocalyptic Madrid (see *mise-en-scène*, above, on *El día de la bestia*). César's last look back at his dreamed companions Pelayo, Antonio and Sofía is a deep-focus shot, with each on a different plane (and with the digitally-composed Madrid skyline behind). In cinematography, too, spectacle is paramount, a fine example being the crane-shot for the deserted Gran Vía at the start of the film.

Sound is used very effectively throughout the film, including diegetic and non-diegetic music, the latter in a commentative way – very much as in Hollywood film, even imitating its sweeping orchestral style. The film opens and closes with a voice-over accompanying a black screen as protagonist César hears a voice asking him 'open your eyes', which is especially significant in a film so concerned with dreams. On two occasions the absence of sound is used powerfully. When César walks through the eerily deserted streets of Madrid (it is 10 am) only his footsteps are heard, echoing in the unnatural silence of a once noisy metropolis. And when in a noisy bar his scientist-counsellor tells him all the people around him are merely there to serve his dream, he says he only wants them to be quiet, upon which the whole place goes completely silent, confirming that they are only his staged sound effects not real people.

Editing choices are based on typical continuity patterns and optical effects are used to enhance the verisimilitude of the fictional world. The narrative is restricted to César's point of view and we are party to the same frustrating enigma as he is, trying to discover the truth. The plot follows an enigma-resolution pattern, which in fact comprises repeated questions and answers:

Q : Why is César the only person in Madrid? A: It's a dream.
Q : Why is César being interrogated? A: He killed someone.
Q : Why is he hiding his face? A: He was disfigured in an accident.
Q : Who did he kill and why? A: He killed Nuria for taking Sofía's place.
Q : Why has his Sofía been replaced by the woman he thought was called Nuria? A: His dream has made a mistake!

The final resolution (and thus necessary closure) is provided by the explanation that César had in fact died, and his Life Extension company had programmed a virtual reality existence for him to experience until such time (150 years into the future) that he was to wake up and live again in a better world (able to cure his disfigurement).

Though this resolution is highly improbable, the style of the film mobilizes all its technical resources in the service of fictional integrity and verisimilitude. Like much of Hollywood science fiction, stylistic choices are based on an attempt to achieve a willing suspension of disbelief in the audience. *Abre los ojos* has much else in common with Hollywood movies: a car crash spectacular (as rare in Spanish cinema as they are commonplace in US cinema); dialogue which is very assured and clever, and believable in this context, despite not being quite how people in contemporary Spain speak. Even the themes and motifs of the film are closer to Hollywood tropes than to Amenábar's native Spain. The extreme wealth of the characters, so untypical of European films but common in Hollywood, and the 'riches to rags and back' motif reveal much about the film makers' influences, as does the theme of the monster, much more a theme of cinematic fantasy itself and fictional narratives like *The Phantom of the Opera*, than any social reality. This, too, is a common feature of Hollywood cinema, which is nourished more from itself than from the outside world.

We have looked at these two film texts as examples of very different styles, mobilizing different identifiable techniques. But the films have in common a strong association with their respective directors. Now that we have enumerated a number of technical systems by which film texts can be analysed, we will turn, in the chapters that follow, to the broader contexts in which whole bodies of films are studied: in relation to their creators (auteurism) and to film categories (genres) and actors (stars).

Chapter Three
AUTHORSHIP ☐

Who is responsible for a film? Who organizes and controls the film-making process? Who takes credit for the content, form and style of a film? Does a film have an author in the same way that a novel does? By author or authorship, we usually refer to the notion of the director as the 'author' of the film, often using the term 'auteur', from French. A director is usually judged to be an auteur if their work is characterized by distinctive stylistic traits and thematic concerns – or, as is sometimes claimed – a 'personal vision' or 'world view', which can be traced across a number of films. The idea of the film director as the key individual responsible for the form, style and meanings of a film has been with us since the 1910s and 1920s (Hayward, 1996: 20–21). However, during the development of the American studio system, for example, with the shift to large-scale production in the 1920s and 1930s, other figures and institutions were often seen as far more important in shaping the final film product. These included the studio itself, its brand image and aesthetic (e.g. Warner Brothers, which discouraged authorship by imposing a visual and ideological 'house style' in the 1930s), studio heads (e.g. Irving Thalberg, David O Selznick), leading actors (such as Chaplin, Pickford, Fairbanks), as well as screenwriters, cinematographers and editors. Directors were essentially hired hands, contracted to studios for a certain number of pictures; figures such as Orson Welles, Alfred Hitchcock, John Ford and Douglas Sirk gained special status as auteurs only later.

Auteurism usually indicates a certain approach to film criticism which analyses films as the personal expression of the director. The director's individual films are read in relation to a group of films or their film output as a whole, often referred to as an 'oeuvre' or body of work. Such a reading promotes the idea of the director not only as an organizing principle in the production of the film, but also as the creative force behind the whole body of work and its meanings. What are the signs of the auteur, or what Bazin termed the 'personal factor', in film making? Where do they lie? Auteur criticism tends to focus on common elements, repeated patterns, recycled features which give consistency and coherence to the auteur's work. For example, in his analysis of Hitchcock, Truffaut noticed the consistent and repeated use of the red herring in the investigation plot, the black humour, the figure of the 'ice blond' paired with the 'wrong' man and the many cameo appearances of the director himself. In this sort of criticism, knowledge of a director's other films may be crucial in understanding a single film. The auteur critic will therefore be alert to the ways in which the director's work develops over time. The key areas of critical interest tend to be: narrative structure, characterization, thematics and visual style. And it is the last category which has been the main focus for auteur criticism.

Historically speaking, the idea of the talented director as a crucial organizing and creative presence emerged with particular force in post-war Europe, especially in France in the late 1940s and early 1950s. It is usually associated with the notion of the 'politique des auteurs' ('author policy' or 'polemic', a term coined by André Bazin). This was the controversial critical position adopted by young critics (and future film makers) of the French film journal *Cahiers du cinéma* (Cinema Notebooks). In a provocative essay published in *Cahiers* in 1954 ('Une certaine tendance du cinéma français'), François Truffaut delivered a bad-tempered critique of the dominant French studio cinema. He saw it as a quality studio cinema, but overly indebted to high literary culture and stifled by the power of the scriptwriter over the director. In short, film style was always subordinated to the interests of the story. Truffaut demanded a decisive shift of emphasis towards the truly cinematic, i.e. towards film style and the recognition of the craft of the film director or auteur, as seen, for example, in the arrangement and shooting of the *mise-en-scène*. Just as controversially for the times, *Cahiers* critics claimed that certain Hollywood studio directors (such as Hitchcock, Ford, Hawkes, Sirk and Lang) could also be accorded the special status of auteur as opposed to being mere '*metteurs-en-scène*' or technicians. In other words, even commercial contract directors working in a highly industrialized studio system like Hollywood, making standardized genre products, could also be regarded as great artists, as seen through the traces of their own unique personal vision imprinted in their film style. The '*politique des auteurs*' was quickly internationalized and popularized, though given different inflections as it travelled. In the USA, for example, in the 1960s, Andrew Sarris (1968) coined the term 'auteur theory' as a means of approaching US film history by way of studies of individual directors. Ranked into rough league tables (and even segmented as 'pantheon', 'second line', 'fallen idols', etc.), the great directors or auteurs revealed across the whole body of their work, Sarris claimed, a distinctive artistic vision and sensibility.

Over the years, the notions of the film author and auteur criticism have been revised, attacked, discredited and pronounced defunct by various waves of film theory and criticism, mainly under the influence of continental philosophy, linguistics and semiology (See Caughie, 1981). Claims concerning the death of the author have been greatly exaggerated, however. Despite a sustained theoretical onslaught since the mid-1960s, the concept of the film author lives on. In fact, it continues to animate film production, distribution, marketing and film financing, as well as film courses and publishers lists, and so on. The notion of the auteur is still with us, even as the boundaries between art and commercial cinema have become increasingly blurred and as mainstream cinema has adopted many of the formal strategies once confined to the domain of art-house film making. Moreover, we have become increasingly aware that the signs of authorship are available not only as traces in the film text itself but outside it too, through the intermingling of auteurism and commerce.

As Timothy Corrigan (1993: Ch. 4) has shown, auteurs engage in forms of cultural visibility not necessarily connected to their role as directors. Rather, their auteurism becomes transformed into a commercial strategy designed to organize and stimulate audience reception, as well as the distribution and marketing of their films. Here we find a different type of auteurism, one which exists not in the film text but in the domain of film reception and consumption and which is defined by the traces of the auteur left in journalistic and marketing materials. In other words, the auteur functions as a star, exploiting the celebrity image to market, promote and sell their films. In Spain, Pedro Almodóvar is arguably the consummate master at promoting his own films. Thus, our access to the auteur is no longer only through the film, but via the vast intertextual array of secondary textual and non-textual sources which surround the films: promotions, reviews, trailers, chat shows, glossy photoshoots, award ceremonies, festival appearances, websites and so on. The durability of the cinematic author can be explained in part, in terms of technological change and the shift from video to DVD, which has helped immeasurably to enhance the visibility of the director as author. After seeing the film (or even before), we can and do watch some or all of the 'extra' features which accompany the DVD, including director's notes and commentaries, the 'Making of' feature or a video diary. We can also check out the preparation of the script, the process of 'story boarding', production notes, trailers, interviews with the director, photo galleries, filmographies and links to other websites. The extras accompanying León de Aranoa's *Los lunes al sol* (2002), all 110 minutes of them, include a trailer, a 'Making of', an interview with the director, rehearsals, out-takes, storyboards, publicity materials, art gallery, filmographies, technical specs, etc. Such marketing materials arguably contribute towards greater film literacy and powerfully reaffirm the key role of the director. Yet they also greatly enhance our access to the collective enterprise of film making and to a much wider range of candidates for authorship (actors, producers, editors, cinematographers, visual effects supervisors, stunt co-ordinators, etc). Paradoxically, where film theory has tried to break free from the figure of the author, technological change and more recent marketing 'savvy' appear to be reinvigorating the discourse of authorship.

Film authorship has been seen traditionally as having a single point of origin, with film meaning being attributable to a single creative source, the author, usually taken to be the director. Of course, common sense tells us that such a view of film authorship, especially in the modern day, sits uneasily with the complexities of film production, which often involves vast numbers of people, many specialist departments and even important subcontractors, especially where CGI (computer graphics imaging) input is required. In such a collective, collaborative, team-oriented activity as film making, it seems almost counterintuitive to single out one gifted individual as the person responsible for the film (Roberts and Wallis, 2003: 128; Buckland, 2003: 85). So, how can we reconcile the creative agency of a single individual within a working environment which is predominantly collective and collaborative? Arguably, we need a rather more flexible and pluralized concept of the film author, one which re-locates authorship in the historical and social realities of film making practice and gives due weight and importance to the creative interventions other key figures in the process, e.g. actors, screenwriters, producers, set designers, cinematographers, editors, etc. This does not mean that we necessarily abandon the attribution of authorship to a single individual. Critical work on a film director as author, in many cases, may well yield immense critical and intellectual rewards, enhancing and deepening our understanding and appreciation of the films. But it may be difficult to sustain the idea that the director has authored absolutely everything or that they are the sole creative agent. And here, work on an actor, producer, cinematographer or even a production company as author may bring important benefits and add to our knowledge, experience and film literacy. By adopting a more pluralist model of film authorship, it may allow us to analyse the extent to which individual and group creative inputs relate to the workings of film style and just how significant these various creative contributions are.

THE AUTEURIST TRADITION IN SPAIN

Looked at from the outside, say from the vantage point of the USA, Japan or the Middle East, Spanish cinema tends to be located and promoted as part of a wider category of European or 'foreign-language' cinema. In other words, Spanish cinema is broadly defined as non-Hollywood and having funding mechanisms, working practices, cultural status and linguistic diversity that make it distinctive. It is also packaged by international film distributors and presented to mainly art-house audiences as a predominantly auteurist-led cinema as opposed to the generically driven, industrially-based products of Hollywood. This is so, despite the fact that Spanish production totals average around 100 films per year, many of which are commercial genre films. And even if the types of Spanish films distributed abroad no longer appear uniquely art-house (witness the recent release in the UK of Alex de la Iglesia's comedy *La comunidad* [2000] or Emilio Martínez Lázaro's sexy musical *Al otro lado de la cama* [2002]), Spanish cinema is still perceived abroad as very much an art cinema. As a result, Spanish films are sold in foreign markets largely on the basis of their auteurist credentials, usually reflecting the marketing strength of the director's name, be it Pedro Almodóvar, Bigas Luna, Vicente Aranda, Julio Medem or Alejandro Amenábar.

Moreover, reflecting marketing strategies adopted in the 1980s and early 1990s, in terms of their attractions and pleasures, Spanish films continue to be sold on the promise of visual flamboyance, edgy, subversive narratives and torrid scenes of often explicit sexual activity (for example, Penélope Cruz in Bigas Luna's *Jamón, Jamón* [1992] and more recently, Paz Vega as sultry siren in Aranda's *Carmen* [2003] and in Medem's celebration of explicit sexual coupling in *Lucía y el sexo* [2002]). In a recent volume on Spanish auteurist cinema (1999), José Luis Borau, one of Spain's leading auteur directors and Peter Evans (the editor) both argued that Spanish cinema, though boasting strong popular cinematic traditions, owes much of its success and international profile to its auteurs. Also, in its relatively short history in the UK, Spanish Film Studies also devotes considerable time and energy to film auteurs, some of whom have had virtually no impact on audiences in Spain (Allinson, 2003: 143), whilst being canonized and celebrated abroad.

Strictly speaking, and despite the art films of Barcinógrafo in the 1910s and the important work in the 1930s and 1940s of directors such as Florián Rey, Edgar Neville, José Luis Sáenz de Heredia and others, an auteur cinema in Spain began to emerge only in the early 1960s, though we find various signs of 'proto-auteurist' styles and activities being adopted before that. Before the 1960s, Spanish cinema was little known abroad, except for the figure of the exiled Buñuel, who had already been adopted by Bazin and *Cahiers du cinéma* in the early 1950s as the new standard-bearer of Mexican cinema (Azevedo Muñoz, 2003: 76). There were also a small number of Spanish films which had gained a degree of visibility and recognition at foreign festivals. These included Berlanga's subversive comic parody of the *españolada*, *Bienvenido Míster Marshall* (1952), chosen to represent Spain at Cannes in 1953 and awarded a prize for Best Comedy (Fernando Méndez Leite, in Borau, 1997: 142), as well as Bardem's *Muerte de un ciclista* (1955), which represented Spain at Cannes in 1955, and jointly shared the Critics' Prize with Benito Alazraki's *Raíces* (1953). This particular award was a major first step in raising Bardem's international profile as an oppositional film maker and Spanish auteur in the making. It was quickly followed by the award of the International Critics' Prize at the Venice Mostra in 1956 for *Calle Mayor* (1956). With foreign sympathy extended to Bardem as a victim of Francoist oppression (following his brief arrest during the student riots of February 1956 while filming), his prize further enhanced his national and international prestige as Spain's leading dissident 'European' film maker. Sadly, despite his international reputation and considerable influence within the national industry, Bardem's scripts and politically engaged film projects were continually frustrated by censorship. Soon after the collapse of the production company UNINCI (following the scandal over *Viridiana*), and after having filmed in Argentina (*Los inocentes*, 1962), he turned largely to commercial features from 1965 onwards.

As D'Lugo (1994) has argued, and as Bardem's example suggests, the dissident film culture of the 1950s and its allegorical denunciations of Francoism were linked to a notion of the oppositional Spanish film maker as beleaguered auteur. Directors such as Carlos Saura, first through Films 59, and later through Querejeta PC, cultivated sympathetic international audiences at film festivals abroad which, it was hoped, would help generate interest and box office back home. Very often such a strategy worked, but sometimes it did not. For example, Saura's first major feature, *Los golfos* (1959), scripted by Daniel Sueiro and Mario Camus (soon to be a major film maker and *auteur* in his own right) and produced by Pere Portabella of Films 59, was selected as the Spanish entrant for Cannes in 1960. While its 'bullfighter' narrative of social mobility among a gang of young tearaways (thematically vaguely akin to the youth 'delinquency' narratives of Truffaut's *Les 400 coups* [1959] and Godard's *À bout de souffle* [1959]), helped launch Saura's international career as a proto-auteur, its bleak ending merited only a low official classification by Franco's film officials, and therefore a limited distribution, thus turning it into a loss-making project. Moreover, according to Saura himself, *Los golfos* was shown at Cannes in a badly mutilated version, suffering 10 minutes of cuts (See Delgado, in Evans, 1999: 38–54). However, from *La caza* (1965) onwards, an allegory of the civil war based on the premise of a rabbit hunt undertaken by a group of war veterans (awarded a Golden Bear at the Berlin Film Festival), Saura became Spain's leading, internationally acknowledged, auteur. His cryptic, indirect style and his explorations of class tensions within the Spanish bourgeoisie provided an influential template for the oppositional Spanish art film of the 1960s and 1970s under Franco.

Strange as it may seem, the auteur cinema which appeared in Spain in the early 1960s was a cinema created, funded, regulated and promoted by the state for political purposes to improve the regime's image and standing abroad, as it sought to stave off an economic downturn by introducing mild liberalization. Reflecting 'new cinema' movements in other countries in the 1960s (French 'New Wave', 'New German Cinema', British 'free cinema'), the officially-sponsored Nuevo Cine Español was conceived as a new quality art cinema, which would seek to raise production standards and give access to the film industry of young graduates from Madrid's film school, the vast majority of whom were anti-Franco dissidents. Another strand of auteur-oriented film making developed in Barcelona at the same time, under the banner of the 'Escuela de Barcelona', some of whose projects would also benefit from state subsidies. Criticised by NCE film makers as a bourgeois, aestheticist, de-politicized and cosmopolitan cinema, the 'Escuela' practitioners claimed that they were making a rather more modern, European and experimental cinema compared to the dull, conservative, antiquated, realist cinema of their colleagues in Madrid, a '*cine mesetario*', a pejorative term meaning cinema produced in central Spain (Font, 2003: 184).

The policy of an officially sponsored art cinema, for mainly foreign consumption, was articulated by the then Director General of Cinema and Theatre, José María García Escudero. He contrasted a backward, poverty-stricken, technically and artistically inferior, escapist genre cinema in Spain to a new cinema, waiting to be developed, an art cinema, a 'cinema with problems', as enunciated at Salamanca in 1955. Realist in orientation, more thoughtful and more demanding on the spectator, this new art cinema would be aimed at more discerning national and foreign audiences and represent Spain at foreign film festivals. The auteurist approach of such a new art cinema, seen as a guarantee of quality, was also regarded as a means of national regeneration in the film industry, a recipe for modernization and internationalization. And like other national cinema movements of the 1960s, the new art cinema would offer a strategy with which to mitigate to some extent the power and dominance of Hollywood.

As noted in Chapter One, despite its six or seven years of life and with more than 40 films to its credit, the Nuevo Cine Español did not create a vibrant auteur cinema nor significantly transform the cultural image abroad of the Franco regime, let alone cover costs. Yet, even while heavily regulated, the system of state subsidies put in place by García Escudero helped producers like Elías Querejeta, via his production company, to finance a film project almost entirely from official monies, almost without needing to release and commercialize the film. Moreover, this official largesse, though with strings, still allowed Querejeta and his flagship directors, such as Carlos Saura and Víctor Erice, to make the sort of personal, auteurist, allegorical films which would have been unthinkable in any commercial context; films like Saura's *La prima Angélica* (1973) or Erice's *El espíritu de la colmena* (1973). Of course, as Triana Toribio points out (2003: 68–9), auteurism became very much a male preserve. Indeed, the attraction of the auteur label for young, predominantly male, Official Film School film makers (funded by the state), in the context of widespread machismo and sexist legislation, would make it far more difficult for female film makers (such as Pilar Miró and Josefina Molina) to develop a film career as auteurs in their own right.

In the post-Franco period, as the cases of Carlos Saura and Víctor Erice show only too clearly, a number of 1960s oppositional auteurs found it difficult to move beyond the oblique filming styles and coded thematics they had developed under Francoist repression. Yet, political and ideological imperatives during the transition period (1975–82) impinged with even greater force on auteur film makers, who were anxious to denounce the ills of 40 years of dictatorship. Such was the aim of *Furtivos* (made in 1975), co-directed and co-scripted by José Luis Borau and Manuel Gutiérrez Aragón. The film's elliptical, melodramatic, ('*tremendista*') sensationalist narrative of matricide and incest revealed the 'rural paradise' of Franco's Spain as a nightmare. This critique of Francoist values and ideology was continued in *Camada negra* (Manuel Gutiérrez Aragón, 1977) and further developed in a range of historical reconstructions and drama documentaries, such as Bardem's *Siete días de enero* (1978), Miró's *El crimen de Cuenca* (1979) and Uribe's *El proceso de Burgos* (1979) and *La fuga de Segovia* (1981). Another key oppositional auteurist trend during the transition, underlining the traumatic effects of Francoist sexual repression, was reignited with Aranda's *Cambio de sexo* (1976) and Pons' *Ocaña: retrato intermitente* (1978). Here the tropes of transsexualism, transvestism and sex change were used as metaphors for political and cultural change, already hinted at in Armiñán's *Mi querida señorita* (1971). And as provocative and thoughtful explorations of the mobility of sexual identities, they anticipated later films such as Uribe's *La muerte de Mikel* (1983) and Almodóvar's *La ley del deseo* (1986).

As noted in Chapter One, under Pilar Miró, the PSOE's attempt to refashion the Spanish film industry in the 1980s by financially marginalizing major areas of genre cinema (identified politically with the old regime) and promoting higher production values and a better quality, 'progressive', art/heritage cinema, based on literary adaptations, failed to prosper. Though some art films were critical and commercial successes, such as Mario Camus' *La colmena* (1982) and *Los santos inocentes* (1984), many were not, including Saura's lavish, but laborious 'superproduction' *El dorado* (1988). Most of the films selected by government committees and made by the Minister's auteurist colleagues, however well intentioned, educative and morally uplifting, were simply unappealing to commercial audiences. In the 1990s, as we have seen, a younger generation of Spanish film makers managed to connect with the neglected area of younger national audiences by presenting them with high quality but also entertaining cinema. The new directors and emerging auteurs, such as Amenábar, Alex de la Iglesia, Juanma Bajo Ulloa, Icíar Bollaín and Isabel Coixet, have found success by following the example of Almodóvar, largely turning their backs on the themes of the civil war, Francoism and an art cinema forged in the context of political imperatives and ideological commitment. They reject the old model of the politicized, anti-Francoist auteur and prefer to combine the high-brow style of a quality art cinema with popular, appealing, middle- or low-brow material. The result is a marriage of art and commerce and a new quality auteur cinema for larger audiences. In short, auteur cinema in Spain has shifted decisively away from its function as a vehicle of anti-Franco political commitment and opposition. It has rediscovered its role as a form of entertainment and pleasure, geared to real audiences and the market, but it is a cinema which is nonetheless capable of serious, thought-provoking, even politically oppositional functions, as recently seen with Medem's *La pelota vasca* (2003) and the collectively made *Hay motivo* (2004).

THREE AUTEURS: ALMODÓVAR, BUÑUEL AND ERICE

Auteur status is clearly based on the defining marks of identity and individuality in both film content and style. Normally, these need to be repeated across a range of films so that a 'list' of personal or even idiosyncratic features can be identified, thus raising the director above other film makers. However, it is certainly possible to achieve such status on the basis of only one film – as in the classic case of Orson Welles' *Citizen Kane* (1941). But, just as film stars can be as much a product of extra-textual activities, so too film directors sometimes gain celebrity status as a result of their biographies. Spain's most internationally renowned film makers, Luis Buñuel and Pedro Almodóvar, can both be studied in terms of defining features (preoccupations, idiosyncrasies, style); and they each have a biography and a persona which is in some ways a product of self-publicity, controversy and myth. To avoid repetition, we will analyse Almodóvar's work across a matrix of production, themes, characterization, narrative and visual style (all of which could be applied to Buñuel), but our take on Buñuel will focus more on his unusual trajectory as a film maker, rather than on detailed analysis of the texts themselves. Finally, we will look briefly at the career of Víctor Erice, whose status rests largely on one film, as a means of problematizing film authorship itself.

PEDRO ALMODÓVAR

Though his films continue to provoke controversy and divide audiences and critics, Almodóvar remains Spain's most successful, best known film director since Buñuel and, for the majority of commentators, a consummate and undisputed auteur. Paul Julian

Smith described him as the 'one true auteur to emerge in the 1980s' (2000: 5). A self-taught director, Almodóvar began making low-budget, underground features in 1978 with *Pepi, Luci Bom y otras chicas del montón,* which took nearly two years to complete and was followed by *Laberinto de pasiones* (1982) and *Entre tinieblas* (1983). Better than anyone, Almodóvar caught the changing mood and the mentality of the 'new Spain' of the early 1980s. Compared to Carlos Saura or Víctor Erice (auteurs of an older generation deeply marked by the dictatorship, who made dense, oblique, allegorical denunciations of Francoist repression), his early feature films mixed melodrama, the musical, surrealism, horror, the sex comedy and elements of the detective story. They were colourful, abrasive, delirious, funny, transgressive and iconoclastic, strongly inspired by the trash aesthetics and punk ethos of the '*movida*' (Triana Toribio, 2000: 276). Underpinned by political incorrectness and the cult of bad taste (the 'golden shower' scene in *Pepi, Luci, Bom...,* for example), they chronicled the transformation of urban Madrid into the wild, partying capital of Europe, in which outrageous, comic-book characters (masochistic wives, nymphomaniac singers, transsexuals, drug-taking nuns, plus Almodóvar himself in various camp cameos) raised two fingers to convention and good taste. As the party subsided, Almodóvar turned to more mainstream projects in a parodic, neo-realist, Felliniesque, narrative, *¿Que hé hecho yo para merecer esto?* (1984), set in one of Madrid's ghastly high-rise, working-class estates. Here, against a backdrop of cramped living conditions, kitsch décor, bizarre family members, neighbours from hell and incompetent cops, an oppressed housewife kills her husband with a ham bone. In *Matador* (1986), in which a female lawyer is sexually attracted to men because of their bullfighting skills, Almodóvar weaves a torrid tale of love, passion, machismo and death, which probes the roots of Spanish identity in the 'national' sport of the bullfight.

Until now, all of Almodóvar's films contained, in one form or another, gay and lesbian characters. But, with *La ley del deseo* (1987), produced by his newly formed production company El Deseo, he made a rather more personal, introspective film, one in which his film fiction and his personal life seemed to merge. His tale of gay love, passion, transsexualism and murder, less burdened perhaps by his trademark interpolations and digressive sub-plots, helped him capture an international gay audience, while boosting his standing on the international art house circuit. He then gained major national and international recognition and commercial success with his pastiche, Hollywood-inspired, screwball comedy *Mujeres al borde de un ataque de nervios* (1988). With *Mujeres...,* Almodóvar was widely hailed as a woman's director, even describing himself as a feminist. Yet despite massive box office success with *Mujeres...,* which underpinned the long-term viability of El Deseo, plus an Oscar nomination into the bargain, his knack for combining public adulation and commercial success seemed temporarily to falter.

In later films, he turned away from the crazy comedy formula and more towards melodrama. Like Fassbinder, Almodóvar was an admirer of Douglas Sirk, attracted to overblown plots of erotic jealousies and unexpected turns of fate. His next three films, *¡Átame!* (1990), *Tacones lejanos* (1991) and *Kika* (1993), developed these elements but were not unqualified successes, critically or commercially. *¡Átame!*'s lurid tale of an ex-porn star who falls in love with her kidnapper caused outrage in certain progressive and feminist circles and led to accusations of misogyny. Then, in *Kika*, the controversial rape scene (deliberately exploited for its humour) seemed to eclipse the film's emphatic critique of media manipulation, reinforcing an earlier view of Almodóvar as anything but a feminist. Since the mid-1990s, however, with *La flor de mi secreto* (1995) and *Carne trémula* (1997), his film making has regained its international appeal and commercial impetus, culminating in *Todo sobre mi madre* (1999) which consolidated Almodóvar's career and his standing as an international auteur figure. He received a Best Director award at Cannes in 1999, and in 2000, seven Goyas and an Oscar for best foreign film. He was also awarded a second Oscar for the script of *Hable con ella* (2001).

Now in his mid-fifties, Almodóvar stands as the most potent, visible sign of Spain's national and international film-making projection and success. But to what extent does he reflect Sarris's notion of the auteur or 'pantheon director' as one who transcends production and technical matters with a 'personal vision of the world...with its own laws and landscapes' (Sarris, 1968: 39)? Let us consider this question by looking briefly at various aspects of Almodóvar's work, i.e. his subject matter, narratives, characters, styles and themes, beginning with a reminder of his ability to control the production process.

PRODUCTION

Almodóvar has been his own producer since 1987, when he set up *El Deseo* with his brother Agustín and made *La ley del deseo*. He also signs his own films with the rubric '*Un film de* Almodóvar', thereby affirming his authorship and using his own name as a brand. His company has produced 10 of his 15 films and has supported other films by Alex de la Iglesia (*Acción Mutante*, 1992), Isabel Coixet (*Cosas que nunca te dije*, 1996; *Mi vida sin mí*, 2003), Guillermo del Toro (*El espinazo del diablo*, 2001). When making a film, Almodóvar can exert control over virtually all aspects of the production process, precisely the area which normally places the severest limitations on a director. Also, he has written the scripts to all 15 of his films (though with co-writers for *Matador* and *Carne trémula*). In terms of casting, in the 1980s, apart from promoting Antonio Banderas, he assembled a group of excellent female actors, almost creating his own repertory company, who would quickly become national and in some cases international stars. These were the so-called '*chicas* Almodóvar', including Carmen Maura, Victoria Abril, Veronica Forqué, María Barranco, Rossy de Palma, Loles León and Kiti Manver, as well as veteran performers from the 1960s, Chus Lampreave, Julieta Serrano and Katia Loritz. He has also been able to rely on a core of creative and talented technical specialists (see Allinson, 2001: 158). All in all, Almodóvar appears to have created for himself an economic and working environment, a set of actors and technicians and a modus operandi which help maximize his expressivity as a modern, internationally-acknowledged auteur. Is this borne out through his themes, film narratives, style and the consistency of a personal vision?

THEMES AND CHARACTERIZATION

Almodóvar's stories are predominantly concerned with, and told from, the point of view of women who have been wronged or oppressed by men. Some fight back, such as Gloria in *¿Qué he hecho yo para merecer esto?*, or Manuela in *Todo sobre mi madre*; others are prepared to capitulate and comply (Luci in *Pepi, Luci, Bom* or Marina in *¡Átame!*). His stories also include women who prefer to be with other women, as well as women who seek to fulfil perverse sexual desires (masochism, incest, nymphomania, bondage, or even sexually-motivated murder). Such perversions appear perfectly normal and acceptable in the moral universe presented in his films. There are also stories about men who pretend to be women, men who desire other men, and heterosexual men who are capable of close male friendship. In short, Almodóvar's film world combines the story material typical of soap opera, with a cast of characters who represent largely dissident sexualities (See Smith, 2000). It is a world where traditional gender distinctions no longer apply, where women predominate and where no sexual choice is off limits. Sexual identities and practices tend to be socially transgressive. This is a world populated by dysfunctional patriarchal families, oppressed wives, grieving mothers, inept fathers, husbands and lovers, transsexuals, sex offenders, repressed young men, streetwise children and Aids victims. Almodóvar's screenplays tend to reserve the meatiest roles for the more complex female characters, while males (unless feminized like Benigno and Marco in *Hable con ella*) tend to be one-dimensional, comic stereotypes drawn from popular culture: bullfighters, inept and impotent policemen, bad husbands, treacherous lovers. Male figures are broadly failed 'macho' bullies, who represent a flawed heterosexual masculinity, as opposed to the array of positive role models among the female protagonists. Almodóvar's films tend to focus sympathetically on society's losers and outcasts (women, gays, lesbians, transsexuals, prostitutes, drug addicts, and so on), their shifting identities and precarious chances in love and sexual desire. And though his approach has been consistently satirical and parodic, his films are always caring towards the underdog and remarkably free of moralizing, however unconventional or problematic the moral or sexual choices. Overall, while always capable of springing surprises, Almodóvar has consistently explored the same tragi-comic, melodramatic, female-centred terrain (though his latest film *La mala educación*, 2003, is a reprise of the gay subject matter of *La ley del deseo*).

NARRATIVE

In most mainstream narrative films, the film image (i.e. camera movement, camera angles, editing of shots, etc.) is normally motivated by the narrative logic of the script. This cause-and-effect logic generates a narrative whose action is usually projected through psychologically defined, goal-oriented characters. Film style is thus subordinated to the demands of the narrative. Also, the viewer makes sense of the narrative through its appeal to plausibility (its verisimilitude), generic appropriateness and compositional unity (see Chapter Two). Though Almodóvar's films have evolved over the years and have become far more controlled and structurally much tighter, and though they exploit Hollywood generic frameworks, they differ in some respects from both classic and more modern narrative films. As in the art film, the relations they establish between image and narrative are often more tenuous or ambiguous, their causal relations are rather looser, yet their appeal to plausibility and their compositional unity are highly variable and until recently, they have tended to lack realistic, psychologically plausible characters, who pursue defined goals. Moreover, they remain generic hybrids, i.e. impure, carnivalesque, textual constructs, a 'collage' bearing the traces of earlier forms, styles and genres, which often clash. *¿Qué he hecho yo…?*, for example, is a mixture of neo-realism (including social message and real locations) with surrealist and horror-movie touches, such as the lizard Dinero, adopted as a pet and sole witness to Antonio's murder, or young Vanessa, paranormal clone of the character of Carrie (in Brian De Palma's film of 1976), who redecorates Gloria's kitchen using telekinesis. This hybridity works well in some cases, such as the fusion of comedy and melodrama in films like *Entre tinieblas* (Allinson, 2001: 144–57). But it also tends to favour an excess of sometimes inconsequential story material which intrudes into and temporarily stops the flow of the narrative, for instance in the use of the absurd sub-plot concerning the forging of the Hitler diaries in *¿Qué he hecho yo…?*

In films such as *Hable con ella* (2001) and *La mala educación* (2003), the main narration features the stories of several main characters, which flash forward and back in time, in a highly complex manner. This approach is curiously reminiscent of Brecht's use of alienation devices, as exemplified in film by Godard in his 1960s and early 1970s 'counter cinema', via inserts or interpolations to break the 'illusionism' of the representation, to jolt the audience out of its complacency by reminding it that it is watching a film, i.e. a fiction. The intent to make the audience aware of filmic artifice is clearly a sign of authorial intervention and control. It is reinforced in *Hable con ella* by the use of the framing device of the Pina Bausch dance interlude which opens and closes the film, though audiences can be confused as to whether the film has actually started. Similarly in *La mala educación* a framing device is used to 'dupe' the audience into thinking they are watching the main diegesis when, in fact, they are witnessing a film adaptation of it. In short, Almodóvar seems to be moving in the direction of even greater narrative complexity, self-awareness and overt control of his material, and Almodóvar's viewers are thus being encouraged to work much harder in order to figure out the logic of his narratives.

VISUAL STYLE

Some of the most recognizable signs of Almodóvar's authorship reside in his handling of the *mise-en-scène*. In the early to middle-period films which – broadly speaking – prefer studio settings to natural locations, Almodóvar is known for his highly stylized sets, his mixing of the bric-a-brac of low and the artifacts of high culture, plus his love of *haute couture*

(Armani and Chanel in *Tacones lejanos* and Jean Paul Gaultier for Andrea Caracortada's monstrous futurism in *Kika*). Above all, Almodóvar's trademark here is his use of colour, particularly reds, which are strenuously coordinated and combined, reflected and refracted in all manner of props and costumes, make-up and décor (Allinson, 2001: 182–6). Regarding cinematography, Almodóvar's selections seem to emphasize the use of the frame and symmetrical framing, shots in depth and deep focus, frequent impossible shots such as in *¿Qué he hecho yo…?*, from inside the washing machine, which emphasizes Gloria's life of drudgery (Vernon, and Morris, 1995: 66). And most of all, the use of the camera as voyeuristic eye, fetishistically contemplating bodies as well as buildings, via use of high and low angle shots, upward tilts and pans (especially in *La ley del deseo*, *Kika*, *Hable con ella* and *La mala educación*). Editing in Almodóvar has evolved from the stressed and jumpy cutting of the 1980s into the relatively smooth linking of shots into sequences we find in later films. Alongside *mise-en-scène*, sound (see Chapter Two) and the soundtrack are arguably domin-ant in Almodóvar's stylistic tool kit, particularly the narrative use of *boleros* (romantic, Latin-American ballads) or other popular Spanish songs, which function as sympathetic commentary, or are expressive of character moods, feelings or states. Such musical inter-polations are perhaps best exemplified by the songs used in *¿Qué he hecho yo…?* such as '*La bien pagá*' sung by Miguel de Molina. Here, as elsewhere, a song is given significant space in the narrative, which it virtually takes over, disrupting the dialogue and overall narrative flow, as the audience joins the characters to savour the same 'old' songs of the 1940s. Apart from this homage to a popular Republican, cultural icon and exile, Almodóvar contrasts the grubby, nasty kitsch décor of the flat, in the present, with the excessively saturated reds of a song clip set in the past, i.e. a realist setting contrasted with the artifice of the televi-sion '*folklórica*'. Moreover, Almodóvar's own cameo appearance miming the song relates to further marks of authorship, those of citation, intertextuality and internal commentary on other media and artistic and cultural styles, high and low, which characterise all of his films.

Almodóvar's films are highly self-referential and deeply intertextual. Hence his consistent, not to say obsessive, interest in the interaction of various media such as pop art, the press and popular fiction (represented in *La flor de mi secreto* by both the editor of *El País* newspaper and a trashy romance publisher), through to high culture fiction (Truman Capote or Tennessee Williams in *Todo sobre mi madre*). Television is often used, becoming the core of narrative devel-opment in *Kika* – centred on Andrea Caracortada's *Lo peor del día* meaning 'The Worst of the Day', as a target for an ironic take on the hyperreality of television. Above all, Almodóvar is mesmerized by cinema itself. Sometimes this takes the form of quotation – most elaborately in *Todo sobre mi madre* via the parallels with *All About Eve* (Joseph Mankiewicz, 1950) – but also in many other films. And the films often use film making as part of the film narrative. Thus we have professional dubbing actors in *Mujeres…*, the making of 'La visita' in *La mala educación*), the use of film making hardware – cameras, tracks, editing machines, microphones (in multiple films), and the use of the 'film within a film' device (such as the opening of *La ley del deseo*, or more recently, the 'Amante menguante' (The Shrinking Man) in *Hable con ella*).

ALMODÓVAR STUDIES: CONTINUITY AND DEVELOPMENT

An auteurist approach to a director permits analysis of films both chronologically, charting the development of themes and style on a film-by-film basis, and systematically, looking at various aspects in turn and comparing films. Thus, on the one hand, we have the approach of Vidal (1988), Strauss (1996), and Smith (1994/2000) which take the films in chronological order (though the first two are general, interview-based, while Smith's book focuses on questions of gender, sexuality and national identity). On the other hand, we have the books by García de León and Maldonado (1989), Vernon and Morris (1995) and Allinson (2001, 2003), which structure their analysis via thematic and stylistic categories. Together, these approaches reveal development (in technique, style and tone, for example), but also continuities (in subject matter, milieu and themes).

Almodóvar may have become rather more reflective, sober, even serious in his films since the mid-1990s, stylistically more controlled, more concerned with pattern, symmetry and coherence, yet his themes remain fairly consistent and constant throughout his work, themes which resonate not only in Spain but also among international audiences. Love and desire dominate his work: old, new, flawed, rekindled, straight, gay, lesbian, marginalized or repressed, frustrated, disappointed or rendered inactive. Gender and sexuality are key elements, since Almodóvar is concerned with individual freedoms under patriarchy – especially that of the underdog – to fulfil sexual, social and political aspirations. Sexual identity is not fixed but moveable, changeable, as is national identity. As Kinder (1996: 601) argues, Almodóvar has managed to replace in the public imagination the imagery and iconography of the *española* as symbols of national identity with new cultural stereotypes, shifting dissident sexualities from margins to centre as representative of modern, post-Franco Spain. Family and motherhood also loom large in Almodóvar's universe, with clear biographical links to his own family life and his public adoration of his own mother. Hence a preference for the non-patriarchal, female-centred family and the crucial role of mothers, though mothering is something not confined to biological mothers, as Benigno and Marco show in *Hable con ella*. Of course, motherhood and gender as forms of identity are aligned in Almodóvar to performance; all mothers are actresses, i.e. role players, assigned roles in life. Linked to this interest in families and especially in female characters, is an admiration for the melodramatic genre. Perhaps Almodóvar's most characteristic signature lies in his synthesis of melodrama and postmodern citation, the merging of some aspects of classical Hollywood narrative structure with a very self-conscious mode of narration, which produces ironic or parodic distance.

LUIS BUÑUEL

Alongside such figures as Antonioni, Bergman, Bresson, Fellini and Kurosawa, for David Thomson, Buñuel remains 'one of the few towering artists' to deign to take up film as a means of expression. Moreover, according to Thomson, he can be assessed as a Spaniard, surrealist and antagonist of the bourgeoisie, elements which persist across all of his films and which merit close attention (2002: 117). Thomson's dictionary entry on Buñuel is a generous, shrewd and thoughtful tribute to the 'maestro'. It also chimes with what many hispanists, film historians and auteur critics have tended to regard, until recently, as Spain's only 'real' international auteur/star director. Yet the fact is that from the age of 25 (after finishing university), Buñuel spent most of his life and film-making career abroad, as an émigré, refugee and exile, variously based in Paris, New York, Hollywood and Mexico.

Un chien andalou (made in 1928, in collaboration with Salvador Dalí) was Buñuel's controversial irruption into modernist, avant-garde film making and his calling card for the Surrealist group in Paris. A tale of a 'tiff' between two lovers, within an impossible narrative and time scheme (broken up by meaningless intertitles), it features the notorious, unmotivated, sequence in which a man (Buñuel himself) slices through the heroine's eye with a razor, only for her to reappear in the next scene, injury-free (see also Editing in Chapter Two). It was followed by the even more scandalous *L'âge d'or* (1930), another bizarre tale of two lovers, prevented by the woman's parents and a disapproving society from consummating their *amour fou*. Full of erotic and phallic imagery and deliberately blasphemous scenes (the withered bishops, Christ leaving an orgy with sadomasochistic overtones), the film was banned after it provoked attacks from right-wing groups. In Spain, in 1932, Buñuel made yet another controversial early film, the documentary *Tierra sin pan/Las Hurdes* (1933), whose devastating indictment of rural poverty and disease and – by implication – official neglect, caused it to be banned the Republican government.

In the mid-1930s, after working as a dubbing director for Paramount and Warner Bros in Paris and Madrid, Buñuel became executive producer at Filmófono in Madrid, supervising (though also occasionally shooting and editing) popular commercial-genre films. Exiled by the civil war, Buñuel worked in Paris, Hollywood and New York (at the Museum of Modern Art) on propaganda films for the Republic, before losing his job after being denounced as a Communist and atheist in Dalí's autobiography. He went to Mexico in 1946, where he spent the next 36 years and made 20 films in all, including two Mexican-American copros in English, *The adventures of Robinson Crusoe* (1952) and *The Young One* (1960). In his Mexican period, Buñuel is perhaps best known for *Los olvidados* (1950), a tale of juvenile delinquents in Mexico City's slums, shot on location, with largely non-professional actors, i.e. elements which at the time suggested a link with Italian neo-realism. Yet, Buñuel's graphic portrait of violent gangs, cruel mothers and the sexualized dream imagery of adolescents is a far cry from neo-realism's sentimental portrait of the noble, deserving poor. Paradoxically, while the film was heavily criticized in Mexico for its negative portrayal of urban youth, it was very successful in Europe, winning a director's prize at Cannes in 1950 and re-igniting interest in Buñuel's career and film-making reputation. Buñuel (1984: 2002) notes that the French distributors of the film added a curiously moralizing subtitle '*Los olvidados ou Pitié pour eux*' (The Forgotten or Pity Them) to mitigate the harshness of the film's representation.

In 16 more films made in Mexico, Buñuel gave vent to his morbid obsessions and fantasies, inviting audiences to share and question Arturo's insane jealousies in *Él* (1952), Ernesto's murderous desires in *Ensayo de un crimen/La vida criminal de Archibaldo de la Cruz* (1955), Nazarín's absurdly naïve religiosity (*Nazarín* 1958), repeated in *Simón del desierto* (1965) and the inexplicable self-imprisonment of the bourgeois dinner party guests in *El angel exterminador* (1962), another scenario also to be repeated. His Mexican period tends to be underrated and often ignored by critics, but there are clear continuities and recyclings of character and theme: in *L'âge d'or* and *Él*, we find the focus on *amour fou*, unsatisfied sexual desire; in *Los olvidados/Nazarín* and *Viridiana* (1961), the similarities between the cruel portrait of the urban poor and the beggars, and also between the defrocked priest and the pious nun; and in *Ensayo de un crimen* and *Tristana* (1970), the ironic emphasis on the fetishisation of erotic objects. In *Viridiana* (another *succès de scandale*) and *Tristana*, both made in Spain, and in the films of his French period, which culminated in his Oscar for *Le charme discret de la bourgeoisie* (1972), we also find significant continuities. His narratives, for example, are full of digressions, diversions, repetitions and shifts between reality and fantasy (dreams and the unconscious).

Buñuel's plots are based on absurd, unmotivated delays and inexplicable breaks in narrative continuity. *Le charme discret de la bourgeoisie* is about nothing more than a series of dinners, which are interrupted. Its premise, vaguely to do with drug smuggling, is left undeveloped; the film's main focus is on the bizarre power of bourgeois social etiquette gone mad and (well before Tarantino's hip gangster talk) wholly trite and inconsequential conversations on food, drink and style. The narrative never reaches a climax or resolution. If it looks like doing so, Buñuel throws in a dream, a character wakes up and the viewer is left to suppose that the whole tale has been a figment of the imagination. His last film, *Cet obscur objet du désir* (1977) perhaps sums up his film-making formula, where delay, frustration and repression emerge as the foundation stones of desire, passion, sexual pleasure as well as film making. Narrating his tale of erotic desire to a group of passengers (that is, stand-ins for the film audience) on a train bound for Paris, bourgeois gentleman Matthieu reveals that, despite showering his object of desire Conchita with expensive gifts, she refuses his sexual advances (Conchita is played by two different actresses, for no apparent reason). If he then withdraws, she returns, cajoling him back and then humiliating him. Finally, Conchita actually appears on the train, thus triggering once again the absurd, deadly cycle of *amour fou*. In other words, Buñuel appears to liken film narration to teasing or sexual titillation, where the pleasure lies not in finally reaching and seizing the outcome of the piece (as in classical Hollywood narration), but in being prevented from doing so (as in the European art film). There is nothing like repression and delay, it seems, to sharpen the desire to repeat, so strong is the compulsion that even a terrorist bomb is unable to stop the obsessive Mateo from pursuing Conchita at the end of the film.

As Marsha Kinder (1993: 286–92) points out, the traditional critical view of Buñuel – reflected in David Thomson's profile above – as the auteur who is deeply Spanish, deeply subversive because of his surrealism, and a constant scourge of the bourgeoisie, is full of contradictions and ironies. One such irony is that Buñuel is the only survivor of the original Parisian Surrealist gang to have continued making films in this mould throughout his career, as if compelled by some inner psychic need to repeat the same scene (Kinder, 1993: 289). It is not difficult, therefore, to make out an auteurist case for Buñuel, given the remarkable degree of consistency and coherence of style and theme across his films. Another is that, despite his standing as the undisputed incarnation of Surrealist film making and for many the embodiment of Spanish as well as Mexican film making, he was and remained until his own death in 1983, the eternal outsider, the permanent exile. In other words, his outsider, émigré status challenges not only his own national identity (his presumed 'Spanishness' and real citizenship), but also the nationality of the films he made, in terms of their location, funding, casting, language, cultural embedding as well as the meanings they offer, etc. (Kinder, 1993: 287). Yet, despite his nomadic existence and the fact that the vast majority of his films were made outside Spain, as we have seen, he is still regarded (mostly by foreign, Anglo-American critics) as the embodiment of Spanish film making. Such a misrecognition, quite understandably, has caused resentment among many Spanish film makers untouched by 'el maestro' but told he is the greatest, and even a certain distancing from close friends and colleagues such as Saura and Borau, who play down the influence of Buñuel on their work (see Kinder, 1993: 290). Buñuel's exile status has thus encouraged critics and film historians to magnify and exaggerate his impact and influence not only as an icon of two national cinemas and a world-wide film movement but also, in the cultural and political sphere, almost as a one-man anti-Fascist, anti-Franco guerrilla army.

It may well be that Buñuel was consistently subversive in his films and that his surrealism sought to undermine narrative as well as social and ideological conventions. It is also the case that for many critics, the surrealist films established Buñuel's unique personal vision and his assault by shock tactics on bourgeois values with images of animalistic cruelty, aestheticized violence and the cult of the bizarre (the slitting of the woman's eye, the ants emerging from the hand, the cow in the bed, the random shooting of the young boy). Yet, his film-making style was and has remained, if anything, extremely austere, straightforward, economical, fast, based on simple stagings and *mise-en-scène*, long takes and the use of pans to establish spatial information and follow the actors (Bordwell and Thompson, 2003: 418). Of course, the once provocative and scandalous images of Buñuel's surrealist classics have now been drained of much of their venom by commodification and commercialism but also exhausted through Buñuel's own consistent and repeated use of them himself. Also, if his aim was to make audiences see things afresh by using shock tactics, then he appears not to have followed his own advice. For all his attacks on the bourgeoisie, the Catholic Church and the exercise of tyranny, rationalized by his own atheism and admiration for Sade, he was nonetheless fascinated by this same class background (i.e. his own), he remained obsessed by his Catholic upbringing and was happy to temporize and accommodate the Franco dictatorship (for example, accepting the '*interés nacional*' award for *Tristana*, a project on which Buñuel had virtually no problems from the regime). Paradoxically, for a film maker whose films are a testimony to his own cruelties, black humour, homophobia and misogyny, thankfully they are not all full of clones of the ice-cold, repressed blondes such as Viridiana. They are also inhabited by stronger, more purposeful, clever, sadistic female characters who run rings around the effete males they cruelly tease and exploit. We find these not only in Buñuel's French films of the 1960s and 1970s, with examples like Conchita, or in Silvia Pinal's temptress in *Simón del desierto* (1965), made in Mexico. They also emerge even during Buñuel's commercial Filmófono period in the 1930s, in the rural melodrama/ *españolada, La hija de Juan Simón* (1935). Here, the novice flamenco dancer/performer Carmen Amaya plays a gypsy seductress and, though only a minor part, is the main narrative agent of revenge and reversal of power relations in the piece. Usually ignored or relegated to the margins, these four early 'genre' sound films which Buñuel produced, partly shot and edited for Filmófono – *Don Quintín el amargao* (1935), *La hija de Juan Simón*, *¿Quién me quiere a mí?* (1936) and *¡Centinela alerta!* (1936) – may well repay further study and research (see Kinder, 1993: 295–300).

As seen in the examples of both Almodóvar and Buñuel, the traditional method of determining authorship on the part of the film director usually centres on an analysis of evidence and examples taken from the film texts themselves. This is normally referred to as a thematic or stylistic analysis, where the critic seeks out a consistent set of themes and styles which are used and re-visited across a series of films. However, this degree of focus on the film text tends to exclude attention towards the extra-textual and pre-textual practices, which both impact on and shape what we eventually see in a film. So, some attention towards the context of 'working practices' is arguably crucial, given the complex financial, production and legal cultures and contexts of modern and contemporary film making. It is this complexity which makes the notion of the director as author in some ways rather unlikely but in others quite compelling.

So how far can we build into our analysis an awareness of the impact of working practices which both precede and follow the making of the film and impact upon its final shape for release? We have decided to look at the figure of Víctor Erice, who we take for granted as perhaps *the* leading example of a Spanish art film director who is widely regarded as a key auteur (during Francoism and after) but whose authorship is rendered problematic on various fronts.

VÍCTOR ERICE

Marsha Kinder makes the argument that because of the paucity of his film output, Erice cannot be considered as a candidate for authorship (1993: 127). The argument seems counter intuitive at first glance, since Erice is arguably the most highly regarded as well as the most enigmatic of Spanish film makers. Moreover, critical opinion, especially Anglo-American academic criticism, rates Erice extremely highly, to the extent that only he, alongside Buñuel, Almodóvar and Saura are normally accorded their own sections or chapters in surveys and panoramas of Spanish cinema (Hopewell, Higginbotham, Besas, Stone and others). Yet the location of Erice as a 'pantheon' director (to use Sarris's term) is usually made on the strength of only one film *El espíritu de la colmena* (1973). Apart from that, Erice has made one episode in a tri-partite anthology film *Los desafíos* (1969) (along-side contributions from José Luis Egea and Claudio Guerín) and two other features, *El sur* (1983), which represents only half of the planned script, and the dramatized documentary *El sol del membrillo* (1992). In 2002, Erice was removed from *El embrujo de Shanghai*, an adaptation of Marsé's novel of the same name and replaced by Fernando Trueba. Thus, in a film-making career spanning 35 years, strictly speaking, Erice has managed to make only two and a half films.

By any standards, this level of output cannot be regarded as a sufficient 'body of work' on which to establish, and trace over time, Erice's unique visual style, distinctive personal vision or his creative genius. And on such a basis, Kinder appears perfectly justified in denying Erice author status. Yet, in many other respects, the reality is that Erice is already canonized, both within the Spanish industry and Spain's film schools and in the wealth of academic writing and criticism, conference papers and monographs devoted to him, which continue to appear. Given Erice's problematic status as Spain's uncrowned auteur/art film maker, how should we approach his work? In the light of arguments made earlier in this chapter, it is probably no longer acceptable or wise to pursue the metaphysics of the auteur, to celebrate Erice as the master art director. If his status rests on one key film, it is also worth recognising that this film was made in 1972/73, i.e. during late Francoism, a particularly repressive and conflictive period shortly before the dictator's death. Erice's film, in its visual style and engagement with its subject matter, arguably bears the imprint of that period and those circumstances. As Paul Julian Smith has argued (1999: 93–114), while acknowledging Erice's undoubted talent and skill as a director, a more useful approach might be to historicize Erice and his film, thereby opening up a space for the acknowledgement and recognition of other key figures involved in the creative process.

It might be useful to start by filling in one or two points of background to Erice's career in the 1960s, after he graduated from film school in 1963, particularly his work as a critic and theorist in *Nuestro Cine*. Erice was one of the founding members of the new film review (1961–71), for which he wrote well over 50 articles, reviews and manifesto pieces over a six- or seven-year period, between numbers 2 and 46 (1961–65) and sporadic pieces thereafter until 1967. A film polymath, Erice's ideas on film, film criticism and film spectatorship were inspired largely by Guido Aristarco, editor of *Cinema Nuovo*, in turn guided by Georg Lukács' notion of critical realism, i.e. a film realism which went beyond the chronicle of everyday life in order to expose the underlying dynamic causes of social and political inequalities and the need for social change. Hence Erice's admiration for 1960s Italian directors such as Rossi, Pasolini, Zurlini, and his opposition to those of the Nouvelle Vague, whose attachment to 'formal acrobatics' and 'art for art's sake' and their thematic superficiality, rendered them unlikely models in the context of Francoist oppression.

As a student at the Official Film School in Madrid, Erice made four practice films, two in 16mm and two in 35mm. The latter, which remain, are *Páginas de un diario perdido* and *Los días perdidos* (40 minutes), his final-year project. According to Pena (2004: 17–18) *Páginas* is no more than an outline, a set of disconnected sequences, showing the daily routine of three generations of women in domestic interiors where nothing happens. *Los días perdidos* (1962/3), at 40 minutes, is a far more elaborate exercise, influenced by Antonioni's *L'éclisse* (1962) and the tenets of 1960s Italian critical realism, in which Isabel returns to Spain from Paris to attend her father's funeral in Madrid. Isabel is our identification figure and guide to Franco's Spain, which is represented as an empty wasteland, a vacuum, where time stands still and where the crumbling cemetery is emblematic of the decay, abandonment and death of the culture and society. The emphasis on evacuated settings (cemetery, graves, train station) and the 'dead time' endured especially by the younger generations, make of *Los días perdidos* an interesting forebear of the type of art film we find among Nuevo Cine Español directors such as Patino with his *Nueve cartas a Berta* (1965).

Intriguingly, by the time we get to 1969 and the moment of Erice's first major feature collaboration on *Los desafíos*, the politicized, radical, critical realist Erice of the early 1960s is far less in evidence. *Los desafíos* was a project commissioned by two American investors (including Dean Selmer, an actor) and taken up by producer Elías Querejeta, who invited three young Basque ex-Film School students to each take on a third of the film, with Rafael Azcona hired to script all three sketches. While Guerín and Egea happily accepted their scripts, Erice refused to use his and wrote his own, a sign perhaps of the proto-auteur asserting his integrity and artistic independence, but in a commissioned three-hander, arguably misplaced. The outcome was that Guerín and Egea shot their episodes according to the script, while Erice made a curious, fragmentary, almost 'counter cinematic' third section, replete with interpolations and insertions, which overall bore little or no relation to the other two episodes/sections. Moreover, his dominant intertext for a story of two 'swinging' couples (one Spanish, one American) which ends with a murder, was *Planet of the Apes* (1969), from which he borrowed the idea of using a monkey in his episode. Also, Querejeta was forced by censorship to intervene and impose a different ending, to suggest that the murder was not committed by a Spanish hand.

With *El espíritu de la colmena*, Smith is surely right to remind us that the reception of the film was mixed. It was both praised and criticized: for its poetic lyricism, its abstraction, obscurity and poorly motivated characterization. Smith also reminds us of the increasing abstraction of the many critical readings of the film since the mid-1970s, frequently reinforced by a quasi-religious cult of the auteur, a figure transformed into an almost spiritual essence. He cautions us to avoid such metaphysical temptations, arguing the case for grounding the film in its historical and production context and in relation to the various creative contributions which shaped the final film. Let us recall the fact that Erice was one of Querejeta's leading young directors and that the idea for *El espíritu...* probably arose in the context of a commission to do a horror film for Mercurio Films as a means of jumping on the growing bandwagon of Spanish horror of the early 1970s (for example, note that Jess Franco had already made two films on Frankenstein). The early versions of the script (written by Erice and Ángel Fernández Santos) included a frame story, in which Ana as adult returns to the village to deal with the death of her father (a strong echo of *Los días perdidos*). At some point, the frame device was dropped as too long, expensive or unwieldy and the film narrative was re-focused exclusively on Ana as a child, there being no reference to any present at all.

Querejeta's production company had its own 'in-house' team of technicians, thus Erice was surrounded by highly competent specialists. A planned six-week shoot was cut to five weeks. Fernando Fernán Gómez, the film's only star, was available for only one week, as was Teresa Gimpera, thus creating timetabling difficulties. Moreover, lacking enough appropriate footage of night and moon shots, Erice was forced to use some compatible outtakes from Gutiérrez Aragón's *Habla mudita* (1973). As if this were not enough, the film crew reported back to Querejeta their mounting concerns over Erice's ability to control and complete the shoot. They claimed they, and he, had little sense of where the film was going, of any clear narrative direction, given that the actual shooting veered so radically away from the agreed script, perhaps influenced by the degree of improvization between Erice and Ana Torrent (Pena lists 15 unshot sequences [2004: 37]). Most importantly, in terms of visual style and underpinning many of the metaphysical readings of the film was the fact that Erice was not in the habit of using establishing shots. This lack of contextual information made it difficult for viewers to establish correct spatial and temporal relations or ascertain the duration of sequences. Hence the elliptical nature of the film diegesis, in which the temporal markers are all but removed, perhaps not altogether for artistic reasons, but perhaps also for those of economy, lack of footage and pressure to complete.

It is useful to take into account such practical background information, i.e. re-inserting the film text into the context of its making and in relation to the working practices involved. Such detail tends to undercut somewhat the image of the director as auteur/creative genius, replacing it with that of the professional film maker as struggling artist who depends increasingly on the help of others to get him out a hole and complete the film.

Figure 3.1 Ana Torrent in *El espíritu de la colmena*

As Smith has shown (and there is no need to repeat the material here), Erice depended very heavily on the contribution of Luis Cuadrado (his cinematographer) for the film's subtle atmospheres, expressionist-inspired lighting and the studied symmetry of its compositions. He also needed Fernández Santos not only in the initial writing of the script (based on their childhood memories) but also in gauging the effects of dropping altogether the historical frame for the narrative and the on-screen narrator, which forces viewers to reconstruct the story themselves. Also, the supposed magic, lyricism and poetry of *Espíritu* and the amazing performance of Ana Torrent may be no more than the effects of technical decisions and lucky breaks during filmed improvizations where Torrent, though in character, is playing herself.

Finally, it is worth crediting the editor Pablo del Amo and producer Elías Querejeta for their role in the editing process, where they arguably rescued what otherwise was a messy, uncoordinated, incoherent piece of film making, according to Pena (2004: 39–40). As Smith (1999: 112) notes, it is unhelpful to regard Erice as a unique and solitary identity, since there is 'no sense of self without the other', that is without his crew, his producer and, more widely, the industry and the audience.

Chapter Four

GENRE

When we look at the cinema listings in the local paper or DVD store and ask our family or friends what kind of film they would like to watch – a comedy, thriller, horror, western, sci-fi – we are talking about genre. Genre is a French literary term, meaning type, or class. It puts films into generic categories as a means of breaking up a very large field into more manageable units. Our choice of comedy over horror, for example, is likely to be the sort of selection which reflects our tastes or preferences in relation to other sorts of film, though we are aware that most films exploit elements of various generic groupings in combination. We also enjoy anticipating and recognizing familiar generic features (Maltby, 2003: 107). Such discriminations are key variables which film producers must take into account and satisfy in order to make appealing films. Likewise, these choices are useful to those media gatekeepers (journalists, critics, reviewers, etc.), who can indicate publicly whether a film is a classic of its type, whether it challenges particular generic conventions or whether it is merely an effective or ineffective example of its grouping. So, in quite practical ways, the notion of genre allows us to bring together and analyse several linked areas: the film industry, the audience, opinion formers and the wider culture. Genre reminds us of the film industry's need to minimize financial risk and in a sense genre films are 'pre-sold' to audiences since viewers already have experience of a genre before they see a particular instance of the type (Maltby, 2003: 79).

As we saw in Chapter Three, auteurism/authorship emphasizes and privileges the personal factor in film making and sees the film as the product of a highly creative individual (the director), who leaves their unique stylistic signatures on and across a range of films or 'oeuvre'. Genre and the genre film, by contrast, refer mainly to the larger scale, mass-produced, industrialized film output of Hollywood and the commercial sectors in many national and macro-regional cinemas (such as Bollywood). Genre privileges convention and collective meaning (Buckland, 2003: 102), standardized attributes and similarities across a group of films, which make an individual film 'typical' of its group. So, where auteurist study focuses on the unique, the specific, the personal, the unusual and the exceptional, genre study is interested in what is typical, standardized and conventional across a series of films. Hence the term 'generic conventions', that is, the basic attributes and codes or rules (of iconography, setting, character, narrative, thematics, etc.) of a certain 'type' of film such as the comedy, romance, thriller, fantasy, science fiction, musical, etc. Such forms of classification, especially in the early years of the Hollywood studio system, helped studios select their markets, target audiences and thereby orient their production schedules. For example, in the 1930s, MGM was most closely associated with making musicals, while Universal Pictures specialized in horror, fantasy and war movies in the 1930s and melodramas, westerns and thrillers in the 1940s (Hayward, 2000: 371–2).

Of course, a major problem for any film industry is that genre films and their conventions can become repetitive, too predictable and overly formulaic. Spanish film history is littered with examples of hard-pressed producers trying to cash in on a commercially successful, popular formula, such as the filmed *zarzuela* in the mid-1920s, the folkloric musical in the mid-1930s and 1950s and the 'sexy Iberian comedy' of the early 1970s (see Jordan, 2003: 172–5). So, in order to continue to attract viewers, producers and directors need to introduce a degree of variation and flexibility, to combine known elements which have satisfied audiences in the past with different features. These will allow the film to be publicized and promoted as offering something 'new' and such features may extend or even challenge established genre conventions. Within the same generic framework, an individual film needs to strike a balance between the known and the unknown, repetition and difference, familiarity and novelty, stasis and change. In this sense, genres and their conventions are by no means static. As frameworks and sets of narrative and stylistic options, they shift and adapt according to commercial pressures and technological change; they also respond to social and cultural changes, including evolving audience tastes and values.

Historically speaking, since the 1960s, genre has been a key concept in the analysis of cinema as a major form of mass-produced entertainment. As noted above, the term's wide-ranging compass stands in marked contrast to the apparent narrowness and elitism of auteurism (see Stam, 2000: 126–30). Where auteurist critics are mainly concerned with exclusivity, i.e. with relatively few film directors, the notion of genre appears to offer far greater inclusivity, an approach more suited to commercial film making, in Hollywood and in other commercial, industrial and national contexts. (see Gledhill, 2000: 221–43). More importantly, genre allows us to focus on popular cinema in ways in which auteurism cannot. Traditionally, while auteurism has stressed stylistic distinctiveness and personal vision, it has also positioned popular cinema as a lower order, inferior form of film production compared to 'genuine' film art. By contrast, genre criticism has sought to deal not with individual genius but with a standardized industrial process and a differentiated product, analysing Hollywood as a mode of film production within a broader capitalist framework (see Ryall, 1998: 327–38). Yet, to see Hollywood as a generic cinema and thereby a paradigm for commercial cinema across the world may not be sufficiently flexible and nuanced an approach to encompass new contemporary realities.

Genres are no longer linked to specific studios, as they were in the 1930s and 1940s, since the studio system no longer exists. The dominant mode of mass production in Hollywood has changed to the 'package unit' model. Since the 1950s, long-term studio contracts have been supplanted by individual producers organizing film-making projects on a short-term, film-by-film basis (see Nelmes, 2003: 22). At the same time, there have been radical changes in our modes of consumption of film. Increasingly, many of us watch films on television. Compared to watching DVDs in a domestic context, a trip to the local multiplex to enjoy the 'film experience' is becoming less common (though this is not the case in Spain, see Jordan, 2003b). Also, films are no longer discrete, self-contained products, but are accompanied by a wealth of merchandising and tie-ins. So, perhaps our traditional acceptance of genre classifications as separable categories, able to differentiate one type of film from another, needs to be updated. In the so-called late-capitalist, postmodern context of 'bricolage' and 'intertextuality', the notion of genre may be less useful in describing a film or what has now become in effect a multi-purpose entertainment delivery system.

In terms of genre criticism, we usually study a film as a specific type of product or commodity and look at different instances of that product, within and between film groupings, on the basis of similarities and differences. This is genre analysis as classification, i.e. trying to fit films into particular groups, defining boundaries between groups, mapping common elements shared by them and often searching for 'progressive' or 'subversive' categories of film (Maltby, 2003: 108). This sort of work is often complemented by questions such as why certain genres are popular at certain times and not at others, thereby taking into account the historically variable and contingent nature of genres. Of course, genre criticism has a methodological problem here, a 'chicken and egg' dilemma in relation to how we 'construct' the genre. What comes first? Do we begin by isolating the body of films or 'corpus' which we recognize as say, Spanish folkloric musicals, or do we begin by making a list of the main attributes of this genre? The trouble is that the common features of the '*folclórica*' cannot be safely determined in isolation from the 'films themselves', a further category which is by no means watertight or settled. We thus become trapped in a rather circular argument, yet we also recognize that the use of genre, as a way of distinguishing between films, assumes a certain consensus about what a '*folclórica*', melodrama or comedy actually mean. We know a '*folclórica*' when we see one. Or rather, we know a '*folclórica*' even before we see it, since we have already internalized, through our film-viewing experiences, a set of images and terms through which we recognize the type. As Andrew Tudor argues: 'genre is what we collectively believe it to be' (1974: 139).

Genres are rule-governed constructs, at least to some extent, characterized by recycled patterns, forms, styles and structures which transcend individual films and which draw on conventional types of imagery. Yet, an individual genre movie, in order to distinguish itself in the market and attract an audience, needs to extend, challenge and innovate genre conventions (Abrams, Bell and Udris, 2001: 176). Ordinarily, the menu of expected conventions for the science-fiction film would not include slapstick comedy or a western-style shoot-out, but this is exactly what we find in Alex de la Iglesia's *Acción mutante* (1992). Also, in the cop thriller, we would not normally expect a song and dance routine or the macho cop hero stealing deodorant from a convenience store during a robbery, but this is precisely what we get in *Torrente: el brazo tonto de la ley* (1998). In other words, we have become aware that in the last decade or two, more and more Spanish films engage in generic experimentation, they deliberately seek new and inventive forms of generic cross-over or hybridity. This particular trend has been identified as a feature of what is called 'the postmodern' or 'postmodernism'. Postmodern technique usually implies the blurring of distinctions between high and low art, avant-garde forms being mixed with elements of trash or exploitation cinema. It implies much greater openness and indeterminacy, a lack of narrative linearity, a rejection of a unified diegesis and the pre-eminence of style over content. Finally, it upsets traditional notions of stable meaning, which are placed in quotation marks and often given an ironic twist.

Nowadays, we are getting used to generic labels, coined by critics and reviewers, that are multi-accented and multi-hyphenated (e.g. gross-out, teen, comedy-horror-musical). Indeed, the eclecticism of much contemporary cinema involves levels of hybridity and self-conscious intertextuality which challenge any definition of genre as a stable category, with its own stylistic and narrative conventions. In other words, many contemporary commercial films, including many Spanish examples, are increasingly made up of elements appropriated and plagiarized from popular and high-culture film sources, which are then re-constructed in ways which defy any notion of a single genre. Also, when we respond to such films, we tend to focus on not what this or that film means but what it reminds us of, what other films it refers to, resembles or echoes? For example, Alex de la Iglesia's *Acción mutante* (1992), *El día de la bestia* (1995), *Muertos de risa* (1999), *La comunidad* (2000), *800 balas* (2002) are all highly self-conscious, generically hybrid films, packed with references, echoes, allusions to other films and other media. So, for example, to call *Bestia* a horror film tells us little about the ironic inversion of the horrific by the gruesomely comic and the sheer level of semiotic excess of the film. If *Bestia* has helped redefine a certain type of Spanish 'grotesque parodic horror', it has done so by wrenching itself free of traditional modes of story-telling and by linking up with an eclectic range of intertexts from many domestic and foreign generic formations.

In more recent accounts of genre (such as Neale, 2000 and Darley, 2002), the argument put forward is that in the digital age, genres can no longer be seen in the same way as before. In the face of new technological developments, new modes of marketing and (re-) packaging of 'films' and with increased opportunities for self-reference and repetition, the old categories are simply breaking down. In other words, the economic realities of contemporary film production, risk management and catering to media-savvy young audiences, mean that genre is increasingly being replaced by processes such as seriality, i.e. the proliferation of sequels, prequels, follow-ups, series, franchises (e.g. *Star Wars*, *Alien*, *Friday the 13th* (now at Part 10), *Spiderman*, etc.) and by other terms such as blockbuster, effects film, event movie, action cinema. Film genres are also being inserted into much wider networks and relations with other media, involving merchandizing, tie-ins, product placement, franchise arrangements, branding, TV spin-offs, video games, novelizations, etc. Yet, it may still be useful to hang on to the notion of genre, since generic markers are still being used and foregrounded in film marketing strategies, which rely on generic motifs to publicize film products. This is happening in Spain, as the example of the *Torrente* cycle suggests, where the film text is but one albeit important commodified element in a much wider constellation of marketing and promotional devices (see Jordan, 2003b: 191–207).

In the following case studies, we wish to suggest that popular cinema conventions need not be limiting or restrictive, but rather, enabling. They offer a film maker a structure within which he or she can exercise talent and ingenuity, in a range of permutations and variations. Even the strictest conventions allow a degree of flexibility and creative freedom. No film is ever an exact replica or clone of another. Firstly, we hope to show that in the case of Spain's most enduring, indigenous genre, the folkoric musical, film makers, even in the 1960s, were still capable of exploiting its conventions, in novel ways, some more inventively than others. In a further two case studies, drawing on examples from the very different production context of the 1990s, we focus first on Alejandro Amenábar's *Tesis*, as an example of the Spanish horror genre, but of what kind? Then we focus on the astonishing phenomenon of Santiago Segura's *Torrente: el brazo tonto de la ley* (1998), Spain's first home grown 'blockbuster'. We consider the film not only in terms of its national identity and 'Spanishness' but also its generic identity and how this seems to break down under the weight of its intertextual and semiotic excess. We also note in passing that, in the domain of the genre film, perhaps especially in Spain, seriality and the ruthless, exhaustive exploitation of successful formulae via sequels, remakes and imitations, are hardly new or recent phenomena, but punctuate the entire history of Spanish film making.

THE SPANISH MUSICAL FILM

Broadly speaking, film musicals are vehicles for often very complex song-and-dance routines. They privilege spectacle and performance over narrative and focus on the erotic and sensual body movements of male and female performers. They are also highly self-conscious, exhibitionist and narcissistic films, always anxious about motivating performance within the narrative (the classic 'show within a show' device), especially when their main purpose is escapist, utopian entertainment. Their naïve plots revolve predominantly around romance and courtship, inevitably leading to marriage, in which characters who are initially opposites sooner or later attract each other and fall in love. Musicals are thus organised along parallel storylines, through clashes and binary oppositions (based on age, temperament, nationality, sexuality, class, gender) all of which are ultimately resolved. Ideologically, musicals tend to support the status quo; their aim is to 'sell' marriage, reinforce notions of community and family, affirm gender stability and overcome the fear of difference (Hayward, 2000: 251).

Before looking at the work of Manolo Escobar in the 1960s, we think it might be useful to clarify what we mean by the 'musical film' in the Spanish context, in the light of arguments put forward by film historian Carlos F. Heredero (1993:181–91). Heredero approaches the musical film tradition in Spain, using the Hollywood musical as a benchmark. He sees the musical as quintessentially American, arguing that because it successfully blended Broadway musical theatre traditions and commercial genre film making (predominantly the comedy), integrating action, music and dance into a coherent film diegesis, it can be analysed as a broadly distinctive genre, with its own codes and conventions. In the case of the Spanish musical film, however, Heredero is far from certain that this constitutes a distinctive, let alone cohesive, genre at all. He argues that the traditions of Spanish musical cinema are very different from those of the American variety and that such traditions have not produced an autonomous genre capable of generating generic conventions separate from those sources which nourish it (1993: 181). In other words, Spanish musical cinema is a complex hybrid of many other forms, including *zarzuela*, music hall, light opera, Andalusian folkloric song, '*cante flamenco*', the '*cuplé*' (light, often risqué, song), and 'pop'. It also draws upon the narrative and stylistic conventions of melodrama, comedy, the radio/newspaper serial, the picaresque tale and the traditional, exotic, folklore of 'deep Spain'.

Heredero is probably mistaken to regard the Hollywood musical as a fundamentally cohesive, 'pure' form. Like its Spanish counterpart, the American musical has its antecedents, descending from vaudeville, music hall and European operetta (Hayward, 2000: 243), i.e. it too is very much a hybrid genre. Yet, he is arguably correct to suggest that in Spain, musical cinema never really developed a specific set of conventions independently of its popular roots and intertextual sources, especially the '*zarzuela*', with its mixture of dramatic dialogue and musical inserts. Thus, rather than talk about the Spanish 'musical' as a definable, tangible category in itself, Heredero suggests that we talk about film comedies, melodramas, folkloric narratives in which songs and dance routines are inserted or interpolated into the film diegesis, rather than fully integrated into and motivated by the narrative and the characters' emotional states. Thereby, he seems to differentiate between a film musical (i.e. a film in which the performance of singing and dancing numbers is the primary or dominant element which drives the narrative forward, as in the Hollywood form) and a musical film (one in which music and dance are not the dominant, structuring centre of interest but rather, illustrative, decorative and secondary, as in the Spanish case).

Heredero's approach suggests that there is still work to be done in terms of generic clarification. This being so, if our broad definition of the Spanish musical film is not as secure as we would like, then by implication we need to be guided by caution when dealing with important sub-categories in this field, such as the widely used and abused term '*españolada*' and what Heredero labels the '*cine folclórico andalucista*' (Andalusia-inflected folkloric cinema), seen as the most popular and prevalent mode of the Spanish film musical tradition. In some recent writings on Spanish popular culture and musical film, specialists broadly coincide in seeing the term '*españolada*' as rather slippery, open to positive as well as pejorative meanings and historically very variable uses. The term has French origins in the early–mid nineteenth century as a label ('*espagnolade*') to describe a particularly narrow, stereotypical, falsified vision of aspects of Spain's popular culture, as exemplified in Merimée's novella *Carmen* (1845) and Bizet's opera of the same name (1875). The term has also been linked to such Hollywood productions as *Blood and Sand* (1922) with Rudolph Valentino and *The Torrent* (1926), starring Greta Garbo (Crumbaugh, 2002: 266). Borau (1998: 321) helpfully reminds us that Spanish film makers and critics in the 1920s used the term to describe this type of foreign film, not always positively. Paradoxically, they also appropriated the very same term to market abroad their own indigenous versions of folkloric musicals. What is interesting is that while Lázaro Reboll and Willis (2004: 7–8) initially use '*españolada*' as a very wide, cross-generic, portmanteau term to describe exaggerated and 'excessive' depictions of Spanish 'national' character, they also accept Vernon, who is rather more specific, in seeing it as a filmic 'hybrid genre of romantic comedy and/or melodrama, incorporating regional, primarily Andalusian, song and dance' (1999: 249). Given the variability of meaning in the use of the term '*españolada*' (a depiction of national character, a foreign film type, a Spanish film genre?), it might be helpful to be guided by Vernon when referring to this dominant form of Spain's musical tradition on film, or Labanyi, who uses the term 'folkloric musical' as a more specific generic descriptor rather than the more generalist, ideologically inflected, term '*españolada*' (Labanyi, 2000: 169–70).

In terms of Spanish film making, from the 1910s right up to the 1990s, the dominant type of musical film has been the '*folclórica*'. Spain's folkloric musical film was a hybrid genre, based on theatrical, light operatic and music hall precedents, as well as silent, bandit biopics, early bullfighting films, 'latin-lover' melodramas from Hollywood and numerous versions of the Carmen story (see Davies, 2004). Exalting the virtues of a pre-modern, feudal Spain (of hierarchy, religion, machismo, etc.), it developed strongly from the late 1910s and early 1920s onwards, displaying the singing talents of female '*folclóricas*' in such silent classics as *La verbena de la paloma* (José Buchs, 1921), *Carceleras* (José Buchs, 1923), *La revoltosa* (Florián Rey, 1924) and *Malvaloca* (Benito Perojo, 1926). It combined clichéd, Andalusian, rural settings and idealized, stereotypical characters (lower class, female gypsy songbirds, upper class '*señoritos*', wealthy young men, sometimes referred to as '*payos*', i.e. non-gypsies, plus bullfighters, friendly priests, petty thieves, singers and musicians) with fairy-tale, Cinderella plots (the witty and wily female gypsy engages in a romantic adventure with her class superior) and unlikely narrative endings, in which conflicts and contradictions are resolved through a marriage union between unequals. Any resemblance to the 'real' Andalusia of gypsy persecution is purely coincidental, since these products were designed predominantly as escapist entertainment.

The folkloric musical remained popular during the Spanish Republic (1931–36), even though early sound versions were technically very poor by foreign standards. It continued to be made during the civil war (both inside Spain and in studios in Italy and Germany) and was still very popular during the 1940s and 1950s, under the dictatorship, championed by directors such as Ramón Torrado, Luis Lucia and Florián Rey, while being gently satirized by Berlanga in *Bienvenido Míster Marshall* (1952). However, unlike the '*cine de cruzada*', which promoted macho Francoist warriors as 'national' role models, the folkloric musical and its dusky, southern, female sirens were not favoured by the regime's film protection and awards system (see Vernon, 1999: 251). In the 1950s, except for the male, child singing stars such as Pablito Calvo and Joselito and the few male, 'flamenco' inflections of the folkloric musical starring Antonio Molina and Juanito Valederrama, the genre was dominated by female performers, such as Juanita Reina, Carmen Sevilla, Lola Flores, Paquita Rico, etc. In 1957, with the massive success of *El último cuplé* (Juan de Orduña), starring Sarita Montiel, we see a certain shift in the genre, not in narrative terms (the rags-to-riches, Cinderella story remains) but in its more melodramatic, moralistic finale of the fallen woman corrupted by associating with foreign men, its adoption of the '*cuplé*' rather than the folkloric, Andalusian '*copla*', as well as an emphasis on the erotic appeal of Montiel herself. Public nostalgia for the *cuplé* was exploited in well over a dozen imitators of Orduña's hit film (Heredero, 1993: 188), yet times were changing. The record industry was developing, song festivals (such as the Eurovision song contest) were beginning to appear and in the 1960s, in the so-called '*años de desarrollo*' (development years) of mass tourism, Spain began to produce its own 'pop' singers, including the Dúo Dinámico, Los bravos, Raphael, Massiel, Joan Manuel Serrat, Julio Iglesias, Marisol and Manolo Escobar.

In the 1960s, alongside such important young female performers as Marisol, Rocío Dúrcal and Ana Belén, Manolo Escobar was arguably the biggest male singing star in Spain (though he could not dance, unlike Marisol). Such honorific labels as '*cantante bandera*' (flagship singer) or '*la voz de España*' (the voice of Spain) made Escobar not only a national celebrity but also an icon of traditionalist Spanish values in the context of economic liberalization, a trope which all of his films sought to incorporate. Born in 1934, in Almería, the fifth of 10 children, Manolo Escobar moved with his family to Barcelona at the beginning of the 1950s. He combined a day job as a sub-postman with developing a singing career in a flamenco-inspired guitar band with three of his brothers. Spotted by a presenter with Radio Barcelona, the band performed for the radio and very quickly began to make records. Escobar's singing career took off in 1958 and by the early 1960s he had several major hit records such as *Madrecita María del Carmen*, *Tu nombre de Anita* and *Mi carro*. He broke into films in 1962, with a small part in *Los guerrilleros* (Pedro. L. Ramírez), a somewhat shambolic, though commerically successful period piece, mixing action, adventure and intercalated songs sung by Manolo, set during Spain's War of Independence against the French. Given his huge popular appeal in the mid-1960s, he was hired by Galician director Ramón Torrado to star in a trio of successful musical films: *Mi canción es para ti* (1965), *Un beso en el puerto* (1965) and *El padre Manolo* (1966), in which he virtually played himself, embodying characters whose trajectories strongly echoed aspects of his own life story. Moreover, in these *folclóricas*, revamped for the 1960s, the film narratives followed the classic, archetypal, 'rags-to-riches' fantasies of lower-class stereotypes (especially singers and bullfighters) who overcome their humble origins and achieve success, stardom and thereby social and class mobility (see Woods, 2004: 40–59).

Following *Mi canción es para ti*, in which he doubled as a noble peasant singer who overcomes his nasty, arrogant, local rival, Escobar played another singer of emblematic, humble, small-town origins (named Manolo, of course) in Torrado's *Un beso en el puerto*. Here, the narrative explores the clash between a backward, vulnerable, naïve Spain (Manolo) and the lures of neo-capitalist consumerism and modernity (represented through an opening mock documentary which charts the rise of tourism in Benidorm, culminating in the influx of 'foreign others', such as Dorothy, the American visitor and heiress). Manolo works as a petrol pump attendant in a busy, out-of-town *gasolinera*, a sign of the booming tourist industry around Benidorm, Altea and Alicante in the mid-1960s. He owns a scooter and knows basic car mechanics, but dreams of fame and fortune as a singer. Clad in his spotless white overalls, he sings his first major number in a heavily marked Andalusian accent to swooning, lower-class, Spanish housewives, as they dry their washing in the fields. Sacked from his menial job for laziness, he is rescued by his old friend Jaime, who has unexpectedly come into money, has a bright new sports car and a new Cuban lady friend. They all set off for bustling Benidorm, a new consumer tourist paradise, where petty thief Jaime teaches the unwordly Manolo how to hit upon foreign tourists by greeting them with a kiss (as if a long lost cousin), calling them 'Dorothy' (whatever their names) and then making an apology for the mistaken identity, thereby 'softening' their resistance to further seduction. Using the same trick, Manolo gets lucky at the port of Alicante and manages to 'hook' an American tourist actually called Dorothy (symbol of American wealth and echo of Marshall Aid, played however by dyed-blonde, Ingrid Pitt, soon to become Countess Dracula in late-1960s Hammer horror).

The film narrative is yet another re-run of the archetypal Cinderella story of courtship and marriage, though this time it involves a comic inversion of gender relations. That is, lower-class '*folclórico*' singer Manolo miraculously falls in love with upper-class American heiress Dorothy who, despite being promised to another, is equally smitten and set on getting married. The path to happiness is complicated, however, by a series of messy and stylistically archaic comic entanglements, confusions, repeated instances of mistaken identity, as well as moments of Chaplinesque slapstick and farce and lots of chases and pursuits, highly reminiscent of the 'Carry On' films (though without the strong sexual innuendo). Narrative cause and effect are tenuous in the extreme (what motivates Manolo's dream in his prison cell, for example, an interpolation which allows Torrado to mount the only modestly choreographed dance sequence in the whole film?). The settings (the petrol station, the hotel rooms, the beach, the swimming pool area, the dance area, the route for the car ride, the police station, the cells, etc.) all emphasize the dualities involved in the film's male/female binary oppositions, while also functioning as so much tourist propaganda for Benidorm and Spain. Costumes and props repeat and emphasize economic differences (Manolo's little scooter versus Dorothy's huge American car; Manolo's masquerade as rich playboy, very reminiscent of the Tony Curtis role in *Some Like it Hot* [Billy Wilder, 1958] versus Dorothy's 'real' wealth). Supporting characters (such as money-grabbing Carlos, voyeuristic policemen, plus other couples: Jaime and Lulu, German tourist and wife, French family man and wife; Dorothy's father and the friendly, singing '*gitanos*' in the cells) all serve as mirrors and counterpoints or complements to the main couple. And, interestingly, in terms of camerawork, Torrado is remarkably consistent, repeating virtually the same pattern of cross-cutting shots during Manolo's seven vocal numbers, plus a repeat of 'Un beso en el puerto' as a finale.

As an allegory of economic and social change, the film presents Manolo as an embodiment of Spain in the face of '*apertura*' (1960s liberalization), exposed to the potential dangers of tourist consumerism, sexual freedom and modernity (dangers echoed in the lyrics of the main song 'Un beso en el puerto'). Indeed, as a product of a backward economy in the throes of economic modernization, Manolo is a figure many Spaniards would find it easy to identitfy with, as we see him dazzled by a picture-postcard image, in technicolor, of a new tourist-led, consumerist paradise. This is especially so when he comes to realize that his status in the new international tourist economy is 'different'. His function in the new economy is one of performer or entertainer, i.e. that of a subordinate, merely part of a new service class, where he is expected to perform a version of 'Spanishness', which helps reinforce the 'imaginary' folkloric vision of Spain demanded by his tourist clientele. And through his contact with Dorothy, Manolo is also made aware of his class and gender differences, his own strong sense of class inferiority and unworthiness, which is maintained until the end of the film (indeed, he very gallantly withdraws from marriage with Dorothy, because of his inferiority, but she insists on going ahead). Manolo is no illiterate peasant '*paleto*' (country bumpkin), though his character frequently echoes this classic comic stereotype. Given his naivety and good nature, neither is he a dangerous petty thief or evil Iberian seducer, though elements of these stereotypes are also written into his role. And while he tries to exercise a form of sexual '*donjuanismo*' against the foreign tourist invader, his innate nobility as a Spanish '*caballero*' (gentleman) prevents him from acting like a cad. In fact, it is not his testosterone, sexual prowess or macho, pin-up image, which win Dorothy's heart, but a far more subtle, sensitive seduction technique based on singing and male submission. In their courtship, it is Dorothy who takes control, who invites him for a ride in her big car, who gives him his instructions on when and where to meet (which he meekly obeys), generally makes all the arrangements and delivers the kiss, as they overlook the bay at Benidorm. Male submission, and a series of softer, feminized responses, seem to work wonders and lead to marriage and happpiness. The price is his gender subordination, which he happily accepts in exchange for happiness, class mobility and assured economic stability, while still affirming traditional Spanish values through his songs.

In the late 1960s, wishing to capitalize on the popular success of *Un beso...* and *El padre Manolo* (in which Manolo plays a remarkably benign priest who donates his prize money from singing competitions to charitable works), producer Arturo González and Regia films signed him up to star alongside 'pop' performer Conchita Velasco, for four new musical comedies in a row: *¿Pero... en qué país vivimos?* (1967), *Relaciones casi públicas* (1968), *Juicio de faldas* (1969) and *Me debes un muerto* (1971).

We propose to look briefly at *¿Pero... en qué país vivimos?* (1967), as it sets a pattern for the cycle of four successive movies. It also demonstrates the flexibility as well as the pre-dictability of the folkloric musical formula and its adaptability to new social conditions, even in the interests of extremely archaic moral values. Reflecting the impact of the new, modern, consumer society and the arrival of advertising and public relations companies in Spain, the film takes as its pretext a joint publicity campaign on behalf of two drinks companies (one making whisky, the other '*manzanilla*' (dry sherry), in which PR executive Rodolfo Sicilia (Alfredo Landa) is charged with developing a dual marketing strategy. At a loss for ideas and at his wits' end, he is rescued by his more perceptive secretary Rosarito (Gracita Morales), who gives him the idea of a national singing contest (to be entitled *¿Qué canta España?*). Here, drinks products are aligned to public song preferences: the darker, drier, *manzanilla* with traditional Spanish *coplas*, and the lighter-coloured whisky, served with ice, with modern 'pop' favourites. The singing competition, sponsored by the drinks companies, will be held at Madrid's Palacio de Deportes; the result will be decided by combining a direct popular vote of the audience in the sports stadium with a nationwide television vote, region by region (in effect, a pastiche of the Eurovision Song Contest on a national scale). The 'pop' star Barbara (Conchita Velasco) is hired to represent whisky and modernity, whilst national idol of the '*canción española*', Antonio Torres (Escobar) rep-resents *manzanilla* and tradition. Initially unwilling to commit himself, the reclusive and wealthy Torres only enters the fray on condition that, if he wins, he can lop off Barbara's lush brunette '*melena*' (long hair) in exchange for his fee. Symbolic of Torres' machismo, misogyny and rejection of modernity, Barbara's annoying *melena* is the trigger to a 'war of the sexes' which nonetheless is finally resolved with declarations of love and marriage at Torres' imposing country estate.

As outlined above, compared to *Un beso en el puerto*, the film is simply and starkly structured according to a series of binary oppositions, based on male/female contrasts of gender and sexuality. However, the narrative messiness and frequent chaos of *Un beso...* with its multi-ple pairings, contrasts and oppositions among its many supporting characters, is replaced by a clear focus on the film's two primary couples (Barbara/Torres and Rosarito/Rodolfo

Sicilia). The issues of inferiority and unworthiness arising from inter-class differences (between Manolo and Dorothy) are dropped in favour of clashes between equals (both Barbara and Torres are professional singers and very wealthy, though she is greedy, while he is blasé about money; their battles are echoed and reflected in Rosarito and Rodolfo's conflictual, high-energy relationship). Also, the archaic *folclórica* storyline of the lower-class female singer seducing the upper-class *señorito* is partly shifted onto and shared by Rosarito and Rodolfo (though he is an incorrigible womanizer, Rosarito fancies Rodolfo and manages to 'tame' him, with Barbara's help). Also notable is the way the film operates a useful and much appreciated division of labour, cutting between Landa and Morales (who brilliantly take care of all the comedy) and Escobar and Velasco (who do the singing and the rather wooden seduction scenes, accompanied by Escobar's romantic ballads).

If the film contrasts the reclusive, *machista*, atavistic, Antonio Torres (who breeds wolves, likes hunting, keeps stuffed game birds and socializes only with his male guitar band), with Barbara (the ultimate material girl, snobbish, greedy, obsessed by her appearance and the latest lifestyle accessories), it is only to assimilate their personalities on terms set by Torres and accepted by Barbara. In other words, the old Spain reabsorbs the new, tradition

Figure 4.1 Antonio (Escobar) seduces Barbara (Velasco) with a romantic ballad

accommodates but re-fashions modernity in its own image, and here, we find several key affirmations of old Francoist values. The first is that consumerism (as represented by Barbara) is shown negatively, as almost a pathological condition, an illness, which old Spain does well to avoid; also, for Torres, Barbara's modernity and sexuality are encapsulated in her swinging *melena*, which covers her face and which he is determined to remove. The second is that, compared to the national television poll, the direct public vote in the sports hall, following the singing contest, becomes disorderly and chaotic. This is meant to prove that Francoist 'organic democracy' (endorsed expressly by Escobar in his dialogue, when he mentions his own vote in Spain's 1966 referendum) is superior to 'inorganic', pluralist expressions of the public will. Paradoxically (and in a rather self-reflexive manner, which underlines the lack of democratic consultation in Spain), the film also includes several minutes of interpolated, authentic, documentary 'vox pops', shot in Madrid's streets, revealing 'real' public attitudes to Spanish and foreign popular music.

Finally, the film resolution is based on the archaic theatrical device of 'unmasking', during which Barbara reveals her modernity to be a pose, a masquerade and merely wig-deep. Having accompanied Antonio back to his '*finca*', she reveals her real name to be the common Spanish name 'Balbina' not Barbara (this is no more than a modern, foreign invention, a stage name). She removes her impressive black '*melena*' voluntarily (thus avoiding the scissors) and to Torres' consternation, shows it to be a wig, under which is an even longer and more striking platinum blonde, shoulder-length wig. She then removes the second wig, to reveal her own, short-cropped, natural dark hair, the sort Torres admires. Barbara's 'striptease', her removal of her double masquerade, offers a striking and direct echo of the archaic figure of the mixed-blood heroine of the *españolada* tradition, the fair, dark-skinned woman (the '*morena clara*'), emblematic of a split personality as well as a potentially mobile female identity (Vernon, 1999: 254). Yet Balbina/Barbara's baring of the 'real' self underneath her stage wigs conjures away the threat of difference and sexual assertiveness. She thus concedes that her modernity is no more than a masquerade, a false identity hiding her authentic, submissive Spanishness, which she now recuperates and offers as a token and demonstration of her love to Antonio. Remarkably, she rejects her independence, empowerment and career (i.e. her own '*folclórica*' narrative of 'rags to riches') for the duties of a Catholic marriage to Torres, embracing submission, servitude and motherhood. Her renunciation of modernity and embrace of Spanish traditions also endorse the pretty crude, misogynistic, patriarchal vision of Spanish womanhood, enunciated by Torres himself: 'As far as I'm concerned, the woman who doesn't cook, sew or pray... is not a woman...'. Thankfully, Torres' reactionary sentiments are offset by the final sequence of the film, a coda in which Rosarito, having heard by telephone of Barbara's impending marriage to Torres, hangs up, saying to Rodolfo off-screen, in bed: 'Everything's under control. We can go to sleep now'. In other words, lower-class Rosarito too has finally 'tamed' her man (thereby also fulfilling the main female fantasy of the *folclórica* narrative), the twist being that she prefers to live in sin, it seems, with not a hint of marriage plans in sight. This is a welcome, ironic alternative and counterpoint to the saccharine-laden main resolution.

SPANISH HORROR: AMENÁBAR'S *TESIS* AND POSTMODERNISM

Amenábar himself has defined *Tesis* as a '*thriller urbano y juvenil*' (Sempere, 2000: 78), whose novelty resides in the use of a sophisticated investigation plot, led by students, within a university context. Christine Buckley also adopts the term 'thriller' but widens its scope to that of 'horror thriller', a hybrid term which acknowledges the incorporation into the film of a monstrous threat and narrative elements of the slasher movie sub-genre (2002: 8). Here, Buckley draws extensively on Carol Clover's feminist work on the slasher film (1992), notably the figure of the 'final girl' (Ángela) who, while not sexually active, is active in the investigation plot and finally tracks down and defeats the killer. Leora Lev also regards Ángela as a 'likely candidate for final girl status' (2000: 36; 2001: 168). However, while both Buckley and Lev appear to accept Clover's contention that the slasher movie assumes dominant male agency (even if via the final girl figure) and masculine norms of spectatorship, Isabel Pinedo sees the sub-genre as providing an imaginary scenario in which women fight back with lethal force against male aggressors and win. As such, the slasher movie can also be seen to appeal to female spectators while inducing significant anxiety in men (1997:85). As a type of 'horror thriller/slasher movie', *Tesis* thus connects with trends in post-1960s horror, fundamentally redefined by Hitchcock's *Psycho* (1960). The latter located the monstrous in the 'ordinary' modern psyche (Norman Bates) and linked horror with the psychological thriller, thereby helping to inspire the slasher, stalker and serial killer movies of the 1970s, 1980s and 1990s.

As Carter and Weaver have suggested, the dominance of the violent action genre of the 1980s (in the *Alien* and *Terminator* series, as well as in the latter stages of the *Rocky* and *Rambo* cycles, for example) gave way in the 1990s to the serial killer genre and ' a new wave of designer violence' (2003: 65). There emerged extremely graphic images of violence seemingly devoid of motivation, effects or moral frameworks. Tarantino's rise to directorial fame, for example, in *Reservoir Dogs* (1992), and *Pulp Fiction* (1994) no doubt responded in part to his hip aestheticization of screen violence, usually set to catchy pop music tracks. Many other films, such as *Man Bites Dog* (Rémy Belvaux, 1992*), The Silence of the Lambs* (Jonathan Demme, 1992), *Natural Born Killers* (Oliver Stone, 1994, based on a Tarantino script), *Se7en* (David Fincher, 1996) and most notoriously *Henry: Portrait of a Serial Killer* (John MacNaughton, 1986/1990) also seemed to indulge in overly visceral screen violence, heavily sexualized, with an emphasis on seemingly pointless, often, narcissistic and sadistic brutalism. In the face of public criticism concerning the 'effects' of such imagery and its apparent legitimation of perverse sexual gratification, directors defended their movies not as shameless commercial fare, but as serious, knowing, often parodic treatments of media exploitation of violence and public fears of crime and disorder. In other quarters, such movies were said to reflect a certain postmodern temperament, one in which 'postmodern horror constructs an unstable, open-ended universe in which categories collapse, violence constitutes everyday life and the irrational prevails' (Pinedo, 1996: 29). Postmodern horror, in this guise, thus acknowledged the dissolution of dominant ideologies and, as the body counts rose, it also seemed to tap into millenial anxieties of apocalyptic proportions (as seen, for example, in Alex de la Iglesia's *El día de la bestia*).

To what extent does Amenábar's *Tesis* ride this 1990s wave of slasher/serial killer savagery and screen violence? Is it necessarily antagonistic to dominant ideologies, do its depictions of violence seem meaningless and unmotivated, disconnected from wider social and political ideologies? Does this make it a form of postmodern horror and if so, of what kind? These are not straightforward questions and arguably demand far deeper examination than can be given here. As Andrew Tudor has pointed out, the trouble with the notion of postmodern horror is its lack of precision, since nearly all of those qualities seen as distinctively postmodern, (as articulated above by Pinedo, for example) seem to have been exploited in earlier horror films: extreme violence, a sense of overriding danger, irrationality, rage and terror, social upheaval; as well as the more conventional features of the blurring of ideological and discursive boundaries, self-reflexivity, intertextuality, lack of narrative closure, etc. (Tudor, 2002: 105). Moreover, as Tudor also argues, the appeal of horror films is arguably less that of tapping into deep-seated unconscious fears and desires than a set of fictional elements which resonate strongly 'with features of the social experiences of its consumers' (Tudor, 1997: 460), by which he means a social reality which is increasingly unreliable, untrustworthy and where the authorities cannot protect the social order. Hence Tudor's distinction between 'secure' and 'paranoid' horror, the former achieving some degree of narrative closure and the containment of the threat, while the latter is characterized, among other things, by a total collapse of authority and expertise and a more open ending.

In an extension of these ideas, Matt Hills has shown that in our definition of postmodern horror we do not need to dismiss altogether the notions of authority and expertise (2003: 3). Authority, in postmodern horror, says Hills, is not fatally undermined but becomes multiple, dispersed, contested and conflictual, hence his reading of *Tesis* in terms of the clash between academic/institutional knowledge and horror fan knowledge or expertise. Hills admits that both sets of knowledges interact profoundly in the film and feed off one another, while in a number of instances neither can be fully believed or trusted, thus reinforcing the paranoid horror component. However, his aim is to show that fan knowledge can be a means towards character empowerment in the face of danger, and is thus to some extent validated by the film's narrative development and outcome.

In broad terms, Hill's thesis has much to commend it, including the idea that Chema's fan expertise is positively valorized on the whole. However, while certainly readable as a postmodern parable based on the de-legitimation of authority and contestation of institutional knowledges, *Tesis* also shows signs of what Cynthia Freeland calls 'realist horror'. That is, a horror thriller which sets up a reasonably credible, diegetic world, creates terror and unease, promises but largely withholds and denies the spectacle of violence, and contains ordinary rather than fictitious monsters (1995: 128; see also, Black, 2002). At the same time, *Tesis* is profoundly self-reflexive and meta-cinematic in that, through Angela's experiences of both screen and 'real' violence as victim, the film seeks to make a serious point about why we are attracted to the imagery of violence and death. *Tesis* thus comments internally, not only on the sombre issue of our sadistic voyeurism, but on the regimes of representation which purport to deliver to us the 'truth' of our desired images of violence, murder and death via 'snuff'. At the same time, the film also manages to combine a paranoid horror framing (via Angela), involving the collapse of trust and certainty in a 'risk' society, while at the same time proclaiming a kind of 'happy ending' and a classical narrative closure. In other words, the film exploits elements of both paranoid and secure horror conventions in the same narrative. These are mainly to do with the dynamics of character development in the movie and the outcome of the investigation plot.

Ángela Márquez seems an unlikely figure for a student who is writing a thesis on the effects on the family of 'audio-visual violence', in its crudest and most repellent forms.

Figure 4.2 Ana Torrent as Ángela Márquez in *Tesis*

Why the inclusion of the 'family' in her thesis title? She appears to have no personal or political axe to grind, given her outwardly stable and secure middle-class family background in Madrid. This aspect is left somewhat undeveloped. Also, despite the approval of her thesis outline by her benign first supervisor Professor Figueroa, Angela seems unusually reticent to press her friendly mentor on his views and fails to articulate any research questions at all. She thus appears to lack even the most basic academic inquisitiveness. In consultation with her new supervisor, Professor Castro, who takes over when Figueroa dies, Castro's critique of her vagueness and superficiality on the matter of screen violence is devastating, as it is cruel and sadistic. Angela is no fan of her subject; indeed, she is profoundly squeamish and cannot look directly at images of violence, having to impose a form of self-censorship by following the soundtrack only, or covering her eyes when watching the 'snuff' video with Chema. Yet, she seems a little too surprised by the nature of the depravity she contemplates on video, too innocent, too lacking in cynicism and guile perhaps to be a totally credible proxy for the spectator.

If Ángela is figured as the epitome of the naïve, non-fan, research student, Chema is the experienced, video-hardened, horror geek. This is evident in his look, dress, hygiene, taste in music and attitude to work. Lean, unwashed, unhealthy, surviving on junk food, greasy, long haired, with his horn-rimmed spectacles, heavy metal fandom, messy and chaotic lifestyle (as are his lecture notes and flat, unlike his neatly catalogued collection of violent videos), above all Chema is the archetypal student loner, marginalized from the mainstream, friendless and geeky, a weird and wholly unattractive example of the male gender.

It is at the level of the investigation plot where Chema's fan knowledge (or more precisely his technical expertise) provides the first big investigative breakthrough-when he spots the tell-tale signs of the XT500 in the 'snuff' video through its use of the digital zoom, its grainy texture and the edits which obscure the identity of the murderer. Soon after, Ángela spots Bosco using the same model of camera in the cafeteria on his girlfriend Yolanda, a scene whose gender and power relations uncannily echo the 'snuff' *mise-en-scène* and cue the viewer to imagine Ángela's own likely involvement as Bosco's snuff victim later on. Yet, Hills (2003) suggests that Chema's fan expertise is largely confined to the private sphere of his huge flat, bequeathed by his grandmother, an internal, enclosed and claustrophobic space, littered with the bric-a-brac of the horror freak and his private collection of extra strong porn and *mondo* videos. Here we would add that, narratively, there are signs that Chema's interest in extreme videos goes rather wider. In order to get access to and check out the Library stacks and passageways, Chema also offers to trade porn to the University security guards. They refer to him jokingly as 'Freddy Krueger', a direct citation from the *Nightmare* series. In other words, the guards provide a clue which links Chema with a well-known fictional serial killer. This not only appears to implicate him in the distribution of tapes made by the 'snuff' ring operating in the University it also identifies him as a potential murderer of Vanessa. Chema, then, is not only the filmic embodiment of fan knowledge and expertise, as Hills argues (2003: 5). Nor is he simply the locus of 'pure' critical reasoning, as Moreiras Menor argues (2002: 256). He is also flagged up to the viewer as the potential stalker, murderer and author of the 'snuff' movies, especially when he describes Bosco to Angela as '*ese psicópata*', as if deflecting responsibility from himself. (He is right of course, but Ángela is maybe too dim or distracted by Bosco to believe him). As in the case of Castro, these strongly marked and sustained ambiguities suggest no simple binary contest between legitimate and illegitimate academic and fan knowledges (in a sense, Castro has let his artistic and 'fan' impulses get the better of him), or between fan and non-fan expertise, embodied in the student characters. In *Tesis*, and as befits a classically constructed thriller, inspired by Hitchcock, the viewer is kept guessing as long as possible. Boundaries and notions of authority collapse, moral frameworks melt away, character roles, identities and motivations become deliberately obscure and unsettled, often re-assigned to other characters (e.g. Bosco initiates his own investigation plot as a counter to Ángela's research on Vanessa) in order to maximise suspense and uncertainty until the end. In emphasising the relativism of his narrative world and the profound vulnerability (self-imposed?) of his heroine, Amenábar tries as best he can to keep us guessing over the identity of the killer.

THE 'TORRENTE' PHENOMENON

The Torrente phenomenon arguably crystallizes recent developments in Spanish film production, since it offers us an example of a 'low' not 'high' concept film blockbuster, which merges aspects of Hollywood and Spanish genre films in a new transcultural style. The notion of the blockbuster arose in the 1970s, in the context of post-classical Hollywood and concerns over its survival, where film producers looked for smaller numbers of films but with far more box-office impact, extended to intermediate products and spin-offs in secondary markets. It is not clear whether the blockbuster was/is a genre or a form of post-industrial film production, reliant on spectacle, awe-inspiring special effects, i.e. 'high-concept cinema', multi-functional, pre-sold to audiences via star names, the director, genre, effects. What is not in doubt is the primacy of style, where the film consists of a linked series of near self-contained action sequences, stunts/effects, etc., rather than any cause-effect narrative structure. Characterization is hardly deep or complex, but purely functional and routine, a device around which to organize a series of set pieces. Thus, the story, plot and characters are no longer the main attraction but narrative spectacle, dazzling imagery, visual excess, technical virtuosity, stunning effects, as can be traced from say, *Star Wars* (George Lucas 1977), through *The Abyss* (James Cameron 1991) to *Spiderman 2* (Sam Raimi, 2004). In terms of the astronomical budgets and technical sophistication of the Hollywood blockbuster, not to mention the range of secondary markets demanded by producers to recoup their investments, the Spanish version of the type represented by Segura's *Torrente: el brazo tonto de la ley* bears little comparison. But in terms of its own national industry and in relation to its production, marketing, box office, cultural impact and sequels, *Torrente 1* (as we shall refer to it from now on) was a new film phenomenon which deserves our attention.

Torrente 1 was produced by Rocabruno España and Andrés Vicente Gómez (75 percent), with participation from Cartel S.A. (25 percent), a company allied to Vía Digital, Spain's second digital television platform, bitter rival to Canal Satélite Digital (Maxwell, 2000, 170–73). It was made for approximately 375,000,000 pesetas (or 2.25 million euros) in 1997 and shot between July and September of that year. Release was preceded by a vigorous, 'American-style' publicity and advertising campaign via posters, postcards, comics, plus film and television spots (*Academia*, 1999: 64 and 68). *Torrente 1* received no official government subsidy from Spain's National Film Institute ICAA (Instituto de Cinematografía y de las Artes Audiovisuales). Leaving aside marketing costs, in relation to industry averages, the final film budget was hardly excessive by Spanish standards, and fairly modest in relation to averages in other European countries (Brown, 1999: 146).

Released in March 1998 on 139 prints, the film ran all year and by December, in Spain alone, it had grossed nearly 2000 million pesetas (11 million euros), attracting 2.5 million spectators, an all-time national box office record (*Fotogramas*, 1999: 142). In 1999, on the strength of domestic takings, the film was gradually released in many other areas and countries including the whole of Latin America, Scandinavia, Central and Eastern Europe as well as Portugal, France, Italy, Russia and curiously perhaps, Iceland. In 1999, *Torrente 1* became Spain's biggest grossing film in its entire history. It outdid Almodóvar's huge international hit *Mujeres al borde de un ataque de nervios* (1988) and also picked up along the way two national Goya awards for best new director (Santiago Segura) and best supporting actor (veteran Tony Le Blanc); Javier Cámara – who played Rafi – was also nominated for best new actor.

The popular, sleazy, late-Francoist genre cinema that Pilar Miró (Director General of Cinema (1983–85)) detested and thought she had finally killed off in the 1980s constitutes a clear precedent for the type of cinema we see in *Torrente 1*. It re-emerged in the 1990s in a rather different, more potent guise in such spoof horror and grisly comic parodies as Alex de la Iglesia' s *Acción mutante*, La Cuadrilla's *Justino, asesino de la 3a edad* (1994), Fernando Fernán Gómez's, *7000 días juntos* (1994), Alex de la Iglesia's *El día de la bestia*, Alberto Sciamma's *La lengua asesina* (1996), Jess Franco's *Killer Barbies* (1996), Juanma Bajo Ulloa's *Airbag* (1997), as well as Alex de la Iglesia's *Perdita Durango*, *Muertos de risa* and *La comunidad*. Like *Torrente 1*, many of these films take a much harder line against the libertarian agenda of the 1980s and early 1990s under the Socialist government, articulating a far more conservative, reactionary and repressive political, sexual and moral agenda. This is expressed within the context of highly parodic treatments of well-known American film genres, particularly horror, but with a far greater emphasis on bad taste, blood, guts and gore, the grotesque, the abjected body and graphic screen violence (Triana Toribio, 2003: 155).

Thus, *Torrente* emerges from a context and type of cinema which rejects the model of the European art film, while acknowledging the commercial appeal of the (Americanized) generic hybrid and the value of certain indigenous popular film traditions, especially the black comedy, 'spiced up' with violence. More importantly, unlike Almodóvar's Euro-friendly melodramas, films like *Torrente 1* do not travel well and resist easy comprehension by foreign audiences, since their language, style and lack of relevant contextualization make them 'inexportable' (Triana Toribio, 2003: 154). Also, where Almodóvar replaced macho matadors, fascist cops, gypsies and flamenco dancers with outrageous though positively imaged marginal sexualities, the new exploitation comedies of the 1990s ditch the latter's political correctness and inclusivity. By contrast, we find an often hostile counter-reaction to the very 'eroticized marginalia' which Almodóvar's films managed to foreground and 'normalize' for his international art-house audiences. In many films, this aggressive rejection of the hedonism, excessive sexual freedoms and far too permeable moral and sexual boundaries of the 1980s forms part of a wider backlash against the ultra-modernizing, '*progre*' ('politically progressive'), pro-European ethos associated with Socialist Spain (1982–96) (Kinder, 1997: 21–23).

In an interview in 1999, the director Santiago Segura declared that with *Torrente 1* he had set out to make a film which evoked a 'realismo sucio costumbrista' ('gritty/crude social realism'). In other words, an aesthetic based on popular, lower-class characters, speaking their own language, in recognizable, national, social settings (*Academia*, 1999: 65). This suggests that in *Torrente 1*, Santiago Segura sought to focus on signs of a Spanish national identity through its capital city, i.e. the language, culture, local customs, attitudes and trib-alisms of working-class Madrid, particularly through the many football and anti-Catalan jokes, and the protracted attention devoted to setting and character. Moreover, as noted earlier, Segura's concern for such 'dirty realism' clearly connects his work to important traditions in national literature and film making, such as *costumbrismo* (the often exoticized concern for local customs and values), the vicious humour of the Spanish *esperpento* (macabre/grotesque story) and the black comedies of the 1950s and 1960s made by Berlanga, Fernán Gómez, Ferreri, Forqué, and others. In the same interview, Segura also claimed that in its early stages, his film (like his shorts) was little more than a string of anecdotes and gags concerning the character of Torrente. Only later was the cod cop thriller plotline added, allowing the director some useful latitude 'because in that way I could spoof American cop films' (*Academia*, 1999: 65). So, while *Torrente 1* exploits and foregrounds its Spanishness and local *costumbrista* character, the film also relies extremely heavily on a wealth of cinematic detail and citation or what Jim Collins refers to as the intertextual 'array' (1993: 254). That is the overlapping, intertextual fields of (mainly American) film and media images, styles and conventions, which are raided and reworked in line with local cultural needs.

The array clearly reflects the increasingly media-saturated nature of contemporary international (American) and global culture and the fragmentation of mass audiences into clusters of niche and target groups. The filmic exploitation of such 'foregrounded hyperconscious eclecticism' (Collins, 1993: 248), or semiotic excess, is also one way of coping with the unmanageable textuality of the image landscape of contemporary culture. Yet, for most younger Spanish directors, Collins's 'array' is hardly a matter of anxiety or scorn; rather, it constitutes an obvious resource, while forming their educational background and the world they inhabit.

As José Arroyo points out, in a review of Alex de la Iglesia's *La comunidad*, like de la Iglesia, Segura and many of his contemporaries are making a 'new type of Spanish cinema by and for a post-Franco, post-*Star Wars* generation' (2000: 38). Moreover, as Arroyo also argues: '...American cultural imperialism, late capitalist commodification of experience and a hyper-real image culture aren't so much a cause for anguished hand-wringing as simply the context for everyday life and the raw materials for their art' (2003: 38).

Also, as de la Iglesia has shown, the genre film need not imply the tedious, predictable recycling of outmoded formulae nor a negation of authorial inventiveness. José Arroyo argues that: 'At its best, this cinema (i.e. the new Spanish cinema) reminds us that genre is not antithetical to, and may indeed be a vehicle for, personal expression and that film does not aspire to art by bypassing expected pleasures but by surpassing them' (2003: 38).

Figure 4.3 Torrente's climax in the fantasy musical number

With *Torrente 1*, we are made aware that the film is not simply contained by one set of genre conventions, but criss-crossed by many different sets, which intersect and create a highly intertextual, if rather jumbled, and disparate diegesis. We find multiple homages, allusions, skits and echoes of the Bond movies, Spaghetti Westerns, horror and gore movies, Russ Meyer films, the American cop thriller/vigilante movie (specifically *Dirty Harry* [Don Siegel, 1971] and *Taxi Driver* [Martin Scorsese, 1977] as well as the *Death Wish* and *Lethal Weapon* series, plus Tarantino's *Reservoir Dogs*) and, of course, John Woo's violent Chinese gangster/action thrillers, etc., as referenced in the 'flying' shot, during Torrente's final shoot-out. Such 'foreign' citations and reworked fragments are combined with an abundance of nods, winks and references to past Spanish sources including: a Buñuel-inspired taste for freakish characters (e.g. Reme's Down's-syndrome daughter, bottle-eyed son Rafi and busty country cousin Amparo, expelled from the village for her nympho-mania; Torrente's own invalid father; Carlitos, the dwarfish lottery seller; Rafi's low-life friends from the gym); the late-Francoist, sleazy sex comedies (grotesquely parodied in the 'romance' between Torrente and Amparito, especially during the fantasy musical number and Torrente's climactic '*polvo*' ['shag']); and Spanish genre films of the 1990s, including *Todo por la pasta* (Urbizu, 1991) – arguably an influential resource in terms of *mise-en-scène* and narrative outcome – as well as Alex de la Iglesia's *Acción mutante* and *El día de la bestia*, Bajo Ulloa's *Airbag*, plus Díaz Yanes's *Nadie hablará de nosotras cuando hayamos muerto* (1995), echoing the female hostage scenario, and sexual degradation. We must also mention another form of citation: the wealth of cameo performances of well-known Spanish actors and actresses, such as Jorge Sanz, Gabino Diego and Javier Bardem, among many others.

In other words, *Torrente 1* contains a vast menu of references, allusions and poses, virtually all media and cinematic citations, clearly reflecting the viewing tastes and histories of its makers, but also their assumptions concerning the vastly increased cine-literacy of Spanish audiences and the possibilities for entertainment of a wide cross-section of viewing publics, of different generations and film memories. Of course, the overabundance of citation, and thus the emphasis on artifice, can threaten to dominate and crush the film (as in the torture scene in the Chinese restaurant, a virtual repetition – minus musical accompaniment – of the same scene in *Reservoir Dogs,* but also similar to a scene in *Nadie hablará de nosotras cuando hayamos muerto*). Also, drawing attention to the conventionality of the cop thriller with so many obvious modern intrusions might well work against the role of genre in regulating/coordinating memory, narrative codings and audience expectations, leaving the film to be read as a mere string of intertextual gags and references. But perhaps one of the key features of *Torrente 1* is its self-conscious spoofery, and thereby its refusal of the audience's desire to enter the film world as a believable, coherent, disciplined narrative construct. In one sense, lacking such points of identification and anchoring and being thus 'distanced' from the diegesis, audiences may be encouraged to read the film in quotation marks, from a position of ironic detachment, aware at all times of its 'ironic halo' (Collins, 1993: 256).

Also, with regard to *Torrente 1* and its parodic reworking of intertextual sources, across a 90-minute film, he gives them a particularly prominent and often aggressive, 'Iberian' inflection. That is to say, while exploiting many foreign (American) film sources and stereotypes, Segura emphasizes Spanish 'difference', capturing the reference, but heavily foregrounding its re-articulation. Of course, such transformations are not total, since total difference would prevent audiences from recognizing sources and thus engaging in the cinefile 'play' and pleasures of recognizing similarities and differences. Yet, mainly via settings, dialogue, iconography, context, motifs and symbols of pop culture, as well as soundtrack, Segura reaffirms the 'specificity' of his gallery of grotesques, as well as their political incorrectness and pseudo 'counter-cultural' role. For example, one of the most compelling of *Torrente 1*'s prototextual clusters, which merits a brief comment, is the main character of the renegade, vigilante, ex-cop protagonist himself. Based on Segura's own previous creation Evilio, the figure of Torrente is also an amusing, but grotesque inversion of the archetypal 'fascist cop' Dirty Harry Callahan.

Dirty Harry (Don Siegel, 1971) was perhaps *the* founding vigilante/cop, action film of the early 1970s, alongside *The French Connection* (William Friedkind, 1973). The first of five outings for Clint Eastwood in the role, this controversial movie pitted a neo-conservative super-cop hero against a sadistic, psychotic, hippie shooter called Scorpio. The film also located its ideological dilemma within the discourses of post-1968 civil rights legislation, the ineffectiveness of the justice system and the breakdown of law and order, which licensed Callahan to act beyond the law. Having played the violent, brutal and amoral loner in Leone's Spaghetti Westerns of the 1960s, Eastwood was perfect for the no-nonsense, street-wise cop role, patrolling the red-light areas of San Francisco, overrun by crime, prostitution, drugs and 'deviant' lifestyles. Just as vicious, ruthless and sadistic as his quarry, Callahan dispensed with the niceties of procedure to get the job done, even if it meant using excessive force.

In *Torrente 1*, Segura replaces the San Francisco vigilante super cop (tall, 'in shape' and healthy, clean, neutrally dressed, macho, expert marksman) with a flabby, balding, drunken, cowardly greaseball, dressed like a pimp and hopeless with firearms. Torrente is thus the physical and behavioural antithesis of the Callahan model. Yet, he adopts many of Harry's basic attitudes, even if these are grossly overplayed. For example, Harry's supposed blanket racism and sexism and his elemental sadism and cruelty towards 'bad guys' like Scorpio are clearly reworked, but in an extreme and cartoonish, comic-book form. Torrente's pathological bullying and arbitrary nastiness towards his victims (his constant slapping, rabbit punching and breaking of fingers), his use of '*guarra*' and '*zorra*' ('dirty whore') to describe women, and his racism (towards the Chinese waitress, and the joke with the piece of steak, which Torrente uses as a way of escaping the three black heavies) all reflect an appalling level of visceral prejudice and obnoxious behaviour which recall, while radically distorting, the Siegel original. In other words, Segura emulates but massively exaggerates and redirects the similarities and differences between Harry and Torrente, in order to deliver unexpected turns and transformations, e.g. the credit sequence, where Harry's regular large morning coffee without sugar – interrupted by the bank heist – is replaced by Torrente's 10 (or is it 11?) midnight whiskies, before going on duty. Such an aggressive degree of variance is clearly attuned to assumed Spanish audience tastes and to the comic potential of scenes which, elsewhere, might well embarrass if not sicken, in their scabrousness and severity.

In terms of law and order symbolism, Torrente does not carry his own, customized, unofficial gun (his is not a Smith and Wesson '44 Magnum like Harry's) but a standard issue, Spanish '38 CGT special, 'made in Spain … in Vitoria', as Rafi informs him. Interestingly, the nerdy Rafi presents the gun as a symbol of national pride, which Torrente initially seems to ignore; the young fishmonger also dominates the sort of technical specification dialogue used by Callahan himself early in *Dirty Harry*. This indicates not only Rafi's own encyclopaedic, knowledge of and fascination with guns (his 'proto' vigilante character) but also his intellectual and practical superiority over Torrente in the use of arms, and indeed in most other vital departments (e.g. when Torrente and Rafi compare penis sizes like two adolescents in the toilet, or when Torrente ask Rafi if he fancies a *pajilla* ('wank') to relieve the boredom of the restaurant stakeout in the fish van). In other words, despite Rafi's totally inexplicable admiration for Torrente (whom he believes to be a secret CIA agent), the master–pupil/cop–sidekick relationship is ironically reversed, placing anti-hero Torrente at an even lower and more degraded level. Such inversions and redirections, alongside repetitions, extraneous insertions and gross exaggerations are the sorts of standard devices Segura deploys to generate ironic incongruity, the basis of most of his gags. At times, however, as in the reworking of the torture scene from *Reservoir Dogs*, Segura brutally up-ends spectator expectations, providing not only the severed ear element of the original, but also a corkscrew driven into the Chinese waiter's left thigh and then a point-blank 'execution' shot to the head. Such an accumulation of violent images, 'excess' realism and radical shifts of tone jolt the spectator and radically disrupt any complacent immersion in sadistic voyeurism. Indeed, occasionally, Segura seems to wish to punish such audience voyeurism, undermining audience engagement with screen violence that in itself is far too 'realistic' and sickening.

The sequel, *Torrente 2: misión en Marbella*, made for roughly double the previous budget, was released in March 2001 through Segura's new production company Amiguetes Entertainment S.L., in conjunction with Andrés Vicente Gómez's Lolafilms. Though it had to compete with Amenábar's Spanish/English language co-pro *Los otros*, starring Nicole Kidman, in its first weekend *Torrente 2* took nearly 600 million pesetas (3.6 million euros), amounting to the best weekend gross ever for a Spanish film (Triana Toribio, 2003: 155) In a little over 18 months, it had attracted 5.3 million spectators and grossed 22 million euros, or nearly 4000 million pesetas, contributing to an outstanding market share in 2001 for Spanish cinema of 18 per cent. Containing rather more (Bond movie) formulae than native invention, *Torrente 2* reminds us of Collins's argument concerning the mediated nature of contemporary culture, the 'real' as always 'imaged' as a construct via other strategies of re-articulation (1993: 248). Also, in a sense, *Torrente 2* could be seen as a riposte to the hegemony of Hollywood cinema in Spain, perhaps an object lesson in how to develop a form of national cinema, able to compete with dominant American action cinema while retaining clear signs of its own local identity. If Spanish audiences have become over-stimulated into numbness by the semiotic excess of international media culture, then they may be reachable in great numbers only by a deliberate appeal to the grossest forms of hybridized exploitation cinema gone mainstream, as seen in *Torrente 1* and *2*.

Chapter Five
STARS □

We all know who stars are. A performer in any field – music, theatre, film, TV or sport – becomes famous, in part as a specialist in their field, but also as a media personality or celebrity. At different times, certain areas of performance achieve prominence in any culture. In the contemporary period, Spain's ability to attract the best footballing stars has given Real Madrid's so-called *galácticos* (meaning 'belonging to a galaxy of stars') a profile more international than any famous Spaniards from other activities have ever been. But the most famous stars of all time are the ones produced by the world's most successful entertainment trade, the film industry based in Hollywood, California. From around 1910 the names of actors started appearing on film credits, as producers began to realize that audiences were choosing films on the basis of their actors. The print media began to publicize the actors' off-screen lives, and by the 1920s the Hollywood star system had emerged (Abrams, Bell and Udris, 2001: 192). During the studio era, most major Hollywood movies were sold almost exclusively on star image (Roberts and Wallis, 2001: 115), a function of the star as commodity in the industry that peaked in the 1930s and 1940s. In keeping with the industrial ethos of the studio system, the film factory produced the star through promotion and carefully selected film roles, taking the raw material of an individual actor, and fashioning her or him into a star using talent schools, dialogue coaches, beauticians, and marketing/publicity experts. To a certain extent, a grateful and inexperienced young actor was a much happier prospect for studio bosses who could in such cases fabricate an ideal star persona for the purposes of publicity prior to any film appearance (Dyer, 1998: 12). Despite this level of studio control, star status needed the co-operation of the media and of fans to respond to their 'candidates for election' to stardom (Alberoni, 1972: 93). With the decline of the studio system in the 1950s, stars gained more power (no longer tied to a studio); they now make fewer films and they can choose to accept roles or not. But even though the so-called 'star system' no longer operates as a closed, controlled industry, stars continue to exist. It was only long after the heyday of the star system that writers began to engage with the phenomenon of stardom in a critical manner.

Biographies of stars and coffee-table books of lavishly photographed anthologies have long existed, and early explorations of stardom tended to concentrate on the beauty, erotic appeal or even the magical quality of stars (See Dyer, 1998: 16). Star studies as a field of systematic academic study began with film academic Richard Dyer in the 1970s. There were, however, a number of pioneering studies that laid the foundations for some of the work of Dyer and others, Edgar Morin's 1957 book *Les Stars*, translated into English in 1960, being perhaps the most important. Dyer's work focused on stars as images and on the ideological aspects of stardom. The emphasis of this emerging field was on the sociology of screen and social roles and audience identifications, in part as a counterpoint and reaction to the strength of auteurism (Hollows and Jancovich, 1995: 80). At that time, as a field of scholarly work, star studies still tended to focus on classic Hollywood stars of the studio era (Cagney, Garbo, Dietrich, Bogart, Bergman, Monroe and others), who were regarded as crucial points of intersection, bringing together the film industry, textual analysis and audience reception. The film star was clearly an economic factor with capital value, a means of attracting and guaranteeing audiences and sustaining the habit of film going. The linkage to the film star and the promotion of star imagery were the means by which producers sought to minimize financial risk and ensure strong box office returns.

Within this new, interdisciplinary approach to film, several key writers – among them Dyer, Gledhill, King and Geraghty – highlight, though with slight differences of terminology, three fundamental aspects of stardom:

1   production (economic factors, including selection, grooming, marketing, publicity)
2   texts (the films themselves, including the actor's performance)
3   audience (reception, identification and fandom).

Though clearly these factors are inextricably linked, their separation, following Geraghty (2000: 183–5), facilitates a more systematic study of stardom. Importantly, from a methodological point of view, star study is intertextual (working across different films) and extratextual (working across different types of material, in various media). While it is theoretically possible for a star to be created entirely on the basis of screen performances, in practice, every star is made up of the film role(s) they play, a star persona (constructed, as we will see, from a variety of sources) and, ostensibly, somewhere inside all that, a 'real' person. Stars are, as Yvonne Tasker (1993: 74) puts it, 'complex personas made up of far more than the texts in which they appear'. Star persona is based on a paradox: stars must be both extraordinary, in their exceptional careers, but also ordinary, in that they have relationships, families and hobbies like everyone else (Ellis, 1992: 93). Lifestyle (swimming pools, limousines, parties and so on) is as central to the creation of a star persona as acting on screen (Dyer, 1998: 38). Celebrity, or in Geraghty's (2000: 187) words, being 'famous for having a lifestyle' can even stem from negative publicity about a star's personal life. In fact, the effective separation of actors (professionals who perform) from celebrities (famous people) in Spain is one substantial difference – as we shall see – between the Spanish cinema industry and its Hollywood equivalent. For the latter, an actor's meaning for the audience is produced jointly by what they bring as celebrities *and* through their verbal and physical performances.

When studying stardom the most stable primary source we have is the film text, a record of a star's actual performances, usually across a range of films. We can analyse an actor's screen performances in a way that a performance in a stage play, once finished, cannot be scrutinized. On the other hand, investigating a film actor's performances presents us with certain methodological problems. Firstly, we have only the final takes selected by the director or editor from the many filmed takes of any scene, so that much of the performance of any one actor is left on the cutting-room floor. Secondly, the sheer range of manipulative technology in film tends to downgrade an actor's construction of character (as compared to the theatre, for example), leading to a kind of 'de-skilling' of the actor (King, 1991: 170). Thus, much of the debate about star performances is of a qualitative nature, evaluating acting skills *in opposition to* star persona. A key distinction has been made between *impersonation*, where an actor constructs a role using imagination and skills, and *personification*, where the role matches the star persona. ('Personification' is used as a neutral term, unlike the industry's own phrase 'typecasting' which has negative overtones.) Personification often involves an actor with a specific look, a set of conventional elements, such as standard gestural or behavioural patterns, repeated over a number or films (Abrams, Bell and Udris, 2001: 193). They can also be associated with particular genres (John Wayne = the Western), up to the point where they can be seen to 'play themselves' to a certain extent in every role (Geraghty, 2000: 190–1). This kind of actor is brought up to date in the contemporary soap opera, where one actor is associated with a particular character over a long period of time.

In terms of critical reception, impersonation is regarded as superior to personification, because it involves the demonstration of talent and/or skill. King attributes this hierarchy of values to the notion that good acting is based on 'intentionality, or even authorship' (1991: 167–8). Thus, actors like Jodie Foster or Meryl Streep, who are known for studied and careful characterization, are more highly regarded than actors like Meg Ryan or Melanie Griffiths who – whatever their acting abilities – tend to get parts based on *who they are* rather than *what they can do*. But in pure economic terms, the selection of actors based on personification, on what their star persona brings to the role, has been preferred over impersonation skills. In an overcrowded labour market in which many people have acting ability, cultivating a persona (based on skill in personification) brings better results than skills in impersonation (King, 1991: 179). Thus typecasting can be an advantage to actors. Conversely, in a world with so many stars, impersonation skills become more valued. Actors such as Al Pacino, known principally for a certain type of role (personification), add to their credentials by celebrated character performances in more high-brow productions such as a Shakespeare play (*Looking for Richard*, Al Pacino, 1996). And although stars can underact (unlike the supporting cast) because all the attention is on them, some stars counter this with an affirmation of their acting abilities (Ellis, 1992: 104). In assessing acting, realistic or believable performances tend to be valued, in keeping with the prioritization of verisimilitude in mainstream Hollywood cinema. Where the criteria of performance or acting are quite acceptable to Spanish actors, and easily applied to Spanish cinema (as to European cinema in general), the relevance of the star persona and fandom to the Spanish film industry is more debatable, and Spanish actors are far more ambivalent about the role and merits of stardom.

Based on consumption rather than production, the study of stardom and its necessary partner, fandom, has proved more elusive to research, perhaps because of the lack of any lasting 'text' for study. Approaches range from the highly individuated analysis of audience responses, claiming every single viewer responds differently, to totalizing discourses such as psychoanalysis, claiming there is only one possible response, because the cinematic apparatus so firmly controls the process. In the 1970s, the task of academic star studies (i.e. how to explain the appeal of stars) was heavily influenced by various bodies of theory not specific to film (semiotics, intertextuality and psychoanalysis). As such, star studies were undertaken largely in terms of textual analyses of 'stars as sign systems', as bearers of visual, verbal and aural ideological meanings, as vehicles which reconciled social contradictions and also 'naturalized' the 'constructedness' of the film (see Dyer, 1998 and 2004). Star images were also seen as products of intertextuality, a shifting, unstable mixture of filmic and non-filmic texts (i.e. advertising, promotion, publicity, journalism, gossip, magazines, television coverage, interviews, biographies, etc.). Moreover, star images were 'read' and 'consumed' by spectators as vehicles of affective pleasures, fantasies, role models and objects of erotic desire. Stars are people the audience can identify with, relate to and admire. They are a source of vicarious pleasure and identification (doing things we can never do) (Abrams, Bell and Udris, 2001: 200). What mattered was the ways in which spectators identified with and gained pleasure and fulfilment from the star image.

Work on film reception and identification was largely dominated by certain types of feminist-inflected psychoanalysis, which sought to explain visual pleasure in film. Theorists such as Laura Mulvey claimed that pleasure in looking was organized around a division between the 'active male' star/hero (who drives the film narrative forward and is the main mechanism for audience identification) and a 'passive female' star (displayed as erotic spectacle for male gratification) (Mulvey, 1989: 14–26). More recent work on clothing, stardom and identity suggests that the active gaze is not necessarily male but also female, where female spectators engage with female star imagery (Bruzzi, 1997). And in her empirical, ethnographic work on actual female audiences, Jackie Stacey has shown that far from being passive recipients of already coded meanings, female spectators engage in various forms of active spectatorship and use of visual imagery (Stacey, 1994). This type of approach is now being tested on Spanish audiences, as in the study by Esther Gómez-Sierra (in Lázaro-Reboll and Willis, 2004: 92–112) In other words, more recent film theory suggests that audiences in general are active rather than passive consumers of visual imagery and can engage not with one but with multiple points of identification in film. Richard Dyer (1998: 3) refers to the 'structured polysemy' of stars, who can possess a range of different possible meanings. And in the age of the internet it is clear to see just how fan behaviour is now outside the control of the industry, hence the mass of non-official websites which can provide a diverse (and occasionally bizarre) range of responses to particular stars (Abrams, Bell and Udris, 2001: 199).

As well as looking at how audiences react to stars, the academic field of star studies has also demonstrated how stars emerge in response to society. For example, the success of Sylvester Stallone or Arnold Schwarzenegger, during the Reagan years, has been attributed to their reflection of that regime's masculinist, militaristic values (Abrams, Bell and Udris, 2001: 200). This in turn gives way to the less threatening values of the 1990s, associated perhaps with less predatory, though still effective heroes, personified by the likes of Tom Hanks. In the emerging field of Spanish star studies, Chris Perriam, in his book on *Stars and Masculinities in Spanish Cinema* (2003) has studied key male stars from the contemporary period, looking at how they reflect and embody changing representations of gender. Work on stars was also invigorated by the approach of the Birmingham Centre for Cultural Studies, looking at the social meanings of cinematic practices (White, 1998: 123), and the appropriation of certain stars by certain subcultures. A frequently cited example, from Dyer (2004) is the adoption of Judy Garland as a gay icon, despite the resolutely heterosexual world in all her films. Stars can also be seen to become the site for media debates on sexuality, as was the case with Marilyn Monroe (again, see Dyer, 2004).

More recently, the field of star studies has been simultaneously problematized and widened to include (or sometimes exclude) other film industries and other areas of activity. Christine Geraghty has reminded us recently that star studies have perhaps been overly influenced by the critical assumptions and vocabulary used to analyse the classic star figures, working at the height of the studio system (2000: 183–4). The implication is that such frameworks and terminology may not be totally suitable for analysing stars in a post-studio system context, in later periods and, more importantly, in national industries outside America. Moreover, the notion of the film star and stardom has experienced significant widening and problematizing in the last 30 years. Cinema no longer enjoys any special or unique relationship to stardom, given the massive proliferation of 'stars' in music, television, sport, design, politics, etc. Also, in the light of technological change, human film stars have been challenged by the appearance of digital/computer-generated 'star' characters and effects (e.g. PIXAR), which now compete for star billing, such as in *Shrek* (Andrew Adamson and Vicky Jenson, 2001). Yet, despite the apparent loss of specificity of the term 'star', it can still be aligned and anchored to the notions of fame and public notoriety, in different forms and modalities.

STARS IN SPANISH CINEMA

Over the last decade or so, European film making has been criticised for being over-dependent on state handouts, and incapable of making films which consistently deliver mass audiences and are able to compete with American output (Finney, 1996: 53–9). One of many issues raised in relation to the European industry has been the difficulty of creating a viable star system in Europe, one capable of developing stars with pan-European appeal. Finney argues that European films are burdened with too many nationally known actors, trying in vain to generate recognition and visibility in other European countries and beyond. The problem is that, unlike their Hollywood counterparts, very few European performers are able to attract major film finance and generate massive media interest, or operate as insurance policies against risk. In fact, there are signs of a trend towards greater American hegemony and globalization in the way increasing numbers of European films are relying on American stars to ensure good box-office returns. It should come as no great surprise that Alejandro Amenábar's *Los otros* (2001), the best-selling Spanish film of all time, features the international Hollywood film star Nicole Kidman. Other examples are Andie McDowell in *Four Weddings and a Funeral* (1994), Bruce Willis in *Le cinquième element* (1997), Julia Roberts in *Notting Hill* (2000), or René Zellweger in *Bridget Jones's Diary* (2001). If such informed critical opinion doubts the existence of a European 'star system', what does this mean for national cinemas in Europe and their own domestic 'stars'? While Finney claims that the UK and France have in fact possessed star systems historically, inflected by national traditions and circumstances, he is rather disparaging about Spain, suggesting it does not (1996: 63). Does it make sense therefore to talk about film stars in the Spanish case, or indeed about a national 'star system' at all? As Perriam (2003: 1–2) also acknowledges, it is still something of an open question as to how far we can apply the term 'star' to a still relatively small, increasingly European but only occasionally global industry such as that represented by Spanish cinema. Indeed, many Spanish film writers and critics tend to approach the question with caution, placing the term firmly in inverted commas, rather doubtful of its validity, let alone its reality.

By European standards, as we have shown, Spain is now an important industrial player, usually appearing third, behind the UK and France, in terms of annual film production totals (including proliferating numbers of co-productions, especially with Latin America). Yet, in terms of company formation, there are only a handful of production houses making more than four films per year, still on fairly low budgets – by international standards – of 4–8 million euros: Sogecine (18), Enrique Cerezo Producciones Cinematográficas (14), Telemadrid (6), TeleSpan (4), El Deseo (4). Thus the structure and scale of the film making business in Spain remains fragmentary and modest. Audiences for Spanish films are also on the whole relatively small (with the exception of the recent *Torrente* cycle and *Los otros*). Acting talent is abundant and relatively cheap, and risk-taking by producers and investors (including the state and its subsidy systems), while always taken seriously, is largely manageable, via co-productions and multi-financed projects. In other words, not many Spanish commercial (or art) films require serious investments in 'big' star vehicles in order to insure against major financial risk when marketing the products at home and abroad. What has tended to sell Spanish films in Spain, historically, is genres, directors and actors (their 'ordinariness' and closeness to their viewers and fans) and the expectations and viewing pleasures built up by audiences around these. Until very recently, fame for Spanish actors was unlikely to come from glamour or sex-appeal (as our two case studies will demonstrate).

Very few Spanish actors have developed star personae, with associated glitz and glamour, via images which resonate beyond the Pyrenees, without actually going abroad to work and promote images. On their own, Spanish films marketed abroad are simply too few in number and are seen by too few people to achieve the required 'transnational projection' of star acting names and performances. Historically, Spanish 'star' traditions are rooted in the theatre and particularly the music hall, in the folkloric musical. The singer Raquel Meller, 'La Violetera', only gained serious star status in the late 1920s by working in France and then the USA. The same arguably applied to Sara Montiel in the 1950s, via her roles in Hollywood. Francisco Rabal, though he worked in France, was never well known in Europe, let alone the USA and something of a 'star manqué'. In more recent times, those actors who have developed star personae (Antonio Banderas, Javier Bardem, Sergi López, Imanol Arias, Eduardo Noriega, Carmen Maura, Victoria Abril, Penélope Cruz, etc.) have worked in Europe, Latin America and Hollywood, though with mixed fortunes. Moreover, until quite recently, the notion of the 'star' was tacitly reserved by national and foreign opinion formers and critics, not so much for Spain's acting profession, but for an auteur tradition and certain internationally celebrated director/auteurs such as Buñuel, and of course Almodóvar, both of whom have been more famous than their actors. And while it is the case that Almodóvar's global brand name can probably 'open' a film in Spain and even Europe, this is not the case with even the most famous or celebrated of Spanish actors. This includes Antonio Banderas, whose astonishing Hollywood career since 1992 has been built around roles as macho action hero, Latin lover, comedy/family man performer, and yet whose star image permutations still lack sufficient 'recognition' among American and European audiences to open a picture single-handedly.

However, while the above remarks invite caution when talking about stars or a 'star system' in relation to Spanish cinema, Perriam (2003: 2) is undoubtedly right to point out that Spain now possesses a 'matrix of production and consumption' capable of supporting a star system of sorts. In other words, there exists a wide and increasing range of media, promotional and marketing platforms and secondary sources which crucially shape and fashion acting careers, biographies and star images and thus help sustain star profiles. And even in more insular times, popular Spanish cinema did create stars for the domestic market, as Núria Triana Toribio (2003: 84–95) has shown in her study of 1960s child-star Marisol. In contemporary Spain, the range of publicity open to film actors across various media is wide. On the most popular level there is the lifestyle interest through chit chat and scandal in *Interviú* and the gossip magazines *Hola, Diez Minutos, Semana, Dunia, Pronto, La Gente,* etc. The daily and weekly press (*El País, El Mundo,* etc.), especially through their Sunday supplements, provide further coverage. Then there are the specialist film magazines, such as *Dirigido Por* or *Fotogramas* with their 'Top 20' latest young acting talents, and television programming on film such as José Luis Garci's late night show, and *Versión española*, presented by Cayetana Guillén Cuervo. Spanish television (both terrestrial and cable/digital) devotes extensive coverage to the annual Goya ceremonies, and to domestic and international film festivals. And it is true that, more so than before, producers and distributors are exploiting the cachet of their actor's fame and status in order to sell their films, as was the case with Amenábar's *Mar adentro* (2004) starring Javier Bardem, where huge publicity across all media managed to attract viewers to 275 screens in Spain.

Against this burgeoning star industry in its subsidiary forms (the media-propagated star persona) are two historical factors which distinguish Spanish film actors from their Hollywood counterparts (though less so from other European traditions): the importance for Spanish actors of both the professional theatre, and of politics. The high cultural value attached to stage acting (perceived in most Western cultures) is strengthened in Spain by the relative reliability of theatre roles for acting, as compared to the extremely precarious situation of the cinema in Spain. With both industries centred in Madrid (unlike in the USA where film and theatre inhabit opposite coasts of the continent), many actors combine theatre and film roles throughout their careers. The most respected actors in Spain tend to be those who pursue 'great' character acting whether on stage or screen. These actors see themselves as professionals like any other, with the right to a private life. For the most part they shun the trappings of stardom, to the point where such lifestyles are considered almost vulgar. Opening the pages of any of Spain's gossip press will reveal few serious Spanish actors baring their souls or showing their homes. This disdain for the consumption-led celebration of stardom is linked to politics. It is worth noting that most members of Spain's theatre and film acting fraternity belong to a long tradition of liberal, left-wing activism and political radicalism, arising from the outcome of the civil war and 40 years of Francoism. They regard themselves very much as workers and comrades, bound together by a certain history and ethos of oppositional solidarity, collective responsibility and freedom of expression. Ideologically and culturally, therefore, it is somewhat difficult for Spanish actors, working in Spain at least, even if they are so inclined, to accept and display the trappings and visible excess of the star lifestyle and to work according to a highly individualistic and competitive 'star system'. In recent years, the political activism of Spain's film actors has been highlighted by their direct intervention in political debate, such as the demonstration at the Spanish parliament in February 2004, in which Javier Bardem and Mercedes Sampietro, alongside 29 other actors, were invited by left-wing parties to attend debates on the Iraq war. And the Goya Awards ceremony in February 2003 was transformed into an anti-war, anti-Aznar campaign of protest, with every award winner wearing badges or T-shirts with the logo 'No to war'.

How then, can we evaluate individual actors from Spanish cinema in terms of 'stars' as defined by Hollywood models? Geraghty (2000: 187) seems to offer a useful way forward as she seeks to reconceptualize stars and stardom via such terms as 'celebrity', 'professional' and 'performer'. For Geraghty, celebrity is a type of stardom which has little to do with acting ability or talent, and far more to do with fame and notoriety, as represented and generated through the media. Celebrity is not a feature of professional skill but of a 'persona' created through secondary texts, such as gossip in the press and on television. An obvious example is that of Penélope Cruz, the 'other' party in the lives of Tom Cruise and Nicole Kidman, the 'scarlet woman' who allegedly broke up Tom's marriage and then had a two-year relationship with him. Here, it is not Cruz's acting performances as such, but her personal/private involvement and public appearances with Tom Cruise as his consort which have given her massive, world-wide exposure as an international celebrity. Her 'stardom as celebrity' has been constructed and deployed by means of a plethora of secondary texts and media vehicles, through her link with Tom Cruise. Cruise is the biggest star on the planet, from whose mega stardom as 'worldwide celebrity' Cruz has clearly benefited. Not surprisingly, this type of stardom for Cruz need not necessarily involve any spectatorial interest in her films. Here, 'star image' is a function, not of her screen roles and her performances, but of her construction as a celebrity across a vast range of secondary sources. However, study of her screen roles is also profitable, as demonstrated by Peter Evans (2004: 53–63). While Cruz provides an example of a film actor who has benefited considerably from the publicity generated by her private life, contemporary daytime Spanish television provides plenty of examples (we will leave them un-named) of celebrities whose fame dispenses with acting talent altogether: a circle of talk-show participants, 'famous' for being talk-show participants.

By contrast, Geraghty's notion of 'star as professional' is firmly anchored in the film texts themselves and in the star's performance. What counts here is the extent to which the actor's 'real' personality appears accurately aligned with and expressed in their 'performed persona' in the film roles undertaken. In short, how far is the actor 'personified' in the roles they play? How far are they acting 'as themselves'? Classical Hollywood's star system created very strong alignments between actors and performed personae, to the extent of recycling personal traits and tics (e.g. Wayne's acting, postures, his hand and arm gestures). In the post-classical period, as Geraghty argues, stars have been increasingly identified with particular genres, such as the action movie, but also with clearly defined variations and specialities within the genre (e.g. Harrison Ford selects different films and performs rather different action roles from those of Jean Claude Van Damme). This gives rise to specific pleasures associated with specific actors and quite distinct and varied sets of audience expectations. 'Stars as professionals' thus provide audiences with the pleasures of regularity, repetition, stability and consistency of performance in a vast, saturated market of film choices. In some ways, with performances heavily weighted towards specific genres and 'known' performance features, such typecasting can of course be a double-edged sword, with actors unable to break out of their allotted role-type. Examples of this type abound in Spanish cinema, especially in comedy: Rafaela Aparicio, Chus Lampreave, Gracita Morales, José Isbert, Gabino Diego, and, perhaps the best example of this phenomenon, Alfredo Landa.

ALFREDO LANDA (Pamplona, 1933)

Landa is a clear example of Geraghty's second star category, the professional, associated with one particular type of role and performance style, though this amounts to an injustice, given the range of his performances in over 130 films. The son of a Civil Guard Captain, Landa grew up in the Basque city of San Sebastián. While studying Law he became involved in the university theatre group, appearing in some 40 plays, a theatrical training he shares with the vast majority of actors of his generation. After a move to Madrid and three years spent dubbing films into Spanish, he secured a leading part in José María Forqué's 1962 hit comedy *Atraco a las tres*. Critics identify three periods in his film career. The first (1960s) comprises secondary (often comic) roles in films, which range from the acclaimed *El verdugo* (Luis García Berlanga, 1963) to the formulaic comedies of Pedro Lazaga and Mariano Ozores. The second corresponds to a series of extremely popular comedies made principally in the 1970s, in which Landa is the main protagonist. And the third phase, coinciding with the new decade of the 1980s and with Spain's new democracy, sees Landa as a consolidated actor, capable of both familiar comic roles and also fine character performances, culminating in a best actor award at Cannes in 1984 for his role as Paco el Bajo in *Los santos inocentes* (Mario Camus). Despite the recognition in these later years (also including Goyas for best actor in 1987 and 1992), Landa's fame stems overwhelmingly from his lead roles in the salacious comedies of the 1970s. Such is the extent of his association with these films (his 'personification' of the genre, to use King's term [1991: 170]), that these politically-incorrect and immensely successful comedies are referred to collectively as '*landismo*'. Clearly, the label '*landismo*' could only be applied to these films retrospectively and descriptively, by identifying certain features and elements that are common to the genre (for *landismo* is a genre, or at least a sub-genre of the Iberian sex comedy [see Chapter One]). The implications for Alfredo Landa – as an actor propelled to national stardom as a result of these successes – were the total subordination of acting abilities (impersonation) to the function of playing himself (personification). Landa's physical attributes – short stature, balding, a little overweight and not good-looking – were determining factors, as is usually the case with actors in the professional/personification category. His looks effectively rule him out as a glamorous sex symbol or classic hero/leading man (Zunzunegui, 2002: 182). The script, genre and directing, with its easy laughs, caricature and crass humour based on stereotypes, leave virtually no room for character acting.

The prototype for *landismo* was Ramón Fernández' huge hit, *No desearás al vecino del quinto* (1971), which tells the story of Antón, who has created a false, parallel life for himself as a gay beauty salon owner, to cover his real identity as a serial womanizer. (See Jordan, 2003a, for more detailed analysis.) Landa as Antón is first seen in his salon wearing a wig of exquisitely permed red hair, a purple flowered shirt and sporting a poodle named Fifi as an accessory. Blowing '*buenos días*' kisses to his clients, and waving his limp-wristed hands about, he is a grotesque stereotype of campness. While this easy stereotype may well have raised laughter for Spanish audiences in the early 1970s, the main source of humour comes from the audience's recognition that it is Alfredo Landa in the role. Landa's star persona is based on his construction as the painfully average Spanish male. Any aberration from such normality (effeminacy is clearly read as an aberration) produces the transgression of that social norm which the narrative has to resolve, thus restoring the comfortable and comforting normality. It is vital, then, to the comic function of Landa's role here, that he be recognizable as himself. Were the character 'Alfredo Landa' to be completely effaced, say in a realistic, keenly observed portrayal of a gay man (though homosexuality is not actually mentioned in the film), the effect would be lost. Hence, despite the accessories which allow the audience to 'decode' his character as effeminate, his make-up does not disguise the actor Landa underneath. The masquerade is revealed – one imagines much to the relief of audiences who know Alfredo Landa to be 'safe' in his sexual naivety and 'normalness' – when we discover Antón has another life in Madrid. There we find him wearing the trademark suit and tie and with a beautiful woman on each arm. Thus, we discover, his performance of gayness in the salon environment is merely a cover to allow him to 'access all areas' with his female clients without the threat of retaliation from their various male protectors. This conceit sustains a plot complication (both too complex and too infantile to go into here) which is resolved at the end of the film by the restoration of the patriarchal family unit.

Following the enormous success of *No desearás...* Landa, for better or for worse, was obliged to reprise the role of 'ordinary Spanish man in extraordinary situations' in countless versions, entrenching acting through personification and excluding acting as impersonation for a decade. In *París bien vale una moza* (Pedro Lazaga, 1972), Landa's name opens the film ('*Alfredo Landa en...*'). Once again his role is that of the ordinary Spaniard. After the opening images of Paris (over the French national anthem and upbeat 1970s easy listening music), we find Juan on his bicycle in the cobbled streets of Aragón, a plodding Spanish guitar reinforcing the idea of the cultural backwater that is rural Spain. Juan works not only in the ironically-named Siglo XXI (21st Century) village shop, but also as waiter and chef in the local bar, football coach, as well as accountant and general fixer of the local rich patriarch. It is this village big-shot who sends the innocent Juan to Paris. Once again, Landa is cast as the epitome of ordinary Spanish maleness, named Juan (as in Juan Español, an Iberian equivalent of the UK mythical Joe Bloggs). And once again his normality is faced with the challenge of an exotic Other, in this case the exotic sensuality and rich sexual possibilities of an apparently depraved Paris. Juan's first incursion is into the world of Pigalle and the 'streeptease' club. This culminates in him successfully defending himself against two male customers, the violence a prelude to his getting mixed up in a US-style gangster operation – which is signalled by an over-chic style in which Juan/Landa is clearly (and intentionally) uncomfortable. His parody of the gangster is as grotesque and inept as his parody of the camp stylist in *No desearás...* but of course, Landa's star persona *requires* him to be grotesquely out of place when he adopts these

Figure 5.1 Landa's parodic gangster in *París bien vale una moza*

non-normative, non-Spanish roles (see Figure 5.1). His performance is characterized, as usual, by the contorted facial expressions of vaudeville humour and his distinctive use of grunts where they are sufficient for his communicative needs.

Within a couple of years, Landa had become almost a parody of himself, in a genre so crass that it can now appear virtually an exercise in postmodern irony (which it certainly was not). In *Manolo la nuit* (Mariano Ozores, 1973), Landa's protagonist is a grotesque parody of the sexy film star. Even before he appears, he is built up as a sex symbol by the narrator. We see two other, younger, muscular, blond males, whom the narrator refers to as 'Latin lovers'. Then, as he describes '*el racial celtíbero español*' Manolo comes into view, first the legs, which could belong to any man, then the slightly overweight, hairy quintessential Spaniard – Alfredo Landa, of course. Manolo claims that in Málaga they say he's a 'sexy man' like Steve McQueen. Manolo is a caricature of the narcissistic male, uttering disparaging noises (the usual grunts) to row after row of admiring foreign women. Landa personifies the clash between backward Spain, and the exotic (and erotic) appeal of sophisticated European (in practice almost always Paris). This, in turn, reflects the socio-cultural inferiority complex that characterized Spain at the time in its clumsy overtures to come to terms with, and eventually belong to Europe.

Just as Spain would gradually overcome its insecurities and shake off its sexist and xeno-phobic defensiveness, so too Landa was able to break out of his 1970s mould and go on to give varied and acclaimed performances in such films as *El crack* (José Luis Garci, 1981) where he plays an impassive private detective, or *El bosque animado* (José Luis Cuerda, 1987), in the role of a Galician peasant taking up banditry despite his kindness of heart. Núria Triana Toribio (2003: 128) rightly points out that Landa's acting curriculum vitae – both his 1970s comic roles and the later performances – contributed to the star role he brought to the award-winning and successful *Los santos inocentes*. But despite such roles, such is the potency of Landa's personification of the simple Spanish everyman, that it is the 1970s *landismo* comedies for which he remains famous today.

Further reading: Zunzunegui, 2002; D'Lugo, 1997; Aguilar and Genover, 1996; Jordan, 2003a; Triana Toribio, 2003.

Geraghty's third category: 'star as performer' changes the focus from the putative bio-graphical details of a star's personal life decisively onto the work and craft of 'acting'. Here, the discourses surrounding the acting performance are crucial to how stars distinguish them-selves and legitimize their careers/roles in a marketplace full of star celebrities and professional actors. The notion of star as performer is arguably a key factor in validating the professional and cultural status of film stardom since it focuses attention on the film text and the acting performance as privileged sites and measures of value. Emphasis on performance, for example, helps distinguish actors like Carmen Maura (see below), Victoria Abril, Marisa Paredes, Javier Bardem, Antonio Banderas and others from lesser talents. Moreover, in the Spanish context, stardom has traditionally been validated in the perform-ance by an appeal to authenticity and naturalism and the extent to which the actor can immerse himself in the role and make it 'real'. Perriam (2003: 110) describes Bardem's evo-lution as 'acting his way out of *macho* typecasting'. At times, his performances come close to 'method acting', as evidenced in his recent portrayal of tetraplegic Ramón Sampedro in Amenábar's *Mar adentro*, but also as the unemployed shipyard worker in *Los lunes al sol* (León de Aranoa, 2002), and as Reinaldo Arenas in Schnabel's *Antes que anochezca* (2000), for which he was Oscar-nominated. These controlled and understated renderings can be compared with his performances in de la Iglesia's *Perdita Durango* (1997), the excessive and mannered performances in his early, Spanish archetypal roles with Bigas Luna, and with a slightly softer machismo in the Gómez Pereira comedies. (See Perriam, 2003: 93–120). Film stardom is further legitimized through the choice of roles and selection of projects undertaken. 'Serious actors' tend to avoid roles which might compromise their star image as 'serious actor' and choose roles which display the clearly recognizable mannerisms associated with their naturalistic performances (see Perriam on Arias and *El Lute*, 2003: 28–9). Moreover, the 'star as performer' supports the 'serious actor' profile via star interviews in upmarket magazines, including photo shoots, public pronouncements of personal views on politics/morality etc. (e.g. Javier Bardem's acceptance speech against the Iraq War), in an effort to distinguish the star image from that of the celebrity's tittle–tattle or the commercialism of lower-order, commercially driven 'performers'. All in all, the serious actor demands recognition and prestige on the basis of the film text and via a rhetoric of quality, craft, devotion, commitment, i.e. all signs of high cultural and professional status, which are constructed extratextually. And these extra-filmic performances help reinforce the distance and the 'difference' of the 'serious actor' from the talentless celebrities or the lesser professional performers who act (as) themselves. (Geraghty, 2000: 193).

Nevertheless, even the most performance-orientated actors still carry with them a 'baggage' which is the sum of their portfolio of roles (and the extent to which these have been personification and/or impersonation-led) and their celebrity star status. Spanish actor Carmen Maura exemplifies this phenomenon.

CARMEN MAURA (Madrid, 1945)

Within Spain, Maura is a classic example of the all-round star as both talented actress and celebrity, not dissimilar to the Hollywood star model, though in a doubly marginalized Spanish film culture (not dominant Hollywood, nor even dominant auteurist Europe). Born into a well-to-do family, she was active in university theatre and, while running an art gallery, maintained contacts in the theatrical world. By the end of the 1960s she was getting minor parts in films and appearing in the short films made by those in her Madrid circle. Her first major role came in 1977 at the relatively late age of 32 in Fernando Colomo's debut feature *Tigres de papel*. Maura plays a young '*progre*' (left-wing liberal, something of a hippy) coming to terms with the changes in the transition from dictatorship to democracy. Against the backdrop of Spain's first post-Franco democratic elections, Maura's character (also called Carmen) struggles with the clash between her political beliefs and her emotional confusion. Colomo's film holds an emblematic position in Spanish cinema of the time: its apparent spontaneity (naturalistic acting giving the impression of improvisation, though this was far from the truth) and its use of direct sound, provided a model for both Colomo and his so-called '*comedia madrileña*' and also, to a certain extent, for the early films of Pedro Almodóvar. For Maura, the role would establish a persona as the middle-class progressive, disillusioned with the political process in Spain, but not bitter about it. And notwithstanding several dramatic roles, Maura would be increasingly, 'constrained by generic convention' (Evans, 1996: 65), categorized as a comic or comedy-melodrama actress. As the star vehicle for Alex de la Iglesia's 2000 hit *La comunidad*, Maura's performance style – a melding of naturalism and grotesque comedy – still owes much to her formative work in the late 1970s and 1980s.

Her protagonist role in Colomo's second feature, *¿Qué hace una chica como tú en un sitio como éste?* (1978) further established her range of performance styles. As a working woman and mother, she plays the part of Rosa in a fairly naturalistic, understated style, though there are moments of powerful dramatic performance, such as when she is raped by her estranged husband, the desperate, fascist policeman played by Félix Rotaeta, or when he takes away her children. But then, following Colomo's script, Maura is equally at home in the grotesque revenge-comedy final section of the film, in which Rosa murders her tyrannical husband with the help of a hairdryer and some champagne. This extended range of performance styles – from grotesque comedy, through melodrama to the naturalistic – was to make Carmen Maura an excellent vehicle for the hybrid films of Pedro Almodóvar, the director with which Maura became internationally recognized.

In fact, it was Maura who discovered Almodóvar, rather than the other way around. She encouraged the aspiring director to turn his project *Erecciones generales* into a full-length feature film, which, with the new title, *Pepi, Luci, Bom y otras chicas del montón*, would become Almodóvar's first commercial success. Maura plays Pepi, a feisty, ambitious and fun-loving 20-something, living on her wits and on the allowance paid to her by a middle-class father. While the character would help further to establish Maura's persona as progressive, strong-willed female, her performance followed the comic-melodramatic of Colomo and would be reprised, with variations, in her next projects with Almodóvar. In *Entre tinieblas* (1983) she plays a cloistered nun who harbours a deep desire to become an ordinary housewife. Then in *¿Qué he hecho yo para merecer esto?* (1984) she actually plays an ordinary housewife. Maura proves she can play against type in a role which is the opposite of the middle-class progressive. Her performance is exceptional: among a cast of comic stereo-types, Maura alone gives a naturalistic performance which works contrapuntally within Almodóvar's crazy, surreal neorealist comedy melodrama. Her reward was the high-melo-drama part of transsexual Tina in *La ley del deseo* (1987) for which she received the National Cinema Prize. On the orders of the director, she took up weight-lifting to prepare physically for the part (an immersion which recalls the efforts of method actors such as Jodie Foster for her role in *The Silence of the Lambs* [Jonathan Demme, 1991]), and Almodóvar was so pleased with the result that the role was extended beyond what had been envisaged in the script. He has said that Maura's performance in *La ley del deseo* should be studied in acting schools (Vidal, 1988: 215). In 1988 came *Mujeres al borde de un ataque de nervios* in which Maura plays the part of actress Pepa in a Hollywoodesque comedy, which brought her to international prominence but also marked a bitter end to her working relationship with Almodóvar. The breakdown of their working relationship and friendship contributed to the media attention surrounding Maura, but also paved the way for a very different, distant and professional actor-director relationship with Carlos Saura in the multiple prize-winning *¡Ay, Carmela!* (1991).

Saura's celebrated film version of the José Sanchis Sinisterra play *¡Ay, Carmela!* was some-thing of a departure for Carmen Maura. An emblematic actor of the liberal, post-Franco, modern Spain, the role as a folkloric artist ran counter to her star persona, harking back to an age of distinctly unliberated female stars associated with a more reactionary ideology. Unlike the female singing stars of the 1930s and 1940s *españoladas*, Maura came to her role not as a singer learning to act, but as an actor learning to sing. Maura's performance in this film is, then, an example of impersonation, where an actor has to use skill, study and practice to create a role on screen, rather than the more typical personification which characterized the great stars of the 1930s and 1940s (Imperio Argentina, Lola Flores and others). Maura trained with voice and dance coaches for a month before filming (Ponga, 1993: 113). The story follows three Republican variety performers who stray into the Nationalist zone and are forced to stage a degrading burlesque of their former pro-Republic show for an audience which includes soldiers of the International Brigades who are condemned to death the next morning. While Paulino's instinct for self-preservation turns him into a pathetic puppet of his fascist masters, Carmela finds the betrayal of her comrades too much and rebels on the night of the show, leading to a disturbance in which she is shot in the head. Her unwillingness to compromise thus feeds back into Maura the actress's associations with left-wing, democratic ideals.

As film acting in Spain has been so linked to performance, and as so many actors have concentrated on talent and skill rather than star persona, a high profile in other media is usually required for celebrity status. One of the facets to Maura's career which marks her out as a star (at least within a national context), is her early appearance on Spanish television. In April 1981 Carmen Maura appeared on Spanish television's main channel as presenter of the programme *Esta noche* directed by Fernando G. Tola. It turned her into a national celebrity from one day to the next, leading to offers for adverts, more television, and ultimately, Maura's decision to leave the programme and rescue her acting career one year later. But Maura's star persona – and especially her catchphrase '*Nena, tú vales mucho*' – has stayed with her (and with a whole generation of TV viewers). Despite (or perhaps because of) her experience as a national TV celebrity, Carmen Maura's star persona also demonstrates the clear limits that most Spanish film actors prefer to place on their celebrity status. She kept the death of her mother a secret, avoiding publicity, and was dismayed at Pedro Almodóvar's attempt at a reconciliation at the very public Goyas ceremony, an attempt which she saw as a publicity stunt; and her unwillingness to accept second best in the 1992 *Antena 3* programme which, briefly, she co-presented, again with Tola, was confirmation of her rejection of celebrity at any price (Ponga, 1993: 129).

Further reading: Ponga, 1993; Aguilar and Genover, 1996; D'Lugo, 1997; Evans, 1996.

A final note. While Geraghty's schema offers a reasonably flexible and usable set of categories, applicable across a wide range of film cultures, they obviously need to be adapted to the specificities, differences and distinctive inflections which arise in different national cultures. This is particularly acute when faced with the work and star image of the likes of Santiago Segura, for example. His remarkable success as an actor, but also as director of 'trash' hits such as *Torrente: el brazo tonto de la ley* (1997) and *Torrente 2: misión en Marbella* (2001), as well as producer, writer and national celebrity, mean that his 'star' image traverses all three of Geraghty's categories. Moreover, while spoofing mainstream Hollywood genre films as well as domestic television, Segura engages aggressively in cultivating a highly commercial, yet anti-establishment hybrid exploitation cinema. Indeed, his is an anti-star stardom (in purely physical terms he embodies the obverse of the handsome leading man, i.e. he plays the gross-out slob); he also inverts the terms of the star's relation to his craft as 'serious actor' while inhabiting and exploiting to excess the 'star as celebrity' imagery. A unique case, perhaps, which requires further investigation.

Chapter Six

REPRESENTATION

WHY IS REPRESENTATION IMPORTANT?

The films seen by the largest number of people across the world come from the enter-tainment industry based in Hollywood, Los Angeles. Typically (in fact, overwhelmingly), they are produced by rich, white, heterosexual, male, US citizens. But within the many and varied worlds portrayed in these films are contained a wider spectrum of classes, races, genders, sexualities and national identities. Those involved in making films, espe-cially, but not exclusively, producers, writers and directors, have a range of choices involving selection, organization and collocation that have an impact on how such identities are portrayed on film. Since the 1960s, a core element of film studies has been representation, 'the process by which art forms use their various languages to ascribe meaning to objects, places, people and, most importantly, social groups' (Blandford, Grant and Hillier, 2001: 198).

Representation in film has concerned critics and academics engaged in the study of soci-eties and cultures because film is a powerful medium for creating 'shared meanings' between individuals and groups of people. To take just one example, if our perception of the role of black people in society is largely formed as a result of watching movies produced by a culture (that of the USA) with a history of racism, how could such a view *not* be affected by the culture that produced it? The approach to the portrayal of social groups in films can be divided into four categories:

- presence and absence: certain groups at certain times are missing from screen images altogether (e.g. gay and lesbian characters in most films before the late 1960s).
- stereotypes: presence on the screen is sometimes limited to stereotypical, often negative representations, (e.g. Native American Indians as 'savages' in classical Hollywood Westerns).
- positive and negative images: the evaluation of how a social group is depicted over time, sometimes in a negative light, sometimes positive (e.g. blacks can be slaves or servants, thus confirming racist stereotypes, but they can also be lawyers, surgeons or action heroes, confirming their equality with whites).
- specific representational strategies: the techniques, styles and conventions of film making, discussed in Chapter Two, all impact on the portrayal of social groups

(e.g. the camerawork, lighting and editing in classical Hollywood movies
highlights the glamorous, seductive but passive beauty of female stars, while
emphasizing purposeful action in male stars).

Coinciding with (and feeding into) debates around feminism, among others, from the
1960s and 1970s, representation studies became highly politicized, even polarized, and the
cinema was frequently the textual site of these debates.

REALISM AND IDEOLOGY

Although the representation of individuals and groups is common to most forms of media,
art and literature, its role in cinema has come under greater scrutiny because of the film
medium's association with realism. Because it utilizes photography, film is frequently
taken by spectators as a more or less faithful depiction of reality. So strong is this assumption that, as Dudley Andrew (1984: 47) puts it, 'No matter what appears on the screen,
audiences will instinctively shape it into a representation of something familiar to them.'
Films are, of course, not reality, but texts using systems of signs and conventions which
can be analysed. But because they portray worlds which appear 'real', or at least credible
to us, films are profoundly ideological. Ideology can be a set of ideas which gives an
account of the social world, albeit selective and partial. It can be visible (i.e. overtly racist
ideas) or invisible (taken-for-granted notions about gender superiority/inferiority, for
example). Films provide images of the world and its people for mass audiences on a global
scale. They provide models of behaviour to copy (or sometimes reject), and their stories
often polarize individuals and/or groups as good or bad. There is no such thing as an
ideology-free film. While it may be easy to recognize the ideological thrust of overtly
political or propaganda films, such as those produced after the Spanish Civil War which
glorify the victorious fascists led by Franco, most films present certain ideological positions
as 'natural' or 'common sense'. For example, the 'natural' assumption, made in countless
movies, that marriage and motherhood are the greatest achievements open to women, is
an ideological position that some women would challenge.

REPRESENTATION IN SPANISH CINEMA

The study of representation in the cinema has focused on both the production of images
and sounds by film makers, and on their reception by spectators (as individuals) and audiences (as groups). And the field has been hugely expanded by the inclusion of semiotics,
Marxist and feminist theories, psychoanalysis, and cultural studies. Much of the work in
this field has been carried out by analysing mainstream, Hollywood movies in an attempt
to reveal the hidden (and thereby more powerful) mechanisms used to portray social
groups or identities. Investigation of non-Hollywood films, including Spanish cinema, has
tended to prefer auteurist approaches (see Chapter Three), but gradually, the question
of representation has also emerged as a field within the study of world cinema. National
identity is frequently the first focus of attention. But increasingly, class, race, gender and

sexuality are fast becoming core elements in Spanish film studies, especially in the USA and the UK, with such writers as Marsha Kinder and Paul Julian Smith.

A twentieth-century phenomenon, cinema in Spain has, unsurprisingly, reflected the ideological conflicts of a turbulent century of history. Periods of dictatorship, marked by censorship of all media and heavy-handed stereotyping (good and bad characters or social groups), have been followed by periods under much more open, questioning and plural-istic regimes. Although the representation of social groups in Spanish cinema has much in common with other western film cultures (in, for example, its portrayal of women), many studies of representation have centred on what makes Spanish film different from other film cultures. The vast majority of studies on Spanish cinema have focused on questions of national identity, which forms the first section of this chapter, before we move on to look at the issue of representing gender.

NATIONAL IDENTITY

The concept of national identity may at first seem an unproblematic one. We probably have a clear idea what, for example, 'Spain' means. We tend to associate national identity with territorial space, the idea of an historic homeland or *patria*, and the shared identity and beliefs of the inhabitants of that particular geographically and politically-defined space (Smith, 1991: 9). But this shared sense of belonging comprises a range of factors includ-ing history, memories, myths, traditions, customs, languages and beliefs. And, contrary to the rhetoric of many politicians, these shared values are not fixed and eternal, but plural and shifting. The last two decades have seen a re-assessment of essentialist beliefs in homogenous national identities by writers such as Benedict Anderson. For Anderson, national identities, rather than equating to real communities, amount, in fact, to 'imagined communities', '*imagined* because the members of even the smallest nation will never know most of their fellow-members, […] yet in the minds of each lives the image of their com-munion' (1991: 6). Nationhood requires people to feel that they belong to communities with shared cultures, aspirations, and values. Shared languages are also important in the perception of national identities, and this presents a special case of often divided loyalties in Spain, given its bilingual communities in Catalonia, the Basque country and Galicia, and the dual experience of national and sub-national cultures in these (and other) regions. Finally, various forms of the media help to shape cultural and national identity. In the twentieth and twenty-first centuries, film has arguably been the most powerful and most widely propagated cultural form.

Part of the power of cinema lies in the ability either to underline national differences or to understate them. Hollywood producers were quick to realize the economic benefits of films which could be sold as having universal, rather than local, appeal. The apparent universality of mainstream US movies can, of course, mask a more subtle nationalism, whereby the world is asked to buy into distinctly American values. But in general terms,

US cinema has been less interested in asserting cultural difference than many other cinemas across the globe. In the face of a film market so strongly dominated by US products, any attempt to make films elsewhere can be interpreted as an assertion of national/cultural difference. The term 'national cinema' has therefore often been used to refer to any films whose narratives, styles and film languages are somehow different from or in opposition to the hegemonic genres and styles of Hollywood. The cultural context of production has frequently been a distinguishing factor for such 'national cinemas', often in implied opposition to the economic context of Hollywood production. In the USA, the film industry based itself as far away as possible from the nation's cultural capital, New York, allowing its producers to concentrate on purely economic priorities. In Europe, film industries have always been based in cultural and political capitals (Paris, Berlin, Barcelona, Madrid), and therefore in constant contact with 'high culture' (art, literature, philosophy) and with politics. Thus, the immediate post-war period produced Italian neo-realism, and the specific historical and cultural conditions of the 1960s produced French New Wave cinema.

But film can *project* as well as *reflect* national cultures. Politicians have been ready to see film as promoting specific conceptions of national identity. The state can become involved in this cultural enterprise by means of subsidies to certain films. This has often led to attempts to promote a so-called 'cinema of quality', usually inspired by national cultural artefacts such as novels, plays and key historical events. The state can even use film for more explicitly propagandistic purposes, as was the case in Soviet Russia, Nazi Germany, or in Spain after 1939. Under totalitarian regimes like that of Franco in Spain, films which promote values acceptable to the regime can be rewarded; and those which offend the regime marginalized or suppressed. During the dictatorship many films chose to engage in the uncritical recycling of national traditions (for example, in the *españolada*, war films, historical epics or religious dramas). Even under less repressive regimes, the state tends to endorse certain kinds of films rather than others. Spain's socialist governments from 1982 supported adaptations of the 'greats' of Spanish literature, films which would reflect a national literary culture, a legacy less sensitive than the immediate past of the dictatorship. But such state-sponsored cinema has always left room for alternative voices to explore and even satirize national identity. Twentieth-century Spain provides a fascinating case study in the changing representations of national identity on screen.

NATIONAL IDENTITY IN SPAIN AND SPANISH CINEMA

Spain's natural geography works against a strong sense of national identity. It is located between two continents (Europe and Africa), between two seas (the Atlantic and the Mediterranean) and between two climatic zones (temperate and sub-tropical). Its mountains tend to divide one region from another, while its river network (which can often unite peoples) is poor. Allegiance to region or even to town or village has often been stronger than to a sense of nationhood. The history of the Iberian peninsula confirms this diversity. From the eighth century BC to the end of the Reconquest in AD 1492, the Iberian peninsula was occupied variously by Phoenicians, Greeks, Carthaginians, Celts, Romans, Visigoths and Muslims. Only from 1469, when the two kingdoms of Castile and Aragon were united through marriage, can we speak of 'Spain' as a nation in something approaching the modern sense of the term. Even more critical for Spain's sense of nationhood were the momentous events of 1492. As the Christian forces of Ferdinand and Isabella were recapturing Granada by defeating the Muslims, Christopher Columbus was discovering the 'Indies' for Spain, marking the beginning of Spain's great imperial adventure. Maintaining a vast empire and acting as the guarantor of the Catholic Church provided Spain's diverse interests with the motivation to work together as a nation. Invasion by the French in 1808 was a further opportunity to strengthen this sense of national identity, against a common foreign enemy.

The failure of Spain's liberal politics in its project to build a nation state in the nineteenth century (see Mar-Molinero and Smith, 1996: 3–30) was compounded by defeat in a disastrous war with the USA in 1898 in which Spain lost Cuba, Puerto Rico and the Philippines. The end of Spanish colonial aspirations, this so-called 'disaster' also marks the beginning of an anxious period of re-evaluation of Spain's national identity, a problem which remained unresolved at the start of the civil war in 1936. That war was – among other things – a battle between a nationalistic concept of community (hence the name Nationalists) and the more internationalist social and political aspirations of the Republic. Once Franco's Nationalists had won the war in the name of 'saving' Spain from disintegration and from communism, they set about establishing a set of nationalistic values, privileging the military and the Catholic Church, and demonizing communists, socialists and all regionalist (Catalan, Basque and Galician) sentiment. After Franco's death on 20 November 1975, the new democratic regime set about re-establishing the so-called 'historical nations' of Catalonia and the Basque Country with statutes of autonomy. There are now 17 autonomous communities, some of which have their own recognized languages (Catalan, Basque/Euskera and Galician). As the examples that follow will show, Spanish cinema has reflected these variations in the interpretation of national identity.

Changes in associations and representations of Spanishness affect the content of films (their characters, genres and narratives), and also their favoured actors, Imperio Argentina in the 1930s, Marisol in the 1960s (see Triana Toribio, 2003: 7). While the nature of incarnations of Spanishness has varied according to the economic, social and political imperatives of the time, the centrality of questions of national identity in Spanish cinema is constant, at least until the late 1990s. Even before any Spaniard had made a film, the Frenchman Lix had made one in 1896 called *Ejecución de una paella* (Pérez Perucha, 1995: 25), indicating the kinds of folksy, stereotypical versions of Spanishness that would dominate early Spanish cinema. Some of Spain's historical, literary and mythical characters would feature in narrative cinema, including *Don Juan Tenorio* and *Los amantes de Teruel* both in 1909 (Higginbotham, 1988: 3), but more popular aspects of Spanish life prevailed, such as bullfighting, flamenco and *zarzuela*. Into the 1920s, films like *Fútbol, amor y toros* (Florián Rey, 1929) were the norm, though some, like *La aldea maldita* (also Florián Rey, 1929) dealt with social themes. During the years of the Republic, the Spanish film industry was only able to resist the influx of foreign films with authentic and lively images of Spanish life, such as *La hermana San Sulpicio* by Florián Rey (1934) and *La verbena de la paloma* by Benito Perojo (1935). But while the public was happy with these stereotypical representations, critics rejected them as inauthentic. '*Españolada*' as distinct from '*españolidad*' was seen as a foreign version of Spanishness (deriving from the black legend and French Romantic conceptions of gypsy culture) (Monterde, 1995: 213).

After the defeat of the Republic in 1936 (see Chapter One), the direction of Spanish cinema (and its representation of national identity) would be guided by political imperatives even more than by economic ones. The principal priority of the Franco regime, above any ideology or political system, was 'the survival of the regime itself, entirely identified with the survival of its leader, and encompassing the nation as the sum of long-held, nationalistic and conservative religious and social principles' (Monterde, 1995: 181). The conception of history in Francoist cinema matches that of the regime:

> The privileging of politics over economics or social questions; the emphasis
> on the biographies of illustrious figures; a tendency towards the exaltation
> of the hero-leader as the driving force of History and in a paternalistic role
> towards the populace; a Manichean division between 'us' and 'them'
> (whether external or internal enemies); a purportedly erudite inclination to
> list decisive, concrete events; the lack of any hypothesis about or critique of
> idolization leading to the predominance of myth over history. (Monterde,
> 1995: 235)

The first task of a Spanish film industry subordinate to Franco's regime was to confirm the 'righteous' victory of one Spain over another. Hence the arch-conservative, militaristic values of the so-called '*cine de cruzada*' (crusade films) which we will see in *Raza*. But films about the civil war were taboo after the brief flurry of the early 1940s because they were 'perceived as a threat to the monolithic national unity imposed by Franco and to his ongoing process of defascistization' (Kinder, 1993: 38). From the late 1940s and throughout the 1950s, what was missing from representations of Spanish national identity was more significant than what was present: comedies, melodramas and historical epics carefully avoided the difficult topic of Spain's recent past. Even so, some, more critical film makers were able to find ways to criticize the regime, as we shall see. Only after the death of Franco and the removal of censorship could the previously excluded versions of Spanish identities (and others) finally be represented in Spanish cinema.

RAZA (José Luis Sáenz de Heredia, 1941)

No film better illustrates the politically motivated changing fortunes of Spanish national identity than this early Francoist propaganda epic, from a story by General Franco himself, under the pseudonym Jaime de Andrade. Its first version (1941) captures the exaltation and certainty of victory, with Franco's regime riding what looked like a wave of victorious fascism in Europe. By 1950, the film had been re-edited to reflect a post-fascist, newly anti-communist world, as we shall see. *Raza* tells the story of the Churruca family over two centuries of patriotic military glory, culminating in the Nationalist victory in the Spanish Civil War, interpreted as the beginning of Spain's triumphal return to imperialist splendour. Its appeal to patriotism is proclaimed from the opening titles, for this is a 'Great Spanish Superproduction', which is 'supported by the Council for Hispanic Identity (Consejo de la Hispanidad)', the body set up to fund this film and to promote (and enforce) Franco's version of Spanish national identity. Candidate directors were asked to submit a test reel and the favoured director was José Luis Sáenz de Heredia (who just happened to be the cousin of the Falangist founder and martyr, José Antonio Primo de Rivera). The budget of 1,650,00 pesetas (10,000€) was unprecedented for Spanish films at that time and 45,000 metres of film were used for a film that eventually amounted to only 3100 metres (Reig Tapia, 2002: 98). The unique conditions of its production testify to its perceived importance to the regime as part of the project to legitimize the fascist victory and re-build a nation along ideological lines. This ideological project is described by Richards (1996: 151):

> The main ingredients of this nationalist ideological brew were the eulogiz-
> ing of the Spanish peasantry as the embodiment of national virtues; the
> maintenance of private property; a revaluation of violence as 'creative' and
> 'purifying' [...] militarism and martial virtues; and the ideal of a national
> unity and a spiritual and material resurgence based upon the developments
> of myths of Empire, Reconquest and Counter-Reformation.

In 1941 the Franco regime's priority for its nation-building project was justifying the war, hence the need to turn the reality of three years of debilitating conflict into the myth of centuries of empowering crusade (see Donapetry, 1998: 41). The action commences in late nineteenth-century Galicia. The landscape is repeatedly shown in establishing shots to remind us that the fatherland (Patria) itself is at stake. But in the course of the film, many other regions of Spain are referred to, suggesting a degree of unity which in reality has always been lacking in Spain. An apparently wealthy family awaits the return of their sea-faring father. Tradition and religion are quickly established as primary virtues. Don Pedro's first action, when reunited with his family, is to go to church. Family roles are clearly defined by gender: the mother's first concern is for her daughter, then the evening meal (even though she has a cook). While Don Pedro's daughter is described as 'pretty and hardworking' his baby son, we are informed, is a bit of a fighter ('*da mucha guerra*').

War is seen as the greatest role open to men. When Don Pedro describes the noble history of the Churruca family, his narrative is full of expressions that link death and sacrifice with glory and beauty, phrases such as 'glorious death' and later 'beautiful death'. He tells his superior he could not stay at home while there are battles to be fought, 'I would die of shame', he says, again playing on the word 'death'. But he does promise his wife he will pray every day. When he is fatally wounded, he kisses the rosary she had given him in recognition of his love for her and for God. Don Pedro's men shout '¡Viva España!' before going into a battle they know they will lose.

Don Pedro represents a distinctly conservative attitude towards Spain's history and politics. A flashback to the battle of Trafalgar and the death of their ancestor prefigures don Pedro's own heroic sacrifice in the Cuban war of 1898, actions only necessary because of what he refers to as 'bad politics'. These political failings are shown to be history repeating itself in a later section, where we see an undignified debate in parliament, using the real chamber (empty in 1941 since Franco had banned all political parties). By this time, Don Pedro's eldest son, also named Pedro, is seeking a career in politics. He demands his inheritance early to finance his election campaign, his desire for money shown to be a negative trait, already witnessed in his childhood. Little Pedro had asked if their famous ancestor was rich. He is shown as a child already preoccupied with money. He fights with his sister while his other brother José is a good, obedient child. Spain's national identity is further defined along racial lines, the construction of Francoist national identity, much in the spirit of Hitler's ideas on race, especially absurd in the context of Spain with its millennium of racial mixing. Don Pedro attributes the unrest he has seen in the Philippines to 'the same disturbances provoked by foreigners; the perennial rebellions of coloured people'. The soldiers he serves with are described as 'chosen warriors, the highest representatives of the Spanish race'. And, at the end of the film, a glorious parade with José recalling in flashback the words of his heroic father in the prologue, prompts Isabel to tell her little son 'This is our race' ('Esto es la raza'). (The film's racial conceptualization of identity extends to the selection of actors, the blond, blue-eyed Alfredo Mayo playing the good brother José, and the dark José Nieto playing the errant Republican politician.)

The film culminates in the civil war in which José, fighting on Franco's Nationalist side, is captured but miraculously (for God is with the Fascists) survives the firing squad. He proclaims, 'My blood is Spanish' and at his execution shouts '¡Arriba España!' His brother Pedro, who has made the mistake of entering politics and thus finds himself on the wrong side in the war, redeems himself by giving the Nationalists important battle plans. Upon his discovery by the Republican side he had betrayed, and about to face execution, he finds his true 'patriotic' spirit, declaiming the virtues of the Nationalist cause in a 'conversion' speech filmed like a religious vision. The Nationalist celebrations, with something of the spirit of the Nazis' Nuremberg rallies, include a Falangist song, fascist salutes by the crowds, and posters of Franco. Finally we see Franco himself giving a fascist salute.

Figure 6.1 Alfredo Mayo as the good brother José in *Raza*

All this would be changed in the 1950 version *El espíritu de la raza*, six minutes shorter than the original (Reig Tapia, 2002: 111). With the Axis powers defeated, Franco could no longer express his victory in terms of a wider European Fascist movement. This crusade is replaced by the fight against communism. An added textual introduction stresses the universality of the struggle: 'a people who will not accept the annihilation that communism produces', thus equating communism with the death of the nation. One of the aims of internationalist communism was to have been the dismantling of national borders in favour of class comradeship. A small irony is that the sequences on board the Vizcaya warship as it prepares for battle off Cuba owe much to the montage style of communism's most acclaimed propaganda film *Battleship Potemkin* (Sergei Eisentstein, 1926). Another addition is a narrator who covers the ellipsis from the 1898 disaster to the wedding of Pedro's daughter Isabel in 1928 with the following:

> In the family of our story faced with the harshness of a futile sacrifice and
> with the political decline which followed the devastation of the remains of
> the Spanish Empire, the boys became men, their personalities formed under
> the protection and guidance of an exemplary, self-sacrificing, Christian,
> Spanish mother.

Female sacrifice is thus equated with Spanish identity. Then, a further narrator's ellipsis relates the 'political turmoil' which led to the civil war (over a montage of newspaper headlines) or, in the narrator's words, which led the nation 'towards the abyss of communism'. As well as those additions, certain references were removed from the later version: a Falangist song, the fascist salutes by the crowds and by Franco himself, and the posters of Franco. And, perhaps fearful of association with the Nazis' racial policies, the final line 'This is our race' ('Esto es la raza') is replaced by 'This is *the spirit of* our race' ('Esto es *el espíritu de* la raza').

If in 1941 Spain's official, Francoist representation of national identity was uncompromising and monolithic, only 10 years later, some film makers were beginning to posit a much more questioning and pluralistic version of 'Spanishness' at home and abroad.

BIENVENIDO MÍSTER MARSHALL (Luis García Berlanga, 1952)

Bienvenido Míster Marshall is a landmark film signalling a more critical attitude to both Spanish cinema and representations of Spanish national identity, though still within a regime that would tolerate a critique of its version of nationhood only up to a very limited extent. A collaboration between the two most prominent figures within this new, more critical Spanish cinema in the 1950s, Juan Antonio Bardem and Luis García Berlanga, the film problematizes 'Spanishness', a concept so important to critics and politicians of the post-civil war period (see Chapter One). It tells the story of a village in central Spain that attempts to impress rich American visitors with a version of Spanishness based on a mythical Andalusian model (in cinema, the *españolada*). Villagers for whom flamenco is as foreign as the can-can, agree to dress up in Andalusian costume, learn the rudimentary moves of bullfighting and flamenco dancing, and erect false whitewashed walls with geraniums in hanging baskets. What is so remarkable about this critique of Andalusian Spanishness is how relevant it remains, half a century on. Foreign conceptions of Spanish culture, propagated first by the French in the eighteenth and nineteenth centuries, even today remain rooted in the regional cultures of southern Spain. But this film is more than a satirization of this misconception: it has much to say about cinematic versions of Spanishness based on Andalusia, the so-called *españoladas*. Originally conceived as a typical folkloric musical itself, *Bienvenido Míster Marshall* is transformed by Berlanga and Bardem into a musical parody of the *españolada* and a satire on foreign-inspired versions of Spanishness, which the coming decades of mass tourism would soon vindicate. Spanish national identity is set against that of the USA.

The film softens its critique of Spanish society by employing an affectionate, light satirical tone. An extra-diegetic narrator, jovial but gently mocking, introduces us to Villar del Río, a nondescript location that could be anywhere in Spain. We see the open countryside, which was promoted as the soul of Spain by Francoist ideology. The narrator begins 'Once upon a time there was a Spanish village', playing on the dual meaning of 'pueblo' in Spanish: 'village', but also 'people' (the Spanish people): thus the village is a microcosm of the whole of Spain. The narrator's seven-minute introduction to the characters of Villar del Río reads like a list of Spanish stereotypes: the unemployed farmers, the local *hidalgo* (once illustrious nobleman, now penniless), the affectionate (if over-zealous) village priest, the gossips, the town crier, the schoolmistress and the Mayor, don Pablo. The Mayor owns the café, hotel, bus company and half the village, as well as holding political office, which amounts to a critique of the concentration of political power and wealth in the same people. The fact that Don Pablo is only the Mayor 'to fill in his time' suggests politics is only a distraction, in what is, after all, a totalitarian regime with no real democracy. When he proclaims to his villagers, 'let us be optimistic, the good times are about to arrive' one is reminded of the paternalistic speeches of Franco himself. Moreover, Don Pablo is shown to be a most ineffectual leader: his first idea for the reception of the Americans is lemonade or *sangría*, and he relies heavily on other villagers and later on the impresario Manolo. There are other veiled references to politics in the film. On the arrival of the Delegado (the Governor, a representative of the Franco regime at the provincial level), the school children recite the lines they have been taught: 'Viva, viva el señor Delegado'. The town fears the Delegado but sings his praises. His entourage are men in suits, officialdom regimented like an army, reflecting a militaristic attitude to discipline.

But within the village community other, less serious pursuits are to the fore. Football is the focus of passion for the men of the village. This accords with the regime's promotion of football to channel rivalries into sport and away from politics. Then there are the dances in the village square: a *pasodoble*, that most Spanish of dances (deriving from the bullfight). Escapism is the order of the day. At the start of the narrative, Carmen Vargas, 'the greatest flamenco star', arrives in the village as the embodiment of a southern Spanish entertainment form, which is exotic to these Castilian villagers. Satire and parody operate here in equal measure: Carmen is the stereotypically vacuous show-woman: she talks in monosyllables; her songs are melodramatic, but unlike the heroines in the *españolada* films, her life is not dramatic. As the representative of Spain's most flamboyant popular culture, she is, unsurprisingly, first choice in the village's planned spectacle for the US visitors. Her agent points out that 'Americans know Spain through Andalusia' and so it is decided that the whole village will perform this variety of Spanishness. The villagers enjoy the charade of dressing up as typically Spanish: one shot has them reduced to a sea of Cordovan *sombreros*. The streets are covered with cardboard white-washed walls, geraniums planted in an artificial Calle de Rocío with Spanish guitar music, and there is even a love scene at the bars of a false window. This is not only a critique of narrowly-defined notions of Spanishness, but of the *españolada* genre itself, frequently as thin and false as these cardboard walls. Spain's film industry, it is inferred, is a microcosm of the country's underdevelopment.

The villagers are shown to have their own fantasies, based in turn on other cinematic models. The nobleman don Luis's dream of long-departed glories is an opportunity for a parody of the '*cine de cruzada*' (given the naval setting, perhaps of *Raza* itself). But for others, Hollywood cinema is the preferred entertainment medium. This gives the film makers further opportunities both to parody American film genres, and to criticize stereotypical notions of both American and Spanish identity. As the villagers prepare for the arrival of their rich guests, their hopes and fears are sublimated into dreams based on Hollywood movies. Don Pablo's dream is a parody of the Western with the saloon bar, dancing girls and country music, and dialogue in a hilarious gibberish imitating the sounds of US English. In a delightful twist, he incorporates Carmen Vargas into the dream: she proclaims, in a mix of country and western with flamenco, 'Even though I'm from Arizona, I will sing flamenco'. The priest Don Cosme's dream turns into a nightmare: Holy Week music is suddenly cut to frenetic jazz as he is carried off by the Ku Klux Klan. His inter-rogation is clearly inspired by gangster films. But, curiously, his trial by the Anti-American Activities Committee is filmed in an expressionistic style, more reminiscent of 1920s German cinema than Hollywood. Don Cosme's dream relates to an earlier sequence, where he rants against the new superpower. In a public gathering, the schoolmistress lists US production totals. This list is copied by the priest, who enumerates their 'sins': 49 million protestants, 400,000 Indians, 200,000 Chinese, 5 million Jews, 13 million

Figure 6.2 Americanos welcomed in *Bienvenido Míster Marshal*

blacks: a racial (and racist) conception of US national identity. The priest continues: one million divorces, 7000 murders, 17000 rapes, 80000 muggings, 60000 robberies. Though this list is abruptly cut to shots of the help received in Europe by the US reconstruction plan, the priest clearly sets material progress and wealth against spiritual well-being. In fact, Spain never received money from the Marshall Plan itself: labourer Juan's dream of a tractor dropped from the skies by the Three Kings signals that the gifts from the USA are pure fantasy; like Father Christmas, the Americans themselves always and necessarily absent (Rolph, 1999: 14). The central musical number of the film continues the satirical/parodic vein: a genre normally exclusive to the themes and tropes of either Andalusian or popular Spanish stereotypes becomes an intertextual pastiche of a US Spanish cultural encounter, highlighting the clash between developed and primitive societies:

The Yanks have come	Los yanquis han venido
Olé! With a thousand gifts	¡Olé salero! Con mil regalos
To shower pretty girls	Y a las niñas bonitas
With aeroplanes	Van a obsequiarlas con aeroplanos
With free-flowing aeroplanes	Con aeroplanos de chorro libre
Which cut through the air	Que cortan el aire
And with sky-scrapers	Y también rascacielos
Kept fresh in Frigidaires	Bien conservados en Frigidaire
Americans are coming to Spain	Americanos vienen a España
To conquer us	Pá conquistarnos
Long live extravagance	Viva el tronío
Of this great and powerful people	De este gran pueblo con poderío
Olé Virginia and Michigan	Olé Virginia y Michigan
And viva Texas, not bad at all	Y viva Tejas que no está mal
We greet you	Os recibimos
Americans, with joy	americanos, con alegría
Olé mother	Olé mi mare
Olé mother-in-law	Olé mi suegra
Olé my aunt	Olé mi tía
The Marshall Plan is here	El Plan Marshall nos llega
From abroad to help	Del extranjero pá nuestro avío
And with so much cash	Y con tanto parné
We'll have a good time	Va a echar buen pelo
In Villar del Río	Villar del Río
They will give good money	Darán divisas
To whoever best fights the bull	pá quién toree mejor corría
And stockings and blouses	Y medias y camisas
For the most presuming girls	Pá las mocitas más presumías.

Elsewhere, attitudes towards the USA are mixed. They are referred to as 'the representatives of a great people', but also as 'noble but infantile'. In the end, their dash through the village leaves no trace, except for the US and Spanish flags floating in a river: national identity reduced to soggy symbols.

This film remains one of the most penetrating and entertaining investigations into cinematic constructions of Spanish national identity. But it would be the period following Franco's death and the restoration of democracy in Spain that would see both the more radical dissecting of Spanish culture and identity, and the exploration of so-called 'subnational' identities.

MATADOR (Pedro Almodóvar, 1986)

From the 1980s, the films of Pedro Almodóvar have deconstructed many of the themes, tropes, stereotypes and symbols associated with Spanish national identity for audiences within Spain and, more especially, abroad, where his films have become the most exportable representation of post-Franco Spain. Despite the contemporary settings, Almodóvar's films have much to say about Spain's cultural identity, both past and present. His representation of gender amounts to what Marsha Kinder (1997: 3) calls 'a radical sex change on Spain's national stereotype'. And his engagement with some of the key themes and icons of Spanish history and culture is more complex and more ambivalent than the gentle satire of *Bienvenido Míster Marshall.*

Among Almodóvar's 15 feature films (up to 2004), *Matador* is the one which focuses most directly on cultural and symbolic conceptions of national identity and with Spain's past cinematic representations of national identity. It is a film about bullfighting but with no colourful spectacles in the bullring; a film about religion but with no positive spirituality; a film about sex but with no conventional romantic dénouement; and a film about the two Spains, where the modern, progressive version (the one to which Almodóvar himself subscribes, we assume) is promoted rather than the reactionary version. It tells the story of ex-bullfighter Diego, who has swapped killing bulls for sexually motivated murder, and his relationship with the equally death-obsessed María. Their fates are linked in an opening sequence in which Diego explains to his *tauromaquia* students the art of killing bulls, while in parallel montage, we see María following these moves in her murder of a young sexual partner. The subsequent encounters of Diego and María are structured like the stylized *tercios* (stages) of the *corrida*, in which the bullfighter attempts to dominate the bull (Allinson, 2001: 28). The climax (both narrative and sexual) is their mutually-agreed and simultaneous death, but it is María who kills Diego (stabbing him in the neck like a bull) before shooting herself (with a gun in her mouth). Power relations between the sexes are shown to be equal in *Matador*, in marked contrast to previous bullfighting films, and to Spanish cinema as a whole.

147

Matador also depicts the clash between a traditionalist, repressive moral code and a liberal society. Diego's bullfighting student Ángel reacts to a strictly religious upbringing by exhibiting psychotic tendencies and an over-developed guilt complex (which leads him to confess to both Diego's and María's murders). The cause of Ángel's psychosis is his mother Berta, described by Evans (1993: 328) as a 'monstrous, self-mortifying, pre-democratic fascist ideal'. Eva's mother (played by veteran comic actress Chus Lampreave) is the model of a liberal, democratic Spanish matriarch (of which there are many in Almodóvar's cinema). For Almodóvar, these two mothers represent the two Spains: 'one is tolerant, a friend to her child, which symbolizes a Spain that has changed, become humanized and lost some of its prejudices, and the other is the eternally intolerant' (Vidal, 1988: 177). 'Spain Divided' is the title given to his fashion show by designer Montesinos (played by Almodóvar himself in the film): Spaniards are either envious or intolerant, he claims. But as Smith (2000: 74–5) points out, this film also divided audiences. *Matador* earned a state subsidy for its 'special artistic quality' from a Spanish government frequently more interested in projecting art films abroad. But while foreign audiences and critics accepted the film as a reflection of timeless Spanish cultural identity, for Spanish critics, it formed part of a more complex debate about the *corrida*'s role in contemporary Spain, and about the country's cinematic heritage and popular culture. *Matador* might be a favourite on Spanish culture and cinema modules in the Anglo-Saxon world, but its reception and interpretation, more than any other of Almodóvar's films, depends on familiarity with a series of cultural and historical contingencies (see Smith, 2000: 74–5).

OTHER NATIONALITIES: THE CASE OF BASQUE CINEMA

Given the strongly determined and, at times, fiercely policed co-ordinates of Spanish national identity as represented in the cinema, we might expect that sub-national, regional cinemas – principally Catalan and Basque cinemas – would project more flexible, less exclusive, less chauvinist reconstructions of their national identities. In fact, the case of Basque cinema demonstrates that, if anything, its version of national identity is even more rigidly and narrowly defined. Well before the Franco dictatorship, which unsurprisingly hardened the formulation of Basque national identity into a political struggle, Basque audiences, like those elsewhere, were keen to see the customs of their own land reflected on the cinema screen. The focus on local folklore, traditions and sports developed, as early as the 1920s, into an ethnographically slanted documentary tradition. This led to the 1933 documentary *Euskadi*, created by the then leader of the Basque Nationalist Party and based on the racial theories of Basque identity propagated by the nineteenth-century founder of Basque nationalism, Sabino Arana. The high point in this documentary tradition is *Ama Lur* (*Motherland*, Basterretxea and Larruquert, 1968), a rhapsodic hymn to the Basque lands and their customs, the editing of which imitates the free association of images taken from the improvizing Basque poet or *bertsolari* (Stone, 2002: 136). Because of the film's almost 'tourist advert' style, and its insistence on cultural myth rather than history or politics, it was tolerated by the Franco regime. The end of the dictatorship in

1975 brought both opportunities and challenges to Basque cinema. Unlike the case of Catalonia, the Basque country had no industrial or commercial base for a film industry. On the other hand, the Basque language *euskera* was never an impediment to its emerging film industry. Where the Catalan language was seen as *the* marker of national identity for Catalan cinema, thus reducing its appeal, Basque is spoken by so few people that it was never an option for a wide target audience, and remained limited to a small number of experiments in Basque-language films. In 1980 powers relating to film production were devolved to Basque culture agencies. The resulting subsidies made film making in the Basque country very attractive (Jordan and Morgan-Tamosunas, 1998: 186), resulting in something of a boom. The existing mythical versions of Basqueness were joined by a new political cinema, principally interested in re-writing the history of the Basque conflict with the Spanish state, in films like *El proceso de Burgos* (Imanol Uribe, 1979), *La fuga de Segovia* (Imanol Uribe, 1981) and *Operación Ogro* (Gillo Pontecorvo, 1980). By the beginning of the 1990s such myth-based models of Basque film making were so firmly established that they were becoming ripe for parodic re-working.

The film which best encapsulates this almost postmodern questioning of historical, political and, above all, mythical notions of Basque identity is by far the most popular choice on Hispanic film modules in the English-speaking world among all films by Basque directors: *Vacas.*

VACAS (Julio Medem, 1992)

Deep in the forest, which is both backdrop but also protagonist in this film, a solitary *aizko-lari* or wood-cutter practises this ancient art, which the Basques turned into a competitive sport. One could hardly imagine a more authentically 'Basque' opening. But any ethno-graphic expectations of a re-vamped *Ama Lur*-type documentary are quickly re-adjusted when we are introduced to what appears to be a historical drama, set on the Vizcayan front during the Carlist War of 1875. An establishing shot of the Basque landscape shows not a rural idyll, but a land physically scarred by war, the earth cut open by trenches. The authenticity of a mythical Basque homeland is replaced by the verisimilitude of the horrors of war, in images that recall Goya's *Disasters of War* series of etchings. The red berets of the Carlists provide a link to the red berets of folkloric Basque tradition, seen in celebratory documentaries such as *Ama Lur*. But although *Vacas* (Cows) is framed by two civil wars (the Carlist War of 1875 and the Spanish Civil War 1936–9), the conflict which dominates the narrative is one that exists between the Mendiluce and Irigibel families, neighbouring clans in a valley which functions as an allegory for Basque identity (Pérez Perucha, 1997: 923). The rivalry between the two families can be seen as representing wider conflicts and civil wars, but it also encapsulates the destructive power of isolation-ist, racial Basque identity, not so much oppressed by the rest of Spain, as consumed from within by its own incestuous insularity (Stone, 2002: 163). Both the endless repetition of predestined social roles and the lack of a broad gene pool are cleverly illustrated in the film by using the same actors to play various generations of Basque males, to the extent that they appear, as Anne White (1999: 7) suggests, almost as clones. The forest functions as a metaphor for this enclosed world: on more than one occasion, it is the scene of pursuit or conflict, its claustrophobia reflected in subjective camera shots among the undergrowth over a soundtrack of heavy breathing. It is also the site of danger, poisonous mushrooms indicating the malevolence of nature, and the site of mystery, embodied in the '*agujero encendido*' ('lighted pit'), a mythical source of the unexplainable, unreason and ultimately madness. When the civil war breaks out, the men are ordered to the forest, considered to be the natural theatre of war.

The film is divided into four dated parts: '*El aizkolari cobarde*' (The Cowardly Woodcutter, 1875), '*Las hachas*' (The Axes, 1905), '*El agujero encendido*' (The Lighted Pit, 1915) and '*Guerra en el bosque*' (War in the Forest, 1936). While the names of these chapters (and the fact that they are named at all) suggest a mythical structure, the inclusion of dates points to specific historical moments. This is in keeping with a narrative that, as Isabel Santaolalla (1999: 317) points out, does not conceive of history and myth as opposites. Despite the superficially chronological episodes, Medem is not interested in a linear, cause-and-effect narrative, nor is he looking to unravel with any closure the mystery of Basque identity. Specific technical strategies work to reveal the constructed nature of film making, and the constructed nature of national identity. In his use of the camera, Medem replaces the traditionally authoritative presence of the 'objective' camera (used in the ethnographic documentary) with the subjective shot, taking the point of view of not only characters but also, unusually, of animals and even inanimate objects. Dialogue is sparse. Communication is concentrated in action rather than words. Thus, Ignacio's act of loving Catalina is expressed through silently making love to her or quietly abducting her, without ever speaking. Their mutual attraction is established each by looking off-screen to a distant point where, we assume, the other is waiting to be looked at.

Medem's fascination with looking (both with the eye and with the camera) permits an exploration of the physicality of traditional Basque sports, many of which centre on the ritualized display of male prowess. A remarkable feature about the activities, featured in the classic *Ama Lur*, is the almost complete absence of females as participants or even as spectators of these sports and pastimes. The cult of masculinity in Basque society seems at first to parallel that of hegemonic Spanish national identity, with its emphasis on physical power and war. But this conception of identity in terms of gender is also subverted in *Vacas*, where females (girls, women and cows) are most often the spectators of these tests of virility. The protagonist of the first section, Manuel Irigibel, is praised for his manly skills as a woodcutter, but his hand is trembling and he feigns death to escape from the war. Two generations later, his grandson Peru survives a firing squad, but unlike that of José Churruca in *Raza*, his escape is not glorious, nor his attitude to death noble. None of the males in *Vacas* corresponds to social models of morally responsible patriarchy: Manuel

Figure 6.3 Masculinity in Basque society: Carmelo Gómez in *Vacas*

is a coward, Ignacio abandons his wife and children, Juan lusts after his own sister, and Peru abandons his American wife and child in favour of his half-sister, just as he has previously abandoned the art of woodcutting in favour of emigration to the USA.

In its very title, this film suggest a female perspective rather than a male one. The male bull, aggressive icon of Spain's *fiesta nacional* is replaced by the female cow, pacific provider, and here, silent witness of the Basque lands and people. In the first episode, Manuel manages to escape death – literally – climbing out of a cart full of dead bodies. His first encounter after his 'rebirth', naked and covered in blood, is with a cow, solitary witness to this ignoble escape. The cow provides the link to the next section, in which, 30 years later, the still injured Manuel is painting a cow; his woodcutter champion son Ignacio wins an imported cow as a prize; and the subsequent birth of a calf and later the death of the cow are central episodes for the family, both in practical and symbolic terms. Manuel's vision of the world is mediated by an increasingly tenuous grip on reality, and is viewed by him through the eyes of the cow. Later his depiction of the civil war is represented by two cows facing each other; and at the very end of the film, when Peru and Cristina depart for France and escape, they are watched over by a cow. Both the cows and the forest are linked by Santaolalla to the Basque Earth Goddess, Mari, providing a contestation of patriarchal notions of national identity and reverting to 'the original pre-indo-European matriarchal structures of Basque civilization' (1999: 318).

The existence of a film like *Vacas* with a distinctly postmodern attitude to once-essentialist notions of national identities demonstrates just how broad is the range of identities (national, regional, gender, etc.) represented in Spanish cinema today. At the same time, in an environment of global capital, new technologies and increasing homogenization (or Americanisation, as some lament), categories of nationality seem less and less appropriate. Many contemporary Spanish film makers look to cinematic models outside Spain and appear largely unconcerned with questions of national identity (see the example of Alejandro Amenábar in Chapter Four). In a sense, contemporary Spanish cinema has gone some way towards neutralizing national identity as an issue (or at least, as an obsessive one). When we turn our attention to gender, we will see that far from fading, gender representation remains a significant, and sometimes emotive, issue.

GENDER

The investigation of how men and, more particularly, women have been treated by and in the cinema has been important for debates in Film Studies since the early 1970s. Film became a battleground for the women's movement (Nelmes, 1996: 228), and the interrogation of gender in the cinema led to research into representations of nation, race, class and sexuality. Gender should be understood as an ideological construction: while a person's sex is biologically determined, gender is social and cultural. Society has tended to equate sex with gender, leading to assumptions about 'natural' distinctions between the roles and behaviour of men and women. Thus, women are assumed to be physically and economically inferior to men, more emotional, more suited to the domestic sphere, and destined for reproduction rather than production. The ideology that supports this male-dominated world is called patriarchy. Film – as both a reflection of culture and a producer of it – has largely helped to maintain such gender stereotypes. Feminist film theorists have sought both to reveal the mechanisms of patriarchy at work in the cinema, and to propose alternative ways of making films *by*, *for* and *about* women.

Although women appear in films as frequently as do men, the vast majority of these films are made by men, who, whatever their consciously held gender politics, inevitably represent women from a masculine perspective. For this reason, much of the work on gender in cinema – and much of this section – is devoted to the representation of women, that is, to films *about* women. Women do, of course, make films. While some of these women may – perhaps unintentionally – simply replicate patriarchal cinema, other women film makers have attempted to break away from this dominant ideology through some form of feminist film practice. We include here, therefore, a short section on films *by* women. A further category worth considering is cinema *for* women, which many critics have analysed in respect of Hollywood cinema, but which has received little attention by writers on Spanish cinema. More recently, masculinity has become the focus of academics, and this emerging field is briefly outlined in the final section of this chapter.

FILMS ABOUT WOMEN

At the simplest level, films can clearly be seen to reflect the social realities of how men and women live. So-called 'reflection theory', such as the work on Hollywood cinema by Molly Haskell and Majorie Rosen in the 1970s, surveyed films for positive and negative images of women, and concluded that most films distort how women really are and what they really want. This line of enquiry was gradually refined to take into account historical and institutional contexts, how women are represented across different periods, geographical locations and in different genres. For example, in Westerns, women were associated with the home. Sociological readings of this type continue to inform studies of gender in Spanish cinema. More complex (and more controversial) is the contribution of psychoanalysis to theories of gendered spectatorship.

The application of psychoanalysis to Film Studies is based on assumptions that 'the unconscious exists, that we as human beings ('subjects') are by definition largely unaware of much of what happens in our unconscious minds, and that it can be fruitful to analyse what 'hidden' mechanisms are at work in films' (Abrams, Bell and Udris, 2001: 209). That these mechanisms operate mostly at the level of gender is hardly surprising, given that 'the recognition of sexual difference is the cornerstone of psychoanalytic theory' (Stam, Burgoyne and Flitterman-Lewis, 1992: 176). Rather than looking at individual films, exponents of psychoanalytic film theory, such as Baudry and Metz, stressed cinema as apparatus, looking at the way in which the viewer is constructed during the spectatorial process (Creed, 1998: 79), and concluding that the cinema 'produces' its spectators, severely limiting the range of possible responses viewers can have to a film. In a highly influential article, Laura Mulvey claimed that psychoanalytic theory 'offers a causal analysis of women's oppression under patriarchy which can provide the foundation for political action and social change' (Taylor, 1995: 152). Using Lacan's re-working of Freud, Mulvey argued that in classical Hollywood film the spectator is always constructed as male, leaving the spectator no choice but to identify with the narrative's male perspective and thus becoming complicit with his objectification of female characters (Taylor, 1995: 152). According to Mulvey's 1975 article, 'in a world ordered by sexual imbalance, pleasure in looking has been split between the active/male and passive/female.' So while the male characters are active agents of film narratives, female characters are passive, connoting '*to-be-looked-at-ness*'. (Mulvey, 1989: 19). Mulvey advocated the 'destruction of pleasure as a radical weapon': revealing the mechanisms of patriarchal cinema and its objectification of the female would undermine its ideological effects; and a set of new conventions, to replace patriarchal cinema with a feminist counter-cinema, could then be established. Subsequent work on spectatorship questioned the male centreing of discourses, suggesting that, in fact, spectators can alternate between identification with male and female characters. And there were more general criticisms too, of psychoanalytic theory for being monolithic, totalizing, and failing to take into consideration socio-historical contexts, and the fact that some spectators are more resistant to film's ideological workings than others (Creed, 1998: 86). Nevertheless, psychoanalytic theories have shaped the study of gender in cinema more than any other approach.

Spain's patriarchal legacy is, if anything, even more reactionary than the arch-conservative culture of mainstream Hollywood cinema that became the target of feminist theorists. Unsurprisingly, Spanish film culture and the majority of cinematic representations of gender are equally patriarchal. Historically, Spanish society has imposed rigid gender distinctions which consistently privilege the male. Its Islamic heritage, the influence of a highly conservative honour code in the early modern period and, of course, the legacy of predominantly right-wing political regimes and an especially powerful Catholic Church, have all contributed to a strongly patriarchal view of society. In the twentieth century the cinema, as the most popular entertainment form, provides a mirror of social attitudes towards gender, a record of changing values and aspirations. Silent-era films thus reflected a predominantly rural Spain, with a predictably narrow view of gender roles (bullfighting for men, Church for women). While the Second Republic (1931–6) brought an impressive raft of political reforms favouring gender equality (including the right of women to vote and stand for parliament), popular films produced at this time barely seemed to notice the change (although Benito Perojo's 1935 film *La verbena de la paloma* does, at least, show two highly liberated female characters). And though the civil war (1936–39) opened up to women a range of activities normally reserved for men, these experiences were not celebrated in mainstream Spanish cinema, given the outcome of the conflict. With Franco's fascists victorious, the clock would be turned back for women in Spain. As Helen Graham expresses it, 'Francoism projected an ultra-conservative construction of "ideal" womanhood, perceived as the fundamental guarantor of social stability' (1995: 182). The patriarchal family was seen as a microcosm of the corporate order of the state: the father, as head of the household, mirrored the hierarchy of the state, with Franco at its head. This vertical chain of authority was preferred by the regime to horizontal allegiances, relating to class (Graham, 1995: 184). During the immediate postwar period, even film genres appeared divided along gender lines: the so-called *cine de cruzada* war films, such as *Raza* (José Luis Sáenz de Heredia, 1941), which was scripted by Franco himself, re-affirmed traditionally acceptable male values (see section in this chapter on National Identity); and the genres targeted mainly at female audiences extolled the feminine virtues of family (religious dramas or plots involving children), or feminine spectacle (*españolada*). Historical dramas further emphasized females of high virtue in films about Spanish queens: *Inés de Castro* (Leitão de Barros, 1944), *Reina santa* (Rafael Gil, 1946) and *Locura de amor* (Juan de Orduña, 1948) (see Higginbotham, 1988: 22). Folkloric musicals provided the mainstay of Spanish popular cinema aimed at female audiences through the 1940s and 1950s and these evolved into light musical comedies, starring Carmen Sevilla, Lola Flores, Sara Montiel and, later, the child star Marisol (Triana Toribio, 2003: 84–95).

The liberal 1960s, which saw the beginnings of second-wave feminism in the USA and much of Western Europe, was felt little and late in Spain. The regime-backed investment in the film industry, and the attempt to create a more artistic and socially-aware cinema did not bring with it any advances in the position of, or in the representation of, women in Spanish cinema. In fact, the official proponent of what was called the Nuevo Cine Español, José María García Escudero, actually characterized progressive, 'quality' cinema *in opposition to* what he saw as a popular, light-weight cinema for a 'feminized' public, a cinema appealing to emotions rather than rationality (Triana Toribio, 2003: 66–9). This Nuevo Cine was an economic failure and led to the return of a more popular cinema, in the new varieties of Iberian sex comedy and horror (Lázaro-Reboll and Willis, 2004: 12), neither of which can be seen as progressive in their representation of gender, though they did begin, at least, to engage with representations of gender. In fact, in Spain the only concession to the liberalization which followed the 1960s was permissiveness with regard to female screen nudity. The *destape* (see Chapter One) only 'reinforced the traditional specularization of the female form' (Jordan and Morgan, 1998: 113).

From the 1970s and 1980s, Spanish cinema has been opened up to more pluralistic voices, impacting on its treatment of issues around gender. This is partly a result of the efforts of female film makers themselves, beginning with Josefina Molina and Pilar Miró (see below), and partly a result of the greater social freedoms and freedom of expression in Spain. Women's liberation came at the same time (and benefited from) the transition from dictatorship to democracy (Hooper, 1995: 165). Spain's Constitution of 1978 affirms equal rights for men and women. Contraception, adultery and cohabitation were decriminalized in 1978 and divorce was finally approved in 1981 (Montero, 1995: 382). But political rights do not guarantee social equality. John Hooper believes that the changes for women have been uncontroversial because of their low impact on men: women are doing new things but have not abandoned any of the activities traditionally regarded as feminine (1995: 174). Films made about women during the 1980s and 1990s reflect the multiplicity of experiences that characterizes living in a society which remains *at least* as ambivalent as any other in Western Europe about gender roles. Many films can be read as a critique of patriarchy by their depiction of 'negative' images of women. Almodóvar's *¿Qué he hecho yo para merecer esto?* (1984) gives us alternative female role models in the shape of an oppressed housewife, Gloria (Carmen Maura), and her sexually 'liberated' but naïve prostitute neighbour, Cristal (Verónica Forqué). Vicente Aranda opts for a similar dichotomy in *Amantes* (1991) where an engagingly passive young soldier (Jorge Sanz) is forced to choose between his virginal, submissive fiancée, Trini (Maribel Verdú) and his *femme fatale* land-lady, Luisa (Victoria Abril). Carlos Saura's 1983 film *Carmen* takes the fictional gypsy heroine and updates her within a contemporary culture still dominated by *machismo* (Fiddian and Evans, 1988: 83). Spain's two most famous (and controversial) directors, Luis Buñuel and Pedro Almodóvar, also have in common a predilection for female characters. Moreoever, they both exploit, in a knowing, self-conscious way, the patriarchal legacy of the cinema. Their resulting films, however, are quite different. Buñuel delights in cinema's fetishization of the female body, but is far from innocent about his own visual pleasure and freedom as an auteur. Almodóvar, who makes films in an environment of much greater awareness of patriarchy, combines an ironic deconstruction of its mechanisms with an array of strong female protagonists.

VIRIDIANA (Luis Buñuel, 1961)

This film follows the trajectory of a young woman from one model of femininity that is typically open to Spanish women, to its polar opposite. When we first see Viridiana, she is in the confines of a convent, about to take her vows. But her brief contact with the world outside (a world dominated by men) changes her course, and at the end of the narrative she is poised to accept her cousin's indecent proposal to join him in a *ménage à trois*. Buñuel's story is based on a series of audience expectations, each of which are subverted. These expectations relate to both formal and thematic or social codes. Neither Buñuel nor his characters know how to conform to acceptable social (and cinematic) standards of behaviour.

The opening shot of a convent, over Handel's *Messiah* on the soundtrack, suggests a melodrama about priests or nuns, a sub-genre aimed primarily at female audiences which was standard fare in Spanish cinema in the 1950s and 1960s. The appearance of children, for example, recalls the popular hit *Marcelino, pan y vino* (Ladislao Vajda, 1954) involving priests and an orphan in a mystical and sentimental melodrama. But such genre expectations are shattered by this film, which is neither pious, nor concerned with the care of children. The tension between the convent and the venal freedoms of country life is expressed through the editing, suggesting two alternative models for female characters. First, we have a medium close-up shot of Viridiana's face in her habit, suggesting a life of enclosure and contemplation; then there is a cut to a close-up of the bare legs of little Rita skipping, indicating an alternative life of freedom and activity. We gradually discover that even the little girl Rita is not immune to sensuality.

If Buñuel's casting of the glamorous Mexican actress Silvia Pinal were not sufficient to categorize her in overtly erotic terms, then his use of the camera leaves no doubt. Pinal does not have the appearance of a typical Spanish nun, and the camera, which continually finds her in specularized close-ups, is in no doubt that she is to become the object of the male gaze, for her uncle and then for her cousin. When we first see her uncle don Jaime, he is looking at Rita's legs. But Viridiana's beauty, and her uncanny similarity to his dead wife, soon distract him. He compares Viridiana's way of walking and talking with that of his dead wife. Don Jaime takes every opportunity to look at Viridiana and the camera prefers his gaze (upon her) to any other. It lingers long in close-up on Viridiana as she removes her stockings, the fetishization of her body accentuated by showing only the lower half. The camera shares the gaze on Viridiana with most of the remaining characters – female as well as male. She is watched voyeuristically by both Ramona and her daughter, Rita, who joyfully shouts: 'I've seen you in your bed clothes'. And don Jaime says he got up earlier so that he could see more of her. She replies – apparently unaware of any erotic connotations – that she is going to make him a cake that will leave him licking his fingers: 'chupar los dedos' (literally 'sucking' in Spanish).

The editing in *Viridiana* is never incidental: a beautiful shot of Viridiana lit like an angel as she sits in front of her cross and crown of thorns, is then cut to a shot of Moncho milking a cow. Viridiana decides to have a go at milking the cow herself but cannot bring herself to touch the flaccid udders, unmistakably phallic. Buñuel plays with psychoanalytically inspired symbols: phallic symbols, especially, are everywhere in the film. There is even a seemingly Freudian sleepwalking sequence, in which Viridiana, her legs bare, collects ash from the fire and deposits it on don Jaime's bed next to his wife's wedding head-dress. (Viridiana later tells her uncle ashes signify penitence and death.) Don Jaime's psychological traumatic back-story is the death of his wife on their wedding night. We see him in the bedroom with his wife's white wedding outfit, trying on her white shoes and bodice. His request on Viridiana's last night with him before she returns to the convent is for her to dress up in the wedding outfit. The implication – that both women were virgins when they wore the dress – is clearly important for don Jaime. His chosen music for staging this re-enactment is Mozart's *Requiem*, thus making explicit the link between sex and death. Don Jaime drugs Viridiana so that she will not leave. Watched by Rita, he carries Viridiana to the bed and lays her out like a corpse, clearly in memory of his dead wife. He kisses her and opens her dress to kiss her breasts, but recoils from going any further. When Viridiana rejects him and decides to leave, don Jaime hangs himself with Rita's skipping rope, the handles of which bear a striking resemblance to the phallic cow's udders (Edwards, 1982: 147).

Don Jaime's death transforms Viridiana from the virginal girl to the role of the widow housewife. We next see her scrubbing floors, which she regards as a penance. When the Mother Superior demands a confession from her, Viridiana is silent. Viridiana's transformation into a property owner and the protector of a group of beggars (almost a bizarre family) represents an assumption of patriarchal power, but this proves a temporary phase. As an unmarried woman, Viridiana cannot control the beggars, who eventually take over the main house and attempt to rape her. In the carnivalesque banquet which leads up to this violence – one of the most famous sequences in all Spanish cinema – one of the beggars actually dresses up in don Jaime's beloved wife's wedding dress – a grotesque masquerade in contrast to don Jaime's earlier, more sensitive performance with Viridiana. The beggar's dance to Handel's 'Hallelujah chorus' is a direct act of sacrilege against the Church. Buñuel's conclusion is that charity – one of the main occupations of the Church (and more especially of women in the Church) – is destined to fail. And when her benevolent project collapses, Viridiana has only one option left: to turn towards her cousin.

Figure 6.4 Buñuel's Leper (Juan García Tienda) wearing the bridal gown of don Jaime's wife

Jorge is represented as the 'new man' of the period. He is associated with rock 'n' roll, as opposed to his uncle's classical music. He has little time for the Church or its morality, referring to Viridiana as 'shrivelled up by so much religion' ('podrida de beatería'). But his modern, liberal ideas about sex are more liberating for his own appetites than they are for his female prey. He takes advantage of Ramona. In a heavy-handed metaphor, a shot of him looking at her is cut to one of a cat pouncing on a rat. Subsequently, we witness Viridiana looking at herself in the mirror in a different light, as a sexual being for the first time. Rita symbolically throws Viridiana's crown of thorns into the fire. And in the final scene, Viridiana turns up at the door of Jorge's bedroom, her long hair let down and, silently, is shepherded in by Jorge. In an ending imposed by the censors (Sánchez Vidal, 1984: 252) Viridiana sits down with Ramona and Jorge to play cards, the outcome cleverly left to the imagination of the audience. In what amounts to a reversal of the fallen woman melodrama – where the woman is redeemed, usually by sacrificial motherhood – here Viridiana is poised to enter into a life of sin, to become the passive object of Jorge's desire.

Further reading: Sánchez Vidal, 1984; Pérez Perucha, 1997; Edwards, 1982.

TODO SOBRE MI MADRE (Pedro Almodóvar, 1999)

Almodóvar's film output provides a range of representations of gender and sexuality which has led to much academic attention as well as much media controversy. From lesbian and sadomasochist relationships in *Pepi, Luci, Bom y otras chicas del montón* (1980), to the open portrayal of gay relationships in *La ley del deseo* (1987) and *La mala educación* (2004), Almodóvar has held up a mirror to Spain's sexual liberation over the last 25 years. His most acclaimed film, *Todo sobre mi madre*, is a good example of what could be called 'post-feminist' cinema. Acutely aware both of Spain's patriarchal legacy and of the scrutiny to which cinematic representation (of gender, among other issues) is subjected, Almodóvar both contests rigid gender distinctions and simultaneously deconstructs patriarchal cinematic practices. *Todo sobre mi madre* is the story of Manuela, who loses her son in a traffic accident and returns to the city of his father, Barcelona, to break the news to him. But he has undergone a partial sex change, fathered another woman's child and now has Aids. Manuela takes on a caring role, first for the women she meets in the city and then, eventually, for her ex-husband's second baby.

The women – unlike the men – are represented in very positive terms. Single mother Manuela, one of Almodóvar's most endearing characters – supports her son economically and emotionally. Once in Barcelona, Manuela finds herself the centre of a support network of women which is clearly more effective than traditional institutions like the patriarchal family (never portrayed as positive in Almodóvar). These women live largely without the support of men. Huma and Nina are a lesbian couple, Rosa is a nun who works with prostitutes, while her mother looks after a senile husband. Men are largely absent or ineffectual. Excluding males from the film's diegesis is, of course, one way to counter the effects of a patriarchal cinematic apparatus: women are unlikely to become the passive objects of a male gaze if there are no males to objectify them. The female characters are not eroticized. They are all at stages in their lives when the consequences of their sexual history – marriage, pregnancy and motherhood – are more important than any sexual ambition. Heterosexual romance – a cornerstone of most cinema – is absent.

Todo sobre mi madre has many of the features of melodrama – a genre developed very much with female audiences in mind. During the 1970s feminist critics began to look closely at melodrama to evaluate its ideological undercurrents. What interested them was whether melodrama should be interpreted as conservative, educating women to accept the roles assigned to them by patriarchy, or whether it might be open to more subversive readings. Almodóvar's world – partly a reflection of a post-feminist reality and partly an idealization or fantasy, in fact represents a disavowal of patriarchy. Unlike classic melodramas in which 'events are never reconciled at the end in a way which is beneficial to women' (Kaplan, 1983: 26), this film offers a happy ending, in which single motherhood and female friendship have replaced the conventional patriarchal family unit. Manuela does re-assume the maternal role at the end of the narrative. But the typical family – with its housewife mother – is here replaced by drug-addicts, prostitutes and transsexuals. Most radically in terms of gender representation, the patriarch father has changed sex. The presence of trans-sexual characters is one obvious way of representing gender as socially, not biologically, determined. Manuela's friend, the transsexual Agrado, believes that gender is based on desire and transforming her self-image. In her words, 'The more you become like what you have dreamed for yourself, the more authentic you are.' This film – along with others by Almodóvar – typifies the notion that all gender is performance (Butler, 1990: 25). But Almodóvar takes the notion of performance even further. The story is intricately linked with two dramatic texts, Tennessee Williams' play *A Streetcar Named Desire* and Joseph L. Mankiewicz's film *All About Eve*. Manuela – like Eve Harrington in the 1950 melodrama – stands in for another actress. She plays the part of Stella in the Williams play, which she had seen with her son the night he was killed. By making Manuela a stand-in actress and a stand-in mother, Almodóvar makes explicit how much these roles have in common. The director dedicates the film to all actresses who have played actresses in the theatre and on film, and to actors who perform as women. By focusing so strongly on gender as performance, and on the performing arts as the locus for drama, Almodóvar exposes the mechanisms of performance in cinema, and in particular, how femininity has been constructed. This, in the language of 1970s feminist critics, amounts to the destruction of (male) pleasure as a radical weapon (Mulvey, 1989: 15): when we can see that femininity is only an act, we can more easily contest patriarchal representations of women in the cinema.

Further reading: Allinson, 2001; Smith 2000; Edwards, 2001; Colmenero, 2001.

FILMS BY WOMEN

When women make films about their own lives (and also about other women and men), these films can provide a relatively rare 'feminine' perspective. At one extreme, some female film makers might be so compromised by the patriarchal system in which they are working, that any potential for feminist film practice is rendered impossible. This is largely true for women working in the classical Hollywood studio system, as it is for the very small numbers of women who were making films in Spain before 1970. And at the other extreme, following Mulvey's rallying call for the 'destruction of pleasure', would be those who put into practice a feminist counter-cinema, purposefully breaking the conventions of mainstream cinema. In practice, abandoning mainstream cinematic conventions only distanced feminist film makers from their target audience, earning them the label of elitist and 'difficult'. In any case, such feminist counter-cinema has been largely absent from Spain (Jordan and Morgan-Tamosunas, 1998: 120). Most female film makers (and most Spanish female film makers) would fall somewhere between these two extremes. On the evidence in film texts, it is clearly possible to make films with feminist values yet still follow cinematic conventions which make them understandable to wider audiences. A kind of popular feminism characterizes many Spanish films by and/or about women from the 1970s and 1980s onwards.

The Spanish film industry was slow to make room for women. The first female director was the Catalan Rosario Pi, co-founder of Star Film, whose first film as director was *El gato montés* in 1935. In the 1950s, the actress Ana Mariscal turned to directing with the social realist *Segundo López, aventurero urbano* (1952). But it was to be from the end of the 1960s when women would begin to break into the world of film making in Spain, when Josefina Molina was the first woman to graduate from Madrid's Official Film School, soon to be followed by Pilar Miró, Spain's most successful female director. Her film-directing career has included a number of films addressing broadly feminist issues, including *La petición* (1976), her controversial first film; the noirish *Tu nombre envenena mis sueños* (1996) with its female killer; and finally *El perro del hortelano* (1996), a version of Lope de Vega's classic seventeenth-century comedy which features one of the strongest female characters in Spanish drama. The work which most closely followed what could be described as a feminist film practice, however, was Miró's 1980 film *Gary Cooper que estás en los cielos*.

GARY COOPER, QUE ESTÁS EN LOS CIELOS (Pilar Miró, 1980)

The film follows three days in the life of Andrea, a television director who, despite her fierce independence and absolute control over her life, discovers that she has cancer, leading her to reflect on her existence as a professional woman and as an emotional human being. She will not be able to have children after her cancer operation, and even her life may be in danger. Her independent stance prevents her from telling anyone about her illness, even her egocentric and absorbed partner and her vain and critical mother. Her partner, who thinks she is pregnant, is angry that the decision to have the baby is Andrea's alone, but he does not know the truth and Andrea lets him attack her. As she is about to go into hospital, she receives an offer to direct a film. She would have to take over straight away – impossible because of her scheduled cancer operation. So she has to choose between her career and her life.

From the opening scene we get an impression of Andrea's lifestyle: she drives her own car, (significantly a small, functional vehicle, not a status symbol), and we see she is in demand and respected by the professional people (almost exclusively men) around her. These early sequences highlight gender as a constant issue. The initial shots emphasize activity and haste as Andrea is surrounded by men, whose questions she answers decisively, sometimes impatiently. Then, suddenly, she encounters another professional female (and partner of her ex-lover Bernardo) and the pace slows to a standstill. Feminine interaction is ponderous, not frenetic. When asked how her work is going she replies 'getting there', rather than bragging about her recent professional award. While her male colleagues greet her physically – which can be read as objectifying her as feminine – only a female colleague, Begoña, bothers to congratulate her about the award. The recording of Andrea's interview by Begoña (actually on the set of her current TV programme) reveals the mechanisms (and deceits) of recording process. This 'inside view' of the world of the media amounts to a demythification of mainstream cinema (which always hides its mechanics in an attempt to maintain the illusion of reality). Destroying this illusion was a key objective of feminist film practitioners in the 1970s.

The film's theme – a problem which, significantly, is not resolved in the narrative – is the difficulty in maintaining a professional life as a woman, as well as a healthy emotional existence. In professional terms, Andrea aspires to film directing on a par with the major (male, US) directors Ford, Hawks and Hitchcock:

> My future plans are unchanged. They have been the same for ten years. To
> direct a film. Whenever they let me. When I finally find a producer who
> I can convince. Who I can seduce with my tremendous talent. One film, two
> films, twenty films. John Ford directed sixty, Howard Hawks fifty-eight,
> Hitchcock, fifty. I won't accept less.

It is interesting to ask, here, why Pilar Miró, a feminist film maker with a heavily European-influenced film school education, takes her role models for alter ego Andrea from the very different production context of 1940s/1950s Hollywood. Andrea does not, apparently, aspire to the auteur status of a Renoir, a Godard, nor even a Coppola or a Spielberg. Note too, that Andrea's actor hero is Gary Cooper, a classic, male star from a highly patriarchal film industry.

While in the professional sphere, where Andrea appears to be winning the struggle for recognition, her relationships have suffered. And this conflict is physically as well as sym-bolically located in her own body. She sardonically comments to her boss, 'I always make sure my abortions take place after a film shoot'. But this bitter joke masks Andrea's real dilemma, acutely embodied in her recently discovered illness: her own female body ultimately frustrates her professional ambition. In direct contrast to the glamorous female bodies displayed for male visual pleasure in mainstream film, here, Andrea's body becomes the object of the camera in close-ups which stress dysfunction, in the doctor's surgery, and in front of her bedroom mirror; a case of de-specularization of the female body. And as a final challenge to mainstream cinematic practice, the ending of this film is completely open, with Andrea moments away from her operation.

The film's open ending frustrates the experienced movie-goer's need for closure which in most female-targeted films is provided by means of a comfortable melodramatic ending (in which the woman is resigned to the constraints of patriarchal society). And in its technique, *Gary Cooper…* makes few concessions to the viewers (male or female). It is difficult to identify with the main character, whose stubborn silence alienates both those around her and also the viewer; and its introspective tone precludes emotion or dramatic action. In sacrificing narrative closure and melodramatic identification, Miró has gone some way towards the radical aspirations of 1970s feminist film makers, but the result is a film unlikely to move many audiences. An altogether different strategy was taken by another female film maker two decades later.

Further reading: Morgan, 1999; Martin-Márquez, 1999; Ballesteros, 2001; Rabalska, 1996.

TE DOY MIS OJOS (Iciar Bollaín, 2003)

Like both her previous films *Hola, ¿estás sola?* (1995) and *Flores de otro mundo* (1999), Icíar Bollaín's third film is firmly focused on issues of gender. It tells the story of Pilar (Laia Marull), a victim of domestic violence at the hands of her husband, Antonio (Luis Tosar). That both actors received awards for their performances in this film tells us two things: first, that this is a film of strong dramatic performances; and second, that it prefers popular social realism, through identification with the protagonists, rather than the distancing strategies of *Gary Cooper...* 20 years earlier. The realism of *Te doy mis ojos* is measured, dramatically crafted and quite manipulative with the emotions of the viewer. The characters – though credible and compelling – are representatives of certain social types: Antonio is an extreme example of insecurity manifest in aggression; his wife Pilar, the victim whose problems are those of anyone living with domestic violence: economic dependence on her husband, worries about the effects of a separation on her child, low self-esteem and guilt. The minor characters too, are representative: Pilar's sister Ana is the feisty, independent type and her Scottish boyfriend is almost stereotypically a 'new man'. Finally, Pilar's mother has accepted the patriarchal norms of her society and her generation to the point of being blind to her own daughter's physical danger. She wants Pilar to go back to Antonio: 'a woman is never better off by herself'.

When we first see Pilar she is desperately gathering her clothes, obviously making a quick getaway. Such is her haste that she forgets to change out of her slippers and only realizes this when she arrives at her sister's. The discovery of this silly, but unimportant mistake is what drives Pilar to hysterical tears – projecting her fear and desperation onto this minor mishap. Her tears echo as the screen fades to black. Far from establishing any equilibrium, any peace that may be about to be shattered by events, the prologue launches into deep traumatic action – something of a rejection of standard narrative film practice.

Before we even see Antonio we know he is violent, from the state of the family home: broken glass and a broken mirror, food thrown in anger at the walls. Antonio finds it difficult to talk about his feelings, another trope of society's socialization of males. The extent of this problem in (Spanish) society is reflected by Antonio's visit to a men's discussion group, led by a psychologist with the aim of exploring and eradicating domestic violence from these men's lives. The younger (and somewhat hippy) professional male tries to reach his primeval pack of *macho ibérico* stock by recourse to recognizable group therapy strategies such as sharing and simulation. But their attitude to the role play of a household situation is highly revealing: they find it impossible to take it seriously, using laughter as a cover for their insecurities about communicating their feelings. Their responses to the psychologist's prompting shows how they have interiorized various cultural prejudices: that a certain amount of domestic violence is acceptable, that their wives provoke them into lashing out. The antithesis of these culturally and socially regressive Spanish men is Ana's Scottish boyfriend, John, who cooks and does the housework while Ana goes out to work. Almost every time we see John he is with children, entertaining them. The only time we see Antonio with his son Juan is when he aggressively kicks a football at him while asking him probing questions about his mother.

Antonio's anger rises in direct proportion to Pilar's attempts at creating an independent life. As she discovers her talent as a museum guide, he becomes more and more threatened. Moreover, he is completely unable to comprehend even why Pilar wants to do this. He cannot see beyond himself. Such has been the extent of his attempt to suppress his wife's ego that, when Pilar tries to explain to her sister how she feels, she expresses it in terms of a complete loss of identity: 'I need to see myself. I don't know who I am'. The climactic scene where Antonio attacks Pilar, as she is about to leave for a job interview in Madrid, is one of the most difficult to watch in all Spanish cinema. Her humiliation is absolute: stripped naked, locked out on the balcony, she eventually wets herself with fear. This is followed by an almost equally unbearable scene in which Pilar goes to the local police station to report her husband's attack. The male policeman's inability to grasp the situation or to deal effectively with it can only be interpreted as a sign that the institution (like Spanish society as a whole) has not yet come to terms with the problem of domestic violence.

FILMS FOR WOMEN

Most film industries produce some films aimed especially (though not exclusively) at women. In Hollywood, the classic example is 1940s melodrama, a genre which proved exportable to audiences in Spain too, both in the Castilian-dubbed Hollywood versions, and in indigenous Spanish varieties. The re-evaluation, over time, of the pleasures and functions of films made for women makes it important to distinguish, as does E. Ann Kaplan, between three types of female viewer: the historical spectator, at the cinema on the film's release; the hypothetical spectator (constructed by film's textual strategies); and the contemporary spectator, whose reading of the film is inflected by feminist consciousness (Quoted in Stam, Burgoyne and Flitterman-Lewis, 1992: 178). Thus, 'the woman's film' as it was termed by the industry in Hollywood, was long considered a lesser form (when compared to 'male' genres like the Western or gangster film). But for female cinema-goers at the time (melodrama's peak, both in the USA and in Spain, was between 1930 and 1960), it was the only cinematic experience which featured women prominently. When psychoanalytic and Marxist critics turned their attention to melodrama, they saw it as a genre in which women are expected to participate in scenarios of masochism, to suffer along with female victims. The dramas exposed the constraints imposed on women by the capitalist nuclear family, but also served to 'educate' women to accept those constraints as 'natural', 'inevitable' and 'given' (Kaplan, 1983: 25). However, feminist critics such as Laura Mulvey see the struggle itself, when set within a domestic sphere – whatever the outcome for the female characters – as a means of domesticating the male, and thus compensating for 'the overvaluation of virility under patriarchy' (Mulvey, 1989: 40). The study of stars, fandom and female identification has become another area of interest, which is only just emerging as a field of investigation in Spanish cinema studies.

While there have arguably been Spanish films aimed primarily at women since the silent period, the 1950s – before the advent of mass television – was, perhaps, the decade of 'the woman's film' in Spain. The most successful film of the decade also consolidated the biggest star in Spanish cinema, Sara Montiel.

EL ÚLTIMO CUPLÉ (Juan de Orduña, 1957)

The phenomenal success of this film – a record 325 days on screen and 150 million pesetas at the box office – not only secured the future of its female lead, Sara Montiel, but also created the formula for a musical melodrama which took the place of the folkloric musicals of the 1930s and 1940s. In common with most of the classic Hollywood melodramas of the period, *El último cuplé* offers female audiences certain pleasures while simultaneously re-affirming the patriarchal status quo. As is usual, the film was overwhelmingly a male product: scripted, photographed, and directed by men; women were only involved in the wardrobe and make-up departments.

The genre associations of the film are apparent from the opening shot of the bright red stage curtain: the world of performance is the locus of melodrama; and the opening *cuplé* establishes the musical genre immediately. Twenty-four musical numbers will follow, many of them romantic songs with a particular appeal to the women of the time. The location is the El Molino cabaret in Barcelona in the 1950s. Sara Montiel plays former singing star María Luján. After her performance she is visited by a young admirer (much like the scene at the end of Mankiewicz's *All About Eve*, perhaps cinema's greatest stage melodrama). María drinks alone – a sign of her emotional and physical decline. When her ex-impresario, ex-lover Juan appears, it is the cue for the film to tell the story of her life. The resulting extended flashback – absolutely typical in melodramas – forms the main part of the diegesis. Just after the end of the First World War, Madrid chorus girl María is befriended by impresario Juan. She already has a young boyfriend – a humble clockmaker – but is persuaded to turn to Juan to launch her career. Moral choices – which women often face, for instance, between principles and career – are another common feature of melodrama. The story then follows María's professional and romantic fortunes, including an affair with a bullfighter, which is cut short by his death in the ring, until it reaches the starting point. Back in Barcelona, the flashback is now over and the film ends with María's dramatic comeback on a Madrid stage performing 'Nena', after which she dies, exhausted, in the wings.

In common with other entertainment-world melodramas, this film exploits the parallels between on-stage performances and off-stage dramas. María uses the song '*Y tú no eres eso*' to reproach her bullfighter boyfriend. And after his death, her rendition of '*El relicario*' in slow, anguished tones dressed in mourning shows María – the victim – investing her emotional trauma into her performances, another trope of melodrama. María, like most protagonists of classic melodrama, cannot reconcile professional and romantic success. More importantly, women are seen to need men to move their lives forward. María is only persuaded to accept Juan's protection as a means to save her boyfriend from prison. Her first taste of celebrity comes from her victory in a beauty contest judged by a group of old men, which establishes her role as an object to be looked at. Her career is launched, promoted and re-launched by the impresario Juan who is first attracted to her physical beauty, before even hearing her sing. She even finds her female honour fought over in a duel that provides a moment of swashbuckling adventure. Many of the pleasures in the film relate to María's physical attractiveness.

Spectacle and nostalgia provide a range of pleasures for female audiences. The film's very title affects a nostalgia for a lost period, a more carefree age, thus appealing to an older generation of women. And nostalgia is a useful commodity in escapist cinema, because it avoids contemporary social problems. María's flashback to her youth provides the excuse for decades of period costumes from the pre-war years. Costume is a key part of the glamour of both the film and its star. Sara Montiel wears a different outfit for almost every scene – 31 in total. Such a display of excess would be especially attractive to Spanish women at the end of a decade of deprivation, and on the brink of an economic boom which would make clothes and consumerism accessible to the many, rather than the privileged few. A wide range of costumes from various regions of Spain is supplemented by French and Latin-American outfits. The Moulin Rouge was – for 1950s women – the very image of exotic (and perhaps erotic) otherness. Conversely, María's rendition of 'La nieta de Carmen', described by the presenter as 'a very Spanish song', conforms to familiar (and stereotypical) notions of southern Spain. Significantly, María's descent into the sordid world of Parisian cafés and gambling is coded as foreign and 'other'.

María's unhappy fate can be interpreted as a warning to women who 'want it all': opting for fame and romance does not provide the rewards that traditional wife-and-mother roles offer. But the ultimate frustration of María's desires does not detract from the delights along the way. In her choice of the *cuplé*, with its sometimes suggestive lyrics, she signals an earlier period with a less constrained social role for women (Woods, 2003: 43). *El último cuplé* presents to Spanish audiences a model of active female sexuality that had been masked by the promotion, since the end of the civil war, of virgins and mothers as being the only options open to women during the early Franco period. María chooses her men, rather than being chosen by them. Judging by the record-breaking impact of this film, and the rise of Sara Montiel as a result, the new feminine model for a film star clearly struck a chord with the Spanish public.

Further reading: Pérez Perucha, 1997; Woods, 2003.

STUDIES IN MASCULINITIES

From the 1980s, Film Studies began to look at masculinity. Scholars moved away from essentialist notions (of masculinity as a 'natural', 'given'), towards the idea that masculinity is an effect of culture, a construction (Cohan and Hark, 1993: 7). This approach was applied retrospectively, scrutinizing nearly a century of defensive masculine hegemony, but also coincided with a contemporary 'crisis in masculinity' (Cook, 1982: 38–46) due to a variety of factors (such as unemployment, the decline in traditional 'male' jobs, and the successes of feminism).

Spanish cinema offers an excellent example of the changing fortunes of masculinity in the cinema. Spain's patriarchal hegemony has been even stronger than that of many other Western nations. Some seven centuries of Islamic rule, followed by a further seven centuries of the Reconquest, privileged the strongly masculinist values of war. Franco's regime reinstated those militaristic, nationalistic values so in evidence in films such as *Raza* (see section on National Identity, in this chapter). But by the 1950s the Spanish state (not unlike post-war nations such as the USA and the UK) required the reintegration of males into more domestic, family structures (in themselves patriarchal, but no longer militaristic). From the transition onwards, the representation of masculinity in Spanish cinema has been much more problematic. In very recent times there have been attempts at a broadly realist depiction of masculinity in crisis in social-issue films such as *Barrio* (1998) and *Los lunes al sol* (2002), both by Fernando León de Aranoa. No less troubling for a generation of apparently insecure Spanish males are the more stereotypical, sometimes ridiculous examples of *machista*, anxious, confused or female-dominated males in Almodóvar's films. Almodóvar – over time – has given us a spectrum of shades of masculinity. His contemporary Juan José Bigas Luna, in his so-called 'Iberian Trilogy' *Jamón jamón* (1992), *Huevos de oro* (1993) and *La teta y la luna* (1995), prefers a stereotypical, almost grotesque version of Spanish masculinity (alongside its equally clichéd feminine equivalents). Of these three exuberant, fascinating, and for some, notorious films, the first has deservedly received the most attention.

JAMÓN JAMÓN (Juan José Bigas Luna, 1992)

The film's 'gendered and oversexed' (Deleyto, 1999: 273) perspective on Spain begins with the very first image, the silhouette of a gigantic bull's testicles on an advertising board for the Spanish brandy, Osborne. Male genitalia and 'cognate phallic imagery' (Morgan and Jordan, 1994) dominate. The conflict in the film is between two males pursuing the same female, Silvia (Penélope Cruz, in her first major role), but also between two differentiated models of masculinity. Raúl (played by the suitably beefy Javier Bardem) is associated with masculine prowess, symbolically but also physically. When we first see him, he is practising bullfighting; long-shots over the sound of the bullfighters' animalistic grunts alternate with close-ups of Raúl's erection under his shorts. (Bullfighting turns him on, and we subsequently see him and a friend fight a bull naked in a more explicit recognition of erotic enjoyment.) His crotch forms a link to the next sequence in the busy underwear factory, as we get a second close-up of Raúl modelling the briefs (brand-name Sansón), and we hear the factory owner Conchita assert that women buy men's underwear and that women will be attracted to 'a good bulge'. Raúl is constructed as a hyperbole of Spanish *machismo*: the ham warehouse where he works and lives is a show-case of hyper-Spanish and hyper-masculine associations: phallic *chorizos*, the name Conquistadores, Raúl admiring his muscles and sampling the produce washed down with beer from the bottle as he listens to heavy metal music. The name 'Conquistadores' is no coincidence: Raúl's masculinity is predatory and, above all, it is based on consumption. His motorbike is a projection of both his virility and of his desire to possess. And his favourite consumable – apart from garlic, which, he says, is good for 'bullfighting and for shagging' – is ham in its multiplicity of Spanish forms. He pursues Silvia with *jamón* (which he says is an aphrodisiac) and even refers to her as 'jamona'. And the garlic and ham come together (quite literally) in his uncouth plan for attracting the attention of Silvia: he inserts an irritating clove of garlic into a pig's anus, sending it running wildly towards the road so that he can help to catch it; he also makes a very good impersonation of a pig's grunt through Silvia's letterbox.

Equally ham-obsessed, but in every other aspect different, is José Luis. At the start of the narrative he is going out with the beautiful and submissive Silvia. He too is a consumer, but with infantile tastes: his breast-fixation is a means of bringing together all his favourite appetites as, he claims, Silvia's breasts taste one of *tortilla*, the other of *jamón*. He expresses the wish to marry Silvia so that she does not ever make *tortillas* for anyone else. The only son of a rich industrialist family who make underwear, José Luis is useless as a business-man. His sole idea is to produce panties for dogs on heat. His version of *machismo*, unlike that of Raúl, is childish macho posturing: José Luis and his friends compare penis sizes, speculate about sexual prowess, and see how far they can urinate, before going to a brothel. Once inside, José Luis only confirms his immaturity. All this is easily explained by his relationship with an overbearing mother Conchita (another Spanish gender stereo-type) whose affection for José Luis is blatantly sexualized.

But this exaggerated predatory matriarch (who ends up falling for Raúl, whom she initially has paid to tempt her son away from Silvia) forms part of a triad of stock female characters. The director describes them in the titles as '*la hija de puta*' (Silvia), '*la puta madre*' (Carmen, Silvia's prostitute mother) and '*la madre puta*' (Conchita). Just in case this cultural legacy (inherent in the Spanish language) is missed, José Luis' father, Manuel explains it: 'All women have something of a whore in them'. Silvia is a hyperbole of submission: she confesses to José Luis that she is pregnant, pleading 'I don't want to be a problem for you' and telling her mother, 'If I can't marry him I'll kill myself'. But once Raúl's weightier tradition of masculinity is revealed to her, Silvia is unable to resist. Her final confrontation with José Luis is under the shadow of the Osborne bull and its enormous testicles, which José Luis angrily (and symbolically) pounds until they fall to the ground (Silvia points out it is José Luis who lacks balls). When it rains she takes the testicle-shaped metal and shelters under it until she meets Raúl in the bar. Subsequently, we see them making love underneath the now castrated Osborne bull. The resolution of the conflict can be nothing less than a fight to death between the two males, a struggle between two kinds of Spain, in which Raúl's weapon (a leg of *jamón*) shows who will prevail.

Although it has been attacked for a lack of critical edge or even for its 'indulgent complacency' (Morgan and Jordan, 1994: 63), *Jamón jamón* is a gift for those who want to deconstruct notions of both gender and national identity, because it presents prototype characters, situations and cultural icons in an overblown form.

Further reading: Deleyto, 1999; Morgan and Jordan, 1994; Aguilar, 1998; Perriam, 2003; Evans, 2004.

Chapter Seven

FILM STUDIES AND
FILM THEORY

Well before becoming formalized and taught in specialist film schools or university departments as Cinema/Film/Screen Studies, the public's fascination for the cinema developed
informally in newspapers, magazines, film clubs, literary societies and cafés. For well over
50 years, film makers, journalists, writers, intellectuals and all manner of aficionados and
cinefiles chatted, debated and wrote about the new medium. Most of this interaction was
haphazard and unrecorded, though a number of directors and aficionados published
important, now 'classic', books and essays on film and film making which were aimed at
a cultured reading public, among them Delluc, Epstein, Moussinac, Arnheim, Kracauer,
Balázs, Eisenstein, Pudovkin, Vertov, Kuleshov, etc. (see Andrew, 1976; Abel, 1984). By
the 1950s, from the Parisian Cinématheque and its ranks of intellectuals and cinefiles,
auteurism as a critical movement took hold, with *Cahiers du cinéma* becoming a crucial
auteurist mouthpiece. Gradually, in universities in Europe and America, in mainly English
and Romance Languages departments, films slowly began to infiltrate the curriculum.
They were allowed in as adjuncts to literary study (often in the form of the literary adaptation) or as examples of a growing trend in the European 'art movie', exemplified by such
directors as Fellini, Antonioni, Buñuel and others. A 'proto' Film Studies began to emerge,
strongly wedded to literary studies and based largely on an auteurist approach. The
romantic idea that the creative individual was responsible for the film work fitted com-
fortably into a literary studies culture which was still based on notions of canons of great
authors with unique sensibilites and personal visions. By the mid-late 1960s, however,
under the influence of French structuralism and semiology, some university academics in
Europe sought to revise and systematize the field in order to enhance curricular credibility and respectability for the study of an essentially 'popular' medium. It was this attempt
to 'discipline' film studies, in a more rigorous 'scientific' manner, which ushered in what
we now refer to as modern Film Theory.

Film Theory is a vast and variegated canvas, embracing a huge range of concerns and
approaches, and revealing a diversity of styles and types of writing. In basic terms, it has
to do with 'any line of enquiry dedicated to producing generalisations pertaining to, or
general explanations of, filmic phenomena or... accounting for any mechanisms, devices,
patterns and regularities in the field of cinema' (Bordwell and Carroll, 1996: 41). In other
words, Film Theory is concerned with general, systematic thinking about the nature of
film and finding explanations for any significant patterns and regularities (or irregularities)

therein. Film Theory poses questions such as: What is cinema? What is film? How do films create meaning? Can we regard the film maker as an author? What is film realism? What forms of film narration are there? What is film style? What do film viewers want from a film? What do they do when they watch a film? How do we make sense of films? Clearly, different types of theory (formalist and neo-formalist, cognitive, psychoanalytic, feminist, reception theory, etc.) will approach the same question in different ways, guided by different cultural and ideological assumptions. In this sense, there is no ultimate right answer to questions relating to film. At its best, Film Theory can be a valuable, enlightening problem-solving activity; at its worst, it can become intimidating, dogmatic and self-indulgent, and sometimes so relativistic as to be unproductive (see Carroll, 1988).

In the 1970s, following the political turmoil arising from May 1968 and the defeat of the French left, left-wing film scholars in the UK and USA drew increasingly on various strands of non-filmic theorizing, from linguistic, literary, philosophical, psychoanalytic and cultural theory being developed in France. This dialogue between early Film Studies and French theory helped establish 'Film Theory' as a legitimate domain of intellectual activity in many universities, while strongly influencing practical forms of film analysis. However, in retrospect and reflecting an often naïve and uncritical admiration for the ideas of Althusser, Barthes, Foucault and Lacan, film theory soon consisted of rather predictable, routinized summaries of these continental 'penseurs' and their revered, canonical texts. Such summaries usually framed somewhat doctrinal readings of how Hollywood functioned as a tool of capitalist exploitation and female oppression. In this mode, Film Theory and Film Studies were arguably co-opted into a left-wing, intellectual assault on American capitalism and its cultural hegemony across the world. According to film theorists such as Metz, Comolli and Narboni, cinema was an ideological apparatus, a symbolic system engaged in maintaining social and psychic relations of domination, subordination and oppression over a predominantly passive, spectatorial, viewing 'subject'. Further afield, as seen in journals such as *New Left Review*, *Screen* and *Camera Obscura*, the task of the left film critic (e.g Mulvey, Heath, Wollen and others) was to 'unmask' dominant (i.e. American, capitalist) ideology in mainstream Hollywood cinema, while drawing attention to instances of allegedly subversive, revolutionary cinema (Godard was the default radical film maker, par excellence). What became known as Screen Theory soon came to dominate Film Studies, a field captured and held very successfully by the Marxist Left for well over a decade (see Wollen, 1972 and Bordwell, 1989).

Since then the hegemony of continental theory has waned considerably. With the collapse of Communism and the Soviet Union in the late 1980s, Marxist analysis has become somewhat implausible, even discredited. And though vital to the development of feminist Film Theory, 1970s Screen Theory has been revised by its practitioners and widely questioned for its perceived model of cinema (static, ahistorical, anti-empirical, based on unconscious, hidden processes of reception, by definition unavailable to direct analysis) and its reductive notion of the spectator as a passive recipient of textual meanings, already 'positioned' as ideological 'subject' of the cinematic apparatus. The pseudo-scientific, totalizing ambitions of Screen or Grand Theory have given way to what has been called 'Post-Theory' (Bordwell and Carroll, 1996). That is, smaller scale projects, more modest, middle-level theorizing, aimed not so much at 'big' issues like culture, subjectivity, ideology or the (lack of) class struggle, but at more specifically filmic ones, such as early cinema, colonial and postcolonial film, film historiography, film narratology, genres, spectatorship and reception studies (especially audience memory and fandom). And while a revamped Screen Theory is still influential and in evidence in significant areas of scholarly work, in broader terms, we note a substantial shift away from conventional theory-driven, scholarly analyses of films, towards other ways of making sense of movies. Internet chat rooms, fan sites, e-magazines and web journals now make available new spaces for more pleasurable, imaginative, subjective writing, where film analysis can be a more creative, pleasurable exercise compared with the routine, ritualized application of often obscure, sometimes unintelligible theory.

SPANISH FILM AND FILM THEORY

Reflections on film as the new modern visual medium of the twentieth century began in Spain with the medium itself. The first film magazines appeared in Spain around 1907 and they reveal the impact of the Lumières' invention, with such titles as *Artístico Cinematográfico, Cinematógrafo Ilustrado* and *Cinematógrafo*. Yet such magazines contained only the vaguest hint of what we would now regard as Film Theory. In fact, they were mainly light, glossy, trivial, heavily illustrated publications in search of the general reader, promising glamour, gossip, fashion, gushing profiles of actors and emerging stars and contained no recognizable film reviews as we would understand them. Even so, popular journalism of the 1900s and 1910s continued to celebrate film's ability to record movement (of marching soldiers, admiring crowds, schoolgirls leaving school, the faithful leaving church) and create fantasy and alternative worlds. By the early 1910s, in new film magazines such as *El Mundo Cinematográfico* (founded 1911) and especially *El Cine* (founded 1912), we begin to find treatments of more topical issues such as health and safety and protection of minors; and the very variable quality of film projection and reports on the many experiments taking place (largely abroad) to combine sound and film. One anonymous contributor warned theatre owners that they 'should begin to tremble' in the face of cinema's technical innovations and the power of the new medium (García Fernández, 2002: 310–11).

The first important and reasonably sustained film publication in Spain was *Arte y Cinematografía* (1910–36), for a long time another generalist magazine, published in Barcelona. It combined copious advertising, with news and gossip concerning early film stars. Its audience was mainly female, which it attracted through its high quality, glossy photography, yet its title clearly reflected a view of the cinema as rather more than a mere fairground attraction or escapist refuge. Indeed, as early as 1913, though reflecting a certain residual imperialist outlook, the magazine linked the industry's weakness in Spain to the loss of its Latin-American markets, which naturally 'belonged' to the mother country because of cultural and spiritual ties (Triana Toribio, 2003: 28–9). Interestingly, from 1923–4, *Arte y Cinematografía* also began publishing supplements and special numbers, which became important sources of information and statistics for the film industry as a whole (Cánovas Belchi, in Borau, ed. 1998: 90–91).

It is perhaps worth emphasizing again that in the 1900s and 1910s, Spain was a rather hostile environment to the development of a film culture and an intellectual acceptance of the new medium. This was particularly so in relation to the question of cinema's artistic value and its status as a medium worthy of intellectual curiosity. In broad terms, govern-ments of the day mistrusted the industry and refused to provide fiscal support or state protection from foreign competition. The introduction of film censorship in 1912 and 1913 led city councils and local authorities to apply controls to film exhibition far too harshly on too many occasions (García Fernández, 2002: 265–67). Also, Spain's respectable middle classes largely turned their backs on the cinema, seeing it as morally disreputable and artistically inferior to more traditional public entertainments. In this, as noted earlier, they were guided by an often militant and hostile Catholic Church, quick to condemn the cinema as a source of immorality, disease, depravity and subversion. In response, some writers emphasized the utopian possibilities of cinema and its awe-inspiring power, while some distributors and exhibitors formed defensive trade associations, such as the Mutua de Defensa Cinematográfica, set up in 1915. However, on balance, the negative discourses (which were also hostile to film as a mimetic, revelatory, documentary medium, suspicious of narrative cinema and contemptuous of the viewing 'masses') overwhelmed the more positive, progressive, utopian attitudes well into the 1920s.

The film theory of the silent era posed the obvious questions: is cinema an art or a mere mechanical recording? As an art, what are its main properties and how do these compare with other arts such as painting, theatre, sculpture etc? What makes film realism different from the 'real world'? What are cinema's psychological implications? What do spectators do (mentally) when they watch a film? Is cinema an instrument of aesthetic importance, to promote beauty, to make the spectator see the world afresh? Is its purpose political, to intervene in the social world and promote political change? Where does cinema's artistic value reside?

If early film theory beyond the Pyrenees was able to focus more readily on cinema's artis-tic and aesthetic qualities, and rapidly legitimate the new medium as an art, in Spain, during the 1900s and 1910s, debates on Spanish cinema were diverted by more pressing national concerns. These tended to be couched in terms of an economically undeveloped, marginalized, post-imperial nation, capable only of generating a film industry which was technically and artistically backward, overwhelmed by foreign competition from France and the USA and struggling to catch up. Moreover, film production in Spain was dominated by poorly-made genre cinema: principally comedies, melodramas, folkloric musicals, serials and the odd 'art' film, but mostly based on foreign models and sources. Such dependency and the resulting 'imitation' effect meant that by the time Spanish film companies managed to make tolerably acceptable examples of a foreign film genre, the latter had moved on in its country of origin, thus making sales of impoverished Spanish versions all but impossible. In short, Spanish journalists, writers, intellectuals, cinefiles and film theorists had to wrestle with a troubling inferiority complex, grounded in Spain's grim economic realities, political and international marginalization and artistic dependency.

Yet, despite these huge obstacles, as noted earlier, we do find signs of an intellectual film culture developing in the 1910s and early 1920s, partly influenced by the arrival of many foreign directors escaping the effects of the First World War and partly by Spain's geographical proximity to France. This resulted in a number of co-productions, some more favourable to France than Spain (e.g. Emile Bourgeois' version of the Columbus story, made in 1916 and shot in Spain; also, the co-pro *L'inhumaine/La barraca de los monstruos* [J. Catelain, 1924], made by Atlántida Films of Madrid and Marcel L'Herbier's company *Cinégraphique*). Within Spain, there were also small but growing numbers of writers and intellectuals who sought to defend the domestic film industry, some by making films themselves (for example, the celebrated Valencian novelist Vicente Blasco Ibáñez adapted his novel *Sangre y arena* for the screen, which he part-financed and co-directed with Max André in 1916.) Also, the novelist Eduardo Zamacois made two documentaries, one on the famous bullfighter *Belmonte* (1916), the other on his writer contemporaries, entitled *Mis contemporáneos* (1920). Another writer, Jacinto Benavente, not only wrote film criticism, but founded his own production house (Madrid Cines) and even directed a version of his own successful stage play, *Los intereses creados* (1918). At the same time, certain critics and writers such as Federico de Onís and Alfonso Reyes (of Mexican origin, nicknamed 'Fósforo') began writing recognizable film columns and reviews in magazines and daily newspapers (Onís in the review *España* from 1915 and Reyes in the daily *El Imparcial* from 1916) where, among other issues, they campaigned to preserve the freedom of the cinema from state control and censorship. More film magazines began to appear, including one by film historian Juan Antonio Cabero who founded *Cinema* in 1918. By the early 1920s, Barcelona had become the capital with the most film magazines in circulation, including new arrivals such as *Cine Revista* and *Cine Popular*. Yet these were not specialist publications, nor could they draw on support from any extended film club network where non-commercial films could be screened and debated with invited speakers and cinefiles and enthusiasts writing reviews and commentaries, etc. Such a 'film culture' would develop only towards the end of the decade.

Nevertheless, by the mid-1920s, we begin to see the publication of some of the earliest essays and monographs on Spanish cinema: Ernesto Gómez Carrillo (of Guatemalan origin), *En el reino de la frivolidad* (1923), José Roman, *Frente al lienzo. Ensayo crítico* (1924) and Alfredo Serrano, in *Las películas españolas* (1925), the first extended work on the economic structure of Spain's film industry. On the whole, such writing and early reflections on film were pretty vague, anecdotal and ad hoc, though clearly aimed at supporting cinema's modernity and establishing its difference from other static media, such as painting and sculpture. Yet there was little evidence of systematic thinking, compared, for example, with the likes of early film critic Ricciotto Canudo in his article of 1911, 'The Birth of the Sixth Art' (in Fowler, 2002: 19–24), or Hugo Munsterberg, Harvard philosopher and author of *The Photoplay. A Psychological Study* (1916). The latter cogently emphasized the role of technical change in the transformation of 'trite episodes' into visual art as well as a notion of the spectator as an active agent in the reception process. Nonetheless, we do find signs and hints of later theoretical issues and problems peeping through in certain magazine articles, as in a piece published in *Almanaque de El Cine* (1925), by José Roges, dealing with 'La mise-en-scène en las películas españolas' (García Fernández, 2002: 312–14). Echoing Jean Epstein and Louis Delluc in France, the article discussed the importance of the '*metteur-en-scène*' as the key figure in film production and also the grandeur of Spain as a prime but little-used film location. Also, Delluc's pioneering work on the revelatory nature of cinema by way of '*photogénie*' was addressed by Carlos Fernández Cuenca in 1927 in a short book (self-financed) entitled *Fotogenia y Arte* (Pérez Perucha, 1995: 101). In 1930, Luis Gómez Mesa (soon to be film critic for Unión Radio) published rather general, anecdotal accounts of *Los films de dibujos animados* (1930), plus *Variedad de la pantalla cómica* (1932) and *Autenticidad del cinema (Teorías sin trampa)* (1936). Also, acccording to Pérez Perucha (1995: 162), the literary historian and scholar Guillermo Díaz-Plaja is also said to have published a volume entitled *Una cultura del cinema* (or perhaps entitled *Una estética del cinema*) which we have been unable to verify or confirm.

On the whole, during the 1920s, journalistic and critical writing in *El Cine, El Imparcial* and *Arte y Cinematografía*, among other newspapers and magazines, was still very impressionistic and improvized. It was also over-determined by economic and industrial issues, fixated on the negative effects of foreign competition and market colonization by the USA, the need for greater investment and risk-taking by Spanish film producers, the poor quality and low production values of Spanish output and above all demands for protection for the national cinema (see Aurelio Pico, *Arte y Cinematografía*, no. 302, 1926, reproduced by García Fernández, 2002: 321–2). In the face of such overwhelming odds, very few Spanish films were economically successful at the box office. This is why Spanish film producers frequently hired foreign as opposed to local directors, aware that local audiences might regard foreign directorial names as better guarantees of quality. These concerns culminated in the *Primer Congreso Español de Cinematografía* (First Spanish Film Conference) held in Madrid, 12–20 October 1928, sponsored and promoted by the new film magazine *La Pantalla*.

The Conference arose from the conjunction of four other important factors:

1   The growing appeal and viability of some of the film criticism being published in the daily press, written by the likes of Josep Palau, Sebastián Gasch and Luis Gómez Mesa;

2   The growing status of cinema (foreign art cinema, that is, not Spanish) among Spain's liberal intelligentsia and its university elites, as a serious artistic endeavour and artefact, worthy of intellectual attention;

3   The development of the 'cine club' movement in Spain in the late 1920s;

4   The appearance in the mid-1920s of three new film magazines, *Popular Film* (founded 1926, Barcelona), *Fotogramas* (founded 1926, Madrid) and the short-lived *La Pantalla* (1927–29, Madrid). Also of crucial importance in the equation was the role of *La Gaceta Literaria*, not a film review but a literary and cultural review, begun in January 1927 by avant-garde writer and film maker Ernesto Giménez Caballero (in the 1930s articulate apologist for clerico-fascism). It was the latter who devoted a section of the magazine exclusively to film, anxious to emphasize its modern, avant-garde, high-culture status, as opposed to that of a popular, mass entertainment. And it was Luis Buñuel who was invited to write the column for over two years, often recycling material he had already written for the French magazine *Cahiers d'art*. His contributions ranged widely and included creative pieces and commentaries on poetry, theatre, film scripts and scenarios as well as film reviews and a few pieces on film technique. The writing was well-informed, if rather slight and superficial, though the pieces on the 'cinematic shot' 'découpage' and 'cinema as an instrument of poetry' make interesting reading in the context of French film avant-gardes of the late 1920s (see Buñuel, 2000). Perhaps more importantly, the review was also instrumental in sponsoring Spain's first film club, the *Cine Club Español* based at Madrid's Cine Callao, from October 1928, whose film programmes (21 sessions in all) were largely supplied from Paris by Buñuel.

The main purpose of the Conference was to generate a national debate on the problems facing Spain's film industry, including finance, marketing, foreign exports, competition from abroad, unionization, censorship and the need for state protection. Yet, issues to do with training and film education, entry into the industry, an official newsreel, the role of archives and film libraries would also figure on the agenda. However, in the context of dictatorship conditions (Spain was governed by the 'dictablanda' or benign autocracy of General Primo de Rivera from 1923 to 1930), the event was heavily controlled and censored: the delegates comprised a very heterogenous mixture of liberal-left film enthusiasts and industry professionals, as well as monarchists and Primo's spies. The presentations were reportedly timid and respectful and the final 22 conclusions of the conference rather vague, yet in some ways fairly progressive given the difficult ideological conditions (see García Fernández, 2002: 279–80). Calling for new censorship regulations and greater Hispano-American cooperation as well as local 'cinematecas', citizens' education in cinema, new classification regimes and an official newsreel (among other things), these conclusions were overly optimistic and ignored by the government. Still, the debate on the parlous state of domestic film making continued in the pages of *La Pantalla* in 1929 under the rubric: 'What direction should national film making take?' in which Rafael Marquina invited a number of Spanish directors (including Perojo, Buchs, Rey and Ardavín) to argue at length on the pros and cons of state protection, especially the establishment of a screen quota for Spanish films (yet another burning issue which, sadly, the Primo regime had no intention of taking seriously).

The 1928 Conference was followed in October 1931 by another national conference, this time the *Primer Congreso Hispano-Americano de Cinematografía*, (the First Hispano-American Film Conference) sponsored by the review *La Cámara*. Coming six months after the arrival of the new democratic Republican government in April 1931 and in conditions of demo-cratic freedom, the conference focused far more on the woes of the commercial film indus-try, which was still undergoing the traumatic and costly transition to sound cinema. Spanish film producers were alarmed at the staggering 80 per cent plus market share enjoyed by Hollywood cinema in Spain, their own inability to supply their Latin-American markets with local product and the fact that in Hollywood, New York, London and Paris, increasing numbers of foreign companies were making Spanish sound films, thereby steal-ing their markets. Fears of colonization and a curiously 'imperialist' determination to recapture markets of former Latin-American colonies (which indigenous producers virtu-ally considered their 'lost' possessions) prompted delegates to call upon the government for protection. Again, this call was never seriously heeded, despite the creation in 1933 of a Consejo de la Cinematografía (Film Council), an official body ostensibly charged with helping to broker co-pro arrangements and other forms of transatlantic cooperation.

Meanwhile, the development of a new, intellectual film culture gathered pace in the early and mid-1930s, mainly among cinefiles, university students and a few film producers and directors. The new film clubs provided venues not only for screenings but also for the discussion and promotion of largely non-commercial, European and Soviet art cinema. For example, as noted elsewhere, film producer Ricardo Urgoiti, head of Filmófono (founded 1931), created the Cine Club Proa Filmófono in Madrid (see Chapter One). Other Madrid film clubs included the Cineclub CECI and Studio Nuestro Cinema; in Barcelona, the Mirador and the Cineclub Horizonte; in Valencia, the Cine Club Valencia and the Cine Studio Popular. Added to this, given the new freedoms allowed under the Republican administration, we also find the creation of new 'cineclubs proletarios', linked to trades unions (such as the bank workers) and the Red Cross but mainly to the Communist Party and its youth section. And here, the film club culture, the activism and ability to influence and proselytize young captive audiences arguably underpinned the appearance of a new film journal, the legendary *Nuestro Cinema. Cuadernos Internacionales de Valoración Cinematográfica* (1932–35), founded by Juan Piqueras.

With editorial offices based in Paris and Madrid and a string of contributors from Europe and America as well as Spain, *Nuestro Cinema* – despite its apparent eclecticism – was a Communist Party platform. Its role was to promote Soviet Marxism and a doctrinal notion of the cinema as a political and ideological tool of social revolution: hence Piqueras' commitment to and activism in the '*cine club*' movement as a mode of CP propaganda, recruitment and indoctrination. Moreover, the title of the magazine, *Nuestro Cinema*, relates not to Spanish cinema as such, most of which Piqueras vehemently detested, but is code for Revolutionary Soviet Socialist Cinema, as opposed to decadent Western capitalist cinema (i.e. Hollywood and much European cinema, too, including – perhaps surprisingly – the 1930s Popular Frontist cinema of Jean Renoir). As Triana Toribio suggests, *Nuestro Cinema* seemed to espouse the creation of a 'working class transnational cinema' (2003: 27). That is, a cinema committed to representing contemporary social 'realities', but a cinema conceived of as a tool of propaganda and social change and inspired by a 'realistic aesthetic'. This was supposedly exemplified by Soviet montage cinema, otherwise known in the West for its rather manipulative montage techniques.

The call for a new type of cinematic realism in *Nuestro Cinema* and in other Spanish film magazines of the 1930s, such as *Popular Film*, strongly prefigured post-civil-war debates in Spain on 'cine comprometido/cine social'(committed/social cinema). In the 1950s such debates were typical among anti-Franco opposition intellectuals and film makers as well as falangist dissidents. The issue of film realism was just as alive in the 1960s in relation to the aesthetics and social and political role of the Nuevo Cine Espanol, hotly debated in the pages of *Nuestro Cine*, a new film journal whose name paid homage to the 1930s antecedent founded by Piqueras. Of course, in the 1930s, in the context of the rise of Nazism/Fascism and Soviet-inspired Popular Frontism, the key issue was the type of film deemed most appropriate and effective in the struggle to counteract fascism and defend a broad, democratic, liberal-left coalition. *Nuestro Cinema* defended a Soviet-inspired, proletarian, realist cinema, though inspired by avant-garde aesthetics (notably the work of Eisenstein), which had little or no serious impact in the 1930s in Spain. But this formula is arguably the origin of a tripartite alignment between film realism, political commitment and high culture avant-garde forms, which would dominate opposition film making and film thinking under Francoism for the next 40 years. It would also oppose and reject a popular commercial cinema as a legitimate form of Spanish national cinema because of its alleged falsity and lack of realism, a problem which would also be revisited in the 1980s and 1990s (see Triana Toribio, 2003: 27).

Republican freedoms were essential for the development of a liberal-left intellectual film culture based on the new film clubs, a ready supply of foreign art films, talks by visiting film makers and local working directors and associations of film writers and critics, all of which helped create a new market in film-oriented publishing. The context also encouraged a new Society of Independent Film Critics and Writers (*Sociedad de Críticos y Escritores Cinematográficos Independientes*) founded in 1933, which sponsored various publishing ventures on cinema, supporting works by playwright Benjamin Jarnés, film maker Rafael Gil and critic and historian Manuel Villegas López, arguably one of the key film intellectuals of the Republican period and after. Yet, the same context which witnessed signs of a Republican documentary cinema, highlighted by Buñuel's scandalous and banned *Tierra sin pan/Las Hurdes* (1932) and other important works by Antonio Román, Carlos Velo and Fernando Mantilla (in their documentary shorts on rural Spain, rivers, fishing and farming) also gave rise to the Cine Club del SEU (founded in 1935). This was a new student film club run by Giménez Caballero on behalf of Falange Española, Spain's Fascist Party, screening mainly Italian Fascist propaganda films. These varying options and differences reflect the growing radicalization of Spanish society in the mid-1930s, leading to the Popular Front victory of February 1936 and the outbreak of the civil war in July 1936.

It is perhaps a truism to say that the nationalist victory in the civil war over a legal, democratic Republic, and the resulting military regime under Franco, had profoundly disabling effects on intellectual and cultural life in Spain over the next four decades. Internal repression, censorship, state control over all aspects of cultural production severely hampered and delayed the entry, circulation and reception of foreign works, ideas and films. Dissident Spanish writers, intellectuals and film makers, faced with the virulent anti-intellectualism of the regime and sheer backwardness and conservatism of official cultural forms, looked abroad even more anxiously to certain foreign trends and influences for solidarity, encouragement, ideas and programmes for action, often exaggerating and misconstruing their importance in the process. At home, a new service class created by Falange was appointed to organize cultural life in Franco's 'nuevo estado' (new state).

In terms of 'film culture', the first Francoist film magazine to emerge began in La Coruña, during war time, in 1938, and was founded by falangist Joaquín Romero-Marchent. The mission of *Radio y cinema* (1938–63), as it was called, was to provide the general, wartime, nationalist reader with news and information on radio and film, plus features and gossip on stars, fashion and other trivia. (After seven or eight numbers, the radio dimension of the magazine was abandoned.) It also had an ideological agenda, that of helping to build the emerging 'new state' via the creation of a new cinema, one which rejected the vulgarities of localist and regionalist Spanish folkloric stereotypes embodied in the folkloric musical in favour of films which exalted the values of the new 'race'. Here we find a strong hint of the way some official Francoist film publications would soon be instrumentalized as ideological tools of extreme falangist nationalism and in some cases antisemitism (*Radiocinema*), celebrating the values of the 'new', fascist-inspired traditions over an 'old', liberal-Republican and discredited Spanish film culture. Ironically, despite the inflammatory, modernizing rhetoric of falangist ideologues, the popular, *castizo* (pure/authentic) film types, traditions and genres of the Republic would continue to be exploited and profitably recycled under Francoism.

After 1939, it was *Primer Plano* ('Close Up', 1940–63), strongly inspired by the Italian Fascist film magazine, *Cinema*, which was the regime's main official film magazine. Especially in its first few years, up to 1943–44, the magazine combined the most banal film reviews, reports, interviews and miscellany with propagandist editorials, bombastic manifestos, demands that film become a mass educational tool and, most vociferously, the need for a new cinema of nationalist and racial exaltation. As noted in Chapter One, this was a cinema which should ideally celebrate the military discipline, warrior spirit, purifying violence and religious asceticism of the new Francoist 'hero'. What was needed was not a 'filthy', 'frente populista' proletarian cinema (based on film naturalism), nor the shamefully provincial, folkloric stereotypes of the *españolada*, but genres and forms which captured the essence of the Spanish 'raza' (race) to be found (curiously enough) in the Castilian, land-owning peasantry (see Triana Toribio, 2003: 40–41). Mercifully, in the 1940s Spanish audiences were largely spared 'peasant' films (apart from Florián Rey's remake of the rural melodrama *La aldea maldita* (1930/1942) and *Orosía* (1943). However, as noted earlier, the regime did encourage and finance various forms of 'fascist heritage' movie, drawing on Spanish literary and dramatic traditions, by supporting a *cine de cruzada* (war and siege films) as well as historical epics, bio-pics and religious films.

As Triana Toribio suggests (2003: 41), and it is worth emphasizing again, the regime – had it wanted to – could have simply imposed by force a home-made, propagandist cinema of national exaltation on a war-weary population, fully protected by screen quotas from foreign film competition, while also abandoning compulsory dubbing. It did not do so. Driven more by graft and favouritism than ideology, it was more concerned to reward its friends and supporters in the industry (i.e. mainly film distributors) with import licences than to promote nationalist ideological fervour or develop a national film industry seriously. In other words, the regime deliberately colluded in reinforcing the backwardness and dependency of its own film industry.

Yet even in Spain's intellectual desert in the 1940s, a few vital signs of an internal film culture managed to cling on and survive, though there were few hints of film theory. Not all Francoist film magazines were as crudely doctrinaire or ideological as *Primer Plano*. *Cámara* (1941–52), for example, based in Madrid, directed by Antonio de Lara ('Tono', famous for his collaborations in *La Cordorniz* (1941–78), Spain's leading humorous magazine) was another generalist publication. In the grim and repressive early 1940s, it traded in glamour, glossy photography and escapism, with lush cover pictures of all the big Hollywood stars. Its approach was informative and its coverage wide-ranging, including news, premieres and reviews, as well as special reports on photography, set design and special effects, plus columns from foreign correspondents. Its contributors were drawn not only from among falangist ranks (Carlos Fernández Cuenca, Joaquín Calvo Sotelo) but also included famous writers and film makers who had had experience of Hollywood and MGM in the 1930s, such as José Lopez Rubio and the outstanding Edgar Neville. Meanwhile, in Barcelona, *Fotogramas* (1946–) initially offered the general reader coverage of literature, music and fashion as well as cinema, again on a basis not dissimilar to that of *Cámara*. However, after a change of editorship in the late 1960s (with Elisenda Nadal taking over from her father), the magazine changed its title to *Nuevo Fotogramas*. It provided a platform for greater intellectual '*apertura*' (liberalization) by attracting key dissidents of the Catalan intelligentsia (Terenci Moix, Vicente Molina Foix, Román Gubern, Enrique Brasó), also engaged in campaigns against censorship, and acted as the mouthpiece for the avant-garde film movement, the Escuela de Barcelona.

Almost the only signs of film theory in the 1940s came in a very unlikely form from deep within the School of Industrial Engineers in Madrid (EIIE), where Professor Victoriano López García, Head of the School, film writer and enthusiast and regime bureaucrat responsible for film stock and other related materials, taught a course in cinematography in 1942. This led quickly to the creation of a Cinema Section, equipped with a rudimentary 'set', a photo-developing lab and a film projection room. This was soon followed by the launch of a new, specialist film review in 1944 called *Cine Experimental*. The publication was motivated, it seems, mainly by a desire to promote the skills and professional training in basic photography and film technique which were so lacking in Spain at the time. This was aligned to a conviction that the cinema was an art, dependent on aesthetic and technical choices, requiring intensive experimentation and development in Spain. *Cine Experimental*, though shortlived (1944–46) also provided a rather unique forum in which Falangist writers and critics (such as Ángel Zúñiga, Antonio de Obregón, Carlos Fernández Cuenca) as well as other erstwhile anti-Francoist contributors (Antonio del Amo, Fernando Fernán Gómez) co-existed and wrote essays on professional training, film avant-gardes, amateur and documentary cinema, scriptwriting, cinematography (on the function of the shot), editing and the relations between film and theatre.

In particular, film director Carlos Serrano de Osma wrote about his experiments in film technique, camera work and editing, including an analysis of German Expressionist set design (as exemplified by Pabst) as well as Eisensteinian ideas on intellectual montage, all woven into a rather speculative theory of 'cine telúrico' (telluric cinema). Gubern remarks on Serrano de Osma's 'curious aesthetic dissidence in relation to official cinema', and in films made in the late 1940s, a highly stylized cinematography which led to 'almost surreal moments' (1995: 229). Most importantly, *Cine Experimental* provided the embryo and catalyst, the collaborators and the platform for the creation of Spain's official film school (Instituto de Investigaciones y Experiencias Cinematográficas) which opened its doors in February 1947.

The IIEC (which opened two years after the IDHEC in Paris), as noted earlier, was, in principle, an official mechanism for regulating access to the film industry. However, as Heredero suggests, its team of teachers (including Falangists such as Carlos Fernández Cuenca and ex-Communists such as Antonio del Amo) was remarkably open and its overall atmosphere and outlook was liberal and pluralist, despite a paltry initial budget of 100,000 pesetas (Heredero, in Borau, 1998: 465–7). Very quickly, with its earliest intakes of students including Bardem and Berlanga, Florentino Soria, José Gutiérrez Maesso and Eduardo Ducay, the IIEC became a focus of intellectual and political dissidence which would form the core of the intellectual opposition to the regime in the 1950s. Indeed, Ducay would be a key figure in re-launching the film club movement in Francoist Spain, which he did from Zaragoza in 1945–6, and without whose example and precedent the re-emergence of film clubs in the early 1950s, including that of Salamanca, might have been far more problematic. Also, it is worth recalling that the opening of the IIEC came shortly after cinefiles and collaborators of Piqueras, like Ricardo Muñoz Suay, were released from jail (1945) for their communist affiliations in the civil war and returned to active, anti-Franco dissidence while working in the film industry. Apart from his work as scriptwriter, assistant director to Berlanga and Bardem and film producer in UNINCI (a PCE front), Eduardo Ducay also wrote film criticism for liberal-left magazines such as *Índice* and *Ínsula*. Moreover, along with Bardem and Muñoz Suay, he would help re-launch the intellectual opposition in the mid-1950s and deliver a blow, in public, to the regime, from the rather inocuous setting of a student film conference in Salamanca (in May 1955).

Even by the turn of the 1950s, Spanish cinema was still dominated by a rampant escapism, provided by Hollywood but also reinforced by the patriotic pomposity and mystifications of an official heritage cinema. Emerging from the regime's new film school (IIEC) and from the rapid rise of the cine-club movement in the early 1950s across Spain's universities, we find a mix of left-wing radicals, liberals and disgruntled Falangist film enthusiasts arguing for a far more socially-engaged and responsive realist cinema. Their model for a new realism was Italian neo-realism, already in decline in its country of origin. Where the Marxist and liberal left saw in neo-realism an effective tool of 'revelation' of hidden social realities and political consciousness raising, Falangist admirers appropriated the trend's naturalism and documentarist style for its proximity to a tough 'national' realist literary tradition, shared by other 'Latin' or 'Mediterranean' races and cultures such as Italy. A degree of tacit official support for a new film realism, if not for the Italian trend itself, had already been highlighted by the *Surcos* affair, which cost García Escudero his job as Director General de Cine y Teatro. Even the boss of the SNE (Sindicato Nacional del Espectáculo/National Entertainments Union), Jesús Suevos, on his return from Cannes in 1951, had canvassed the idea of a 'neorrealismo a la española', by which he meant a mild, non-political, non-confrontational version, which gradually crept into films of the mid and late 1950s, such as *Cómicos* (Bardem, 1954) and *Calabuch* (Berlanga, 1956) (see Triana Toribio, 2003: 58–9). Yet, as the *Surcos* scandal also illustrated, the regime was not ready for hard-hitting, graphic film realism, anxious as it was to prevent unpleasant, corrosive images of contemporary social realities to contradict official triumphalism.

Italian neo-realist cinema was virtually unknown in Spain until 1950, when Rossellini's *Roma città aperta* (1945) was screened in a private showing at the Italian Institute, Madrid, to students of the IIEC. Also in 1950, De Sica's *Ladri di biciclette* (1947) was shown commercially in Madrid and Barcelona to the delight of Falangist cinephiles such as Josep Palau writing in *Destino* and leftist cinefile Eduardo Ducay in *Ínsula*. But whereas Palau appropriated the film as a realist alternative to a 'despotic Hollywood', Ducay brushed aside its sentimentality and poeticization of the real in favour of its subject matter and its convincing representation of grim daily realities (urban unemployment and conflictive father/son relations). These meagre samples of the Italian trend were followed up in 1951 by a First Week of Italian Cinema, held in Madrid, organized by Unitalia Films, followed by another week in 1953, both of which were successful. There were highlights such as *Paisà* (Rossellini, 1946) and *Mirácolo a Milano* (De Sica, 1949) but the organizers (very likely on orders from Spanish officials) omitted to screen such vital classics as Rossellini's *Sciusià* (1946) and *Germannia anno zero* (1947) as well as Visconti's *Ossessione* (1942) and *La terra trema* (1944).

In a little under three years, numerous Spanish cinefiles, students, intellectuals, writers and scholars (i.e. intellectual elites) from different ideological standpoints were able to see, inside Spain, a not unreasonable sample of Italian neo-realist films, though by no means fully representative. Nonetheless, this injection of neo-realism inspired the creation of a new specialist film journal, *Objetivo* (1953–55), sponsored by the editor of *Índice* (Juan Fernández Figueroa), who brought together an editorial team comprising Bardem, Muñoz Suay, Ducay and Paulino Garagorri, all ex-IIEC students and apart from the latter, all Communists. *Objetivo* – which ran for only nine numbers before being forcibly closed down in October 1955 – offered a range of specialist material, including auteurist pieces on Pudovkin, Welles and Dreyer, as well as items on British documentary cinema, plus reviews and reports on festivals and conferences, etc. Yet, in its consistent emphasis on film realism and its focus on Italian neo-realism in particular, the journal followed almost to the letter, the outlook, positions and line adopted by the Italian film review *Cinema Nuovo*, run by Marxist critic Guido Aristarco. Number 1 of *Objetivo*, for example, contained lengthy pieces on the work of Vittorio De Sica and especially of scriptwriter Cesare Zavattini, plus programmatic articles by Marxists Giuseppe de Santis and Carlo Lizzani, regarded as templates for cinematic and political renewal in Spain. Number 3 contained pieces which linked film realism and literature and a certain left-leaning realist literary tradition in Spain, a set of relationships which had been more generally debated at the Parma Cinema Conference of 1953, and attended by Muñoz Suay. So enthused was Muñoz Suay by the debate that the *Objetivo* team decided to organize a similar conference themselves to be held in Spain. They published the Call for Papers and an agenda for the Salamanca

Conference in Number 5 of *Objetivo* (May 1955), which also contained a rather tendentious reading of the political and 'revolutionary' significance of Italian neo-realism by Carlo Lizzani. The conference (some of whose papers were published in Number 6) was organised locally by the Cine Club Universitario de Salamanca, led by Basilio Martín Patino. The latter had already established the new film magazine *Cinema Universitario* in March 1955, very much a successor to its Madrid cousin and in line with the radical left editorial outlook of *Objetivo*, with its support for a politically-inspired testimonial realism. Moreover, it is worth noting that *Cinema Universitario* published contributions not only by Zavattini, but also by Sartre, Georges Sadoul, Joris Ivens as well as essays on Gramsci and Azorín.

The Salamanca Conference was arguably the culmination of a process in which an intellectual, PCE-inspired, anti-Francoist opposition movement subverted – for the first time in Spain – a public debate for political purposes. Looking back, García Escudero likened the manoeuvre to the infiltration of the *Centro Sperimentale* and other official film organisations in Italy by anti-fascists during the 1930s and 40s (see Jordan, 1991: 238). Salamanca also echoed to demands for reform (not only from the left), mainly in terms of replacing a dominant, false and escapist film culture with one devoted to revealing Spain's contemporary 'hidden realities', i.e. the lives of ordinary people in the here and now, via a revelatory, testimonial, non-editorializing film realism, exemplified by Italian neo-realism. In retrospect, one is struck by the passion and determination but also by the naïvety of the anti-fascist infiltrators of Salamanca, especially in their belief that in Spain, a Communist-inspired, non-manipulative, neo-realism might have radical political effects on home audiences. First, such a cinema would never have been allowed, second, even if it were, it would attract few spectators and no box office and third, for all their leftist affiliations, very few Italian film makers were actually Communists and, as Overby argues, even fewer neo-realist films were Marxist-inspired or offered Marxist solutions to social problems (1978: 10–11).

Paradoxically, a certain kind of 'neorrealismo a la española' was allowed to develop in the 1960s. What had been unthinkable in the mid-1950s, now, because of changing circumstances and new foreign-policy priorities, rapidly became feasible. As mentioned in Chapter Three, in line with other European 'new wave' film movements of the 1960s (the Nouvelle Vague in France, Free Cinema in the UK, New German Cinema, etc), Franco's Spain produced its own home-grown trend. As Torreiro puts it, like France, Spanish film making experienced its own domestic revolt against the 'cinema de papá' (Torreiro, in Gubern, 1995: 308). Yet, unlike France, the impulse for reform in Spain's film industry came not from below, in the form of prestigious journals or budding auteur critics, but from above; in fact from the Ministry of Information and Tourism, via the Department for Cinema and Theatre (see Villegas López, 1967: 53). Here, José María García Escudero (briefly Head of Cinema between September 1951 and February 1952), was re-appointed to the post in July 1962. His role was to promote the image of Francoist Spain abroad as liberal, pluralist and culturally vibrant, on a par with its European neighbours. What better exemplar of cultural modernity than a newly emergent, well-made, culturally respectable, Spanish art cinema?

As the architect of this new art cinema, the so-called 'Nuevo Cine Español', García Escudero, in speeches, articles, books and finally legislation, laid down the parameters and ambitions for the new cinema. He was no film theorist, rather he was a regime technocrat, also something of a benign despot, but he was also a genuine film enthusiast, who had engaged intellectually with the field, however narrowly. He had contributed articles to *Objetivo, Cinema Universitario*, and other magazines in the 1950s, and written a number of books on the Spanish cinema. Unfortunately, in such works as *Cine social* (1958), *Cine español* (1962) and *Una política para el cine español* (1967), his disdain for Spanish popular film is almost as palpable as his contempt for Spanish film audiences, whose low-brow tastes and lack of film education he blames for the backwardness of Spanish film production (see Triana Toribio, 2003: 65–9). Not only does he fail to acknowledge the role of the regime in presiding over a repressive and deeply divisive education system, he also fails to mention Spain's lack of democratic freedoms. Not surprisingly, his writing exudes a strongly patrician, cultural snobbery, part and parcel of his Falangist elitism, an attitude which also underpinned his paternalist management of Spain's new art cinema, to be championed by his chosen 'universitarios', i.e. (all male) students from the IIEC/EOC. Yet, in other ways, García Escudero was arguably a reformer in his day, bearing in mind the constraints he was working under. He called for a cinema which confronted rather than evaded social problems, echoing the demands of left-wing critics of the regime at Salamanca for a realist cinema of social issues. Within obvious limitations, he also created spaces and opportunities for new, young, mainly oppositional directors to explore differ-ent approaches, genres and film styles, paid for by the state. He also contributed much to the development and liberalization of a 'film culture' in Spain. Having been president of the Federation of Film Clubs since 1957, he invigorated the university film-club network, allowing greater access to more foreign material. He also rationalized the Filmoteca Nacional (with new screening facilities), in 1967, created new art cinemas in larger towns and cities (*Salas de Arte y Ensayo*) and revamped the official Film School, changing its name to the *Escuela Oficial de Cine* in November 1962. Above all, García Escudero went some way to raising film production standards, produced a small number of important films, and gave young EOC graduates access to the national industry, people such as Víctor Erice, Pedro Olea, Antonio Eceiza, Manuel Summers, Antonio Drove, Francisco Regueiro and Mario Camus (Caparrós Lera, 1999: 127).

Unfortunately, the cinema made in and around Madrid (*cine mesetario*) and Barcelona (under the rubric of the Escuela de Barcelona) failed to generate a serious 'cine de autor' or much in the way of aesthetic renovation in film style or technique. This 'lack' was also felt in relation to theoretical reflection on film practice. Josep María Forn refers to the NCE as an 'etiqueta sin producto' (a brand lacking a product) (Caparrós Lera, 1999: 130). It is also a pity that, despite the new 'art theatres', the Director General of Cinema could not improve the conditions for the growth of art-house audiences at the same time, i.e. an educated, liberal, film-going middle class, which at that time hardly existed.

Among the numerous film magazines and journals of the 1960s in Spain (such as *Cine Universitario, Documentos Cinematográficos, Cinestudio, Temas de Cine*, the fleeting *Griffith* and *Ensayos de Cine*), only two are arguably of any consequence in terms of film theory, and then only tangentially: *Film Ideal* and *Nuestro Cine*, the latter being the more influential publication, especially in relation to the Nuevo Cine Español.

Film Ideal (1956–70), founded by José María Pérez Lozano, grew out of the Salamanca experience of 1955. Initially, it began as a series of information sheets for cine-club screenings which soon became a monthly magazine (1500 copies) and platform for progressive Catholic film intellectuals and enthusiasts. It was anti-Communist and was soon strongly influenced by *Cahiers du Cinéma*. In reviews and reports, its early focus was on thematics rather than form or film style, but this changed after 1961. It showed strong support for the satirical, regenerationist realism of Bardem and Berlanga. But splits in the editorial board in 1961 saw the departure of Pérez Lozano and others to form *Cinestudio*, while the entry of Miguel Rubio (working from Paris) and José Luis Guarner (from the Cine Club Monterols, Barcelona) re-oriented the review towards positions promoted by *Cahiers*. As a result, Guarner began to explore auteurism and the function of *mise-en-scène* as evidence of authorial presence, with effusive studies on Sirk and Walsh, directors virtually unknown in Spain. This new orientation and focus on Hollywood was very attractive to readers, pushing up readership and sales to 12,000 copies per month by the mid-1960s, quite unheard of for a Spanish film review. However, following a further split in 1965, the socialist faction of the editorial board left to form *Griffith*. This provided an opening in the review for new critics influenced by Bazinian writings on phenomenology and the ontology of photographic image (see Guarner, 1971 and Tubau, 1983 and 1984).

By contrast, *Nuestro Cine* (1961–71) played a key role as the launch pad and supportive intellectual/theoretical platform for the NCE. It emerged a year before the official birth of the NCE, under the direction of José Angel Ezcurra, very much in the tradition of *Objetivo* and *Cinema Universitario* (by then in decline, with its final number appearing in March 1963). The journal title, *Nuestro Cine*, was a deliberate homage to the Communist/Republican magazine *Nuestro Cinema*, directed by Juan Piqueras. In terms of editorial board, the journal drew upon a group of young film students from the EOC (including the prolific writer and critic Víctor Erice, José Luis Egea, César Santos Fontenla, Santiago San Miguel and Jesús García de Dueñas), led by theatre critic José Monleón. Contributors also included Claudio Guerín, Pedro Olea, Joaquín Jordá, Ramón Gubern, Antón Eceiza, Alfonso García Seguí and playwright Alfonso Sastre. *Nuestro Cine* was ideologically aligned to the PCE and strongly influenced by *Cinema Nuovo* and *Positif*, journals known to be more concerned with issues of political engagement than formal or aesthetic matters. In this regard, *Nuestro Cine* scorned *Cahiers* and its alleged mouthpiece in Spain *Film Ideal*. In terms of editorial ambitions, in a censored and politically repressed country, *Nuestro Cine* sought to introduce a degree of modernity and internationalism into an otherwise backward and ill-informed national film culture. The journal also saw as part of its political role a focus on Spanish cinema and, initially, to act as cheerleader for the NCE. There was also an ambition to promote theoretical reflection on how to regenerate Spanish cinema and develop a politically committed film practice.

As regards its international remit, the journal tended to focus on Socialist and Third-World cinemas in the 1960s (especially Cuba, Brazil, Argentina, Chile, Mexico, as well as Poland, Hungary, Czechoslovakia and Yugoslavia). Little or nothing was published on German, Swedish, Japanese or Canadian national cinemas, however. And alongside a certain amount of attention to Buñuel, Saura, Berlanga and classic Spanish directors of the 1940s (such as Sáenz de Heredia and Nieves Conde), the journal's support for the NCE was extensive, solid and virtually unwavering, seeing it as an antidote to a Spanish 'cine sin contenido' (cinema without content) (Editorial Note, Number 2, 1961). The journal published shooting reports, scripts, interviews, stills, commentaries and articles, especially in the key years of 1965–66, with the release of Saura's *La caza*, Patino's *Nueve cartas a Berta*, Aranda's *Fata Morgana* and Eceiza's *De cuerpo presente* (in Numbers 51–52). Yet the journal failed to underpin the NCE with a coherent, worked-out set of aesthetic principles or a political programme. Moreover, despite Erice's voluminous contributions (see Chapter Three), the writing and criticism in *Nuestro Cine* rarely reached the depth or sophistication of *Cahiers* or *Cinema Nuovo*. Surprisingly, there was little or no serious acknowledgement of the *politique des auteurs* and the function of *mise-en-scène*; and despite its affiliation to the ideological outlook of *Cinema Nuovo*, very little echo of debates in Marxist aesthetics and realism around Lukács, Adorno and Benjamin. Rather, in *Nuestro Cine*, realist film theory took the form either of translated sections of articles by Aristarco and Zavattini or contributions by Spanish and foreign writers (e.g. García Hortelano, Antonio Ferres, Alberto Moravia) and critics (Gubern, Bozal, San Miguel). In 1965–6, following the 'Mostra del nuovo cinema' at the Pesaro Film Festival, the journal published a series of papers arising from the event, including hints of the '*cine semiology*' now being seen in work by Metz, via Barthes. This could have been a valuable new seam worth exploring, a way of moving beyond the post-neorealist, untheorized 'critical realism' which was still being promoted as an appropriate form of political engagement with the Franco dictatorship. In the end, *Nuestro Cine* produced a mixture of doctrinaire, speculative and programmatic material designed to support the NCE as well as more neutral, revisionist, auteurist pieces on Rossellini, Eisenstein, Huston, Truffaut and Lubitsch. Sadly, it failed to encourage NCE directors to generate a more systematic critical/theoretical debate about their own practice.

Monterde (2003: 115–17) dates the beginning of the end for the journal in 1968, when Vicente Molina Foix, writing in a monographic Number 77–78, devoted to Spanish cinema, introduced the notion of an 'ajuste de cuentas' (settling of accounts) with the NCE, reporting on younger film graduates of late 1960s who were showing frustration and impatience with the trend, a revisionism which was excaerbated in later numbers. It is worth mentioning that oppositon to the 'posibilismo' and accommodationism between the regime and young Spanish film makers, through the NCE and EOC, had surfaced in October 1967 at the legendary Conference of Film Schools held in Sitges. Anticipating the 'Manifesto for a militant cinema' of the *États Généraux du Cinéma Francais*, following the May events in France in 1968, the famously utopian 'Conclusiones' of the Sitges Conference (see Hernández and Revuelta, 1976: 90–91), demanded an independent cinema, an end to censorship and the state subvention system, freedom of exhibition and the democratization of the film-industry union, no less. In demanding the impossible, the 'anarchists' of Sitges threw into sharp relief the limitations of the regime-controlled 'aperturismo' which had allowed the 'new Spanish cinema' to develop. Within two months García Escudero was out of a job, the NCE and the Escuela de Barcelona on the way down and a much tougher, more repressive period was to follow.

As noted earlier in the introduction to this chapter, the late 1960s and 1970s saw major changes in film theory in Europe and America, stimulated by events in post-May 1968 France. New questions arose such as: how does mainstream cinema help to secure the exisiting social structure? What forms should an oppositional cinema take which will break the hold of mainstream cinema and transform film from a commodity into a tool of social change? The new theory saw film as fundamentally political, both as an instrument of oppression and as a tool of social transformation. The spectator of 'dominant' mainstream cinema (i.e. Hollywood) was allegedly 'positioned' by an oppressive filmic apparatus and persuaded to imagine that they had mastery over the film *histoire* (Bordwell, 1996: 16). Such control was said to be illusory, however, since by generating fanstasies or misrecognitions of wholeness and completeness, dominant film aligned itself with bourgeois 'ideology', a process which also appealed to the 'myth' of a unified subjectivity. In short, as Hayward argues, 'Mainstream or dominant cinema, in Hollywood and elsewhere, put ideology up on the screen' (2000: 14).

In retrospect, the 'ideology' model of cinema in the 1970s, so influential in left and feminist circles of the time (often for very different reasons) displayed a number of weaknesses. As noted earlier, these included not only its anti-empiricism and textual determinism, but also its exclusive reliance on unconscious processes of film reception. It thus failed to take sufficiently into account the fact that film spectators also apply conscious forms of knowledge processing and memory retrieval as well as modes of inference, perception and cognition in order to 'read' what they see and hear in their film viewing. Spectators thus 'make' rather than passively 'absorb' or 'receive' filmic meanings (Bordwell, 1989: 3).

Also, as Neale has usefully argued, the ideology model proposed in the 1970s rather caricatures the nature of Hollywood cinema, since it 'tends to downplay the heterogeneity of Hollywood's output, of Hollywood's audiences and the uses those audiences make of Hollywood's films' (2000: 227).

Despite such evident limitations, the 'film as ideology' model was strongly echoed in Spain, even if very little of the specific theoretical work carried out in *Cahiers* and *Screen* was either known or read at the time. Indeed, in the closing years of the Franco regime, many left-wing (Marxist) Spanish critics and writers were convinced of the malign and retrograde ideological effects not only of Hollywood, but also of Spanish popular film. This was particularly true of the so-called 'cine de sub géneros' (sub-generic cinema), including the 'comedia de destape', an offshoot of the sexy Spanish comedy. Critics and academics such as Doménec Font, Carlos and David Pérez Merinero, Carlos Santos Fontenla and José Vanaclocha (1974: 195–284) all railed against a cinema which exploited the sexual repressions of the Spanish public (Vanaclocha, 1974: 266–67). Indeed, virtually all popular commercial cinema under Franco was seen as engaged in a vast, nationwide conspiracy, a campaign of mass deception, especially against the misguided, poorly educated, 'rural' spectator, the basic objective of which was 'la manipulación ideológica' (ideological manipulation) (Font, 1975: 321). There is no doubt that some popular films did fit this blood-curdling description (such as some of the 'factory' products of Masó, Ozores and Lazaga). But at the same time, it is simply far too sweeping and simplistic to claim that Spanish spectators were rudely duped or bamboozled *en masse* by official ideology, delivered by popular commercial cinema. Indeed, it has increasingly become a truism that authoritarian societies generate more sceptical audiences, able to read politically, obliquely and well beyond the apparent formal coherence or seamlessness of dominant film, in a more ironic, detached, critical fashion (see Donald and Donald, 2000: 125). Pam Cook also proposes that, contrary to the 'ideology' model of cinema described above, 'popular cinema problematizes all social categories... (being) based on the premise that spectators may experience the thrill of reinventing themselves rather than simply having their social identities or positions bolstered' (1998: 234).

Paradoxically, in an increasingly politicized environment in Spain, the new film magazine of the early 1970s, significantly entitled *Dirigido Por* (founded 1972 and still appearing), seemed to be swimming against the tide in its unfashionable focus on the film auteur. Indeed, it began as a monographic publication devoted to international auteurs (Chabrol, Kubrick, Pekinpah, Bertolucci, Minelli and others), comprising abundant (though secondary) interview, critical and bibliographical materials, most of it taken from French sources. In 1973 and 1974, other sections appeared (comprising reviews, reports on festivals, notes on soundtracks and more photographs) thereby gradually widening the scope. Directed by Fernando Valls, contributors included people who are now university professors and involved in significantly shaping the field of Film Studies in Spain, e.g. Riambau, Monterde, Heredero, Torreiro and others. But even with the incorporation of younger writers in the 1990s (e.g. José María Latorre, Carlos Losilla, Ángel Quintana), a new critical language sensitive to 'film as language' and film's social and historical implications, and new sections on television and video, the journal seemed not to have advanced very far in updating its outlook or clarifying its founding auteurist stance.

In a wider context, and in relation to the deteriorating state of Spain's film culture in the early 1970s, it is worth noting the closure of the EOC (announced in 1971 and finally achieved in 1976 via the new Education Reform Law). Weakened by political radicalism, repression and the resignations of its most acclaimed teachers (Berlanga, Picazo and Borau), the national film school was incorporated into Madrid's Complutense University, in the newly created Facultad de Ciencias de la Información (from 1972) under the pretentious title: 'Ciencias de la Imagen Visual y Auditiva'. For the rest of the 1970s it was the only department of its kind in the country. Fernando Trueba was a graduate. But during the 1980s, so-called departments of 'Imagen' (Image/Screen Studies) sprang up in many publicly-funded universities (in the Autónoma, Pompeu Fabra and Ramon Llull in Barcelona, as well as in Sevilla, Málaga, and the País Vasco). Also, several new private film schools, practical in orientation and concerned with professional training, emerged (mainly in Barcelona) in order to meet growing demand (such as the ESCAC, Escuela Superior de Cine y Audiovisuales de Cataluña, Barcelona, which opened in 1994). This process culminated in 1995 in the controversial attempt to resuscitate the old EOC via a new institution, the ECAM (Escuela de Cinematografía y del Audiovisual de la Comunidad de Madrid), by way of an agreement between the autonomous government, the national Film Academy and Spain's Society of Authors (Borau, 1998: 311–12).

Despite the Franco regime's attempts to impose an intellectual *cordon sanitaire* on Spain through censorship and more directly repressive measures (which seriously disrupted and delayed access to foreign writings on Film Theory), certain key works were translated and did get through, including Bazin's *Qu'est-ce que le cinéma?* (published in Spanish by Rialp in 1966) and even Aristarco's *Historia de las teorías cinematográficas* (Lumen, Barcelona 1968). Moroever, French Structuralism was already being widely discussed and used in literature departments in Spain from the early 1970s via digests and summaries (by writers such as Jean Marie Auzias). And even if important titles were not available in Spain, they were likely to be so in Spanish translation, via imported editions published in Mexico. (For example, Barthes' *Le plaisir du texte* (1973) appeared in an edition published by Siglo XXI, Editores, Mexico, 1974.) Yet, even taking into account a certain time lag or 'décalage', we have to wait until after the departure of the regime and the appearance of the radical film journal *Contracampo* (1978–87) to see signs in Spain of the sort of film semiology and so-called 'cine psychoanalysis' being developed by Metz and Baudry in the early 1970s, and Mulvey, Heath and Wollen in the UK.

Echoing 1960s notions of 'counter' culture and cinema, *Contracampo* was an important, if irregular and uneven, specialist publication (42 numbers in nearly 10 years), which always struggled to achieve a stable readership (see Losilla, in Borau, 1998: 248–9). Edited by Francesc Llinás, it had its roots in *Nuestro Cine* and its rejection of Bazinian humanist ideal-ism, as well as in the symptomatically titled *La Mirada* (1978–9), a short-lived specialist journal (only four issues), whose focus was on close textual analysis and most of whose editorial board (Joan Miguel Company, José Luis Téllez, Vicente Ponce and others) and contributors (e.g. Román Gubern, Santos Zunzunegui) passed over to *Contracampo*. Apart from much name dropping (Marx, Freud, Barthes, Brecht), the editorial note of Number 1 opposed a strong Spanish tendency towards amateurism, film appreciation and cinephilia with a rigorous focus on film and its industrial context, paying special attention to 'la estricta materialidad del cine mismo' meaning 'the strict materiality of cinema itself' via close readings. The pedagogically committed editors of *Contracampo* developed work on three fronts: on Spanish cinema (reviving ignored or poorly known directors), revisionist studies of classic, largely non-American auteurs (including Eisenstein, Welles/Toland, Hitchcock, Renoir, Walsh, Ophuls, Sirk, Ozu, Ray, Wenders, Godard and Pasolini) and studies on independent, international directors, such as Bertolucci and Woody Allen. Ploughing a furrow already opened up to some extent by *Dirigido Por*, *Contracampo* never-theless attempted to lend its material greater scientific rigour with translations of articles from French sources such as *Communications* and *Poétique* and formalist essays on narratology and film semiotics. In Number 31 (Nov/Dec 1982), following financial difficulties, the mag-azine reduced its meagre coverage of film reviews and news on current developments, thus squeezing its readership. And after a severe reduction in format and quality in Number 34 (Winter 1984), it began to fade. From Number 39 (Spring/Summer, 1985), it was published by the Instituto de Cine y Radiotelevisión de Valencia, where it would end its days. A brief look at Number 34, the key transitional number, reveals (apart from very poor reproduc-tion, fuzzy type and poor photographs) a curious mix of materials. The number is fronted by two pieces of close-shot analysis of the opening to *Citizen Kane* (one translated from the French, written and published by Marie Claire Ropar in *Poétique* in 1972; the other a response in Spanish). These are followed by rather oblique essays on Saura and Eloy de la Iglesia; a recuperation and defence of Max Reinhart; a critique of film studies curricula in university departments of 'Imagen'; a revisionist view of the work of Juan de Orduña and various reports from different film festivals. All in all, *Contracampo* was a curious cross between a proto-academic journal and a more generalist publication, too uncritical and overly dependent perhaps on foreign theoretical sources, whose selections fail to reflect how structuralism quickly segued into post-structuralism and deconstruction in the 1970s.

During the 1980s, apart from various generalist publications, such as *Casablanca* (founded 1981 by Fernando Trueba), *Interfilms* (which first appeared in 1988) and a sister review to *Dirigido Por* called *Imágenes de la Academia*, the only specialist publication of note was *Nosferatu* (founded in 1989, sponsored by the Department of Culture of San Sebastián's

Municipal Council). Linked to the film festival of San Sebastián and seeking to balance generalist material with more theoretically informed work, *Nosferatu* specializes in monographic studies which might help to fill gaps in the film history and critical record for Spanish students and cinefiles. These comprise materials (including interviews) on themes (such as Sex and Violence), national cinemas (Japan), genres (American science fiction and horror), and auteurs (Melville, Fuller, Hitchcock's English films, Wenders, Ripstein, Islamic directors, etc), plus exhaustive bibliographical support.

After many years of neglect and inadequate funding under Francoism, from 1982 and under the auspices of Miró's new policy, the Filmoteca Nacional (National Film Archive) was put on a much sounder financial footing. Though lacking autonomy, it was re-organized as a branch of ICAA (Instituto de la Cinematografía y de las Artes Audiovisuales) within the Ministry of Culture. The Filmoteca became an important source of film publications, through its links with the San Sebastián Film Festival and Cátedra Publishers. Also, under devolution arrangements contained in the 1978 Constitution, new autonomous, regional governments soon began to create their own Filmotecas (Barcelona, Valencia, Andalucía, Galicia, etc.) with opportunities for new publications and new modes of access to national and foreign films. These initiatives helped to create the conditions for highly regarded, theoretically-informed journals such as *Secuencias* (Universidad Autónoma de Madrid) and what must be arguably the most important specialist film publication in Spain today, *Archivos de la Filmoteca* (founded in 1989 by Ricardo Munóz Suay) and in principle a 'revista de estudios históricos sobre la imagen' (Angulo, in Borau, 1998: 77–8). Published by the Filmoteca de la Generalitat de Valencia, in its early years the journal combined rigorous historiographical work on Spanish cinema in line with the recovery and preservation mission of the institution (on CIFESA, NO-DO, as well as Malraux's *L'espoir* and Mexican melodrama) with auteurist studies (Greenaway, Becker, Zulueta), survey essays, film criticism and reviews, embracing the whole gamut of visual and screen studies. Following the appointment of Vicente Sánchez Bisoca as editor/director in 1993, *Archivos* sought to expand its field of enquiry and overcome a tendency to localism by calling upon foreign and international contributions (e.g. David Bordwell, Raymond Borde).

The 1990s in Spain have seen a proliferation of generalist film magazines, including *Cinerama* (begun in 1992), *Cinemanía* (1995), *Nickelodeón* (founded by José Luis Garci, 1995), as well as more vaguely specialist outlets, such as *Film Historia* (1991), *Letras de Cine* (1998), *Rosebud* (1996, devoted to film music), *Banda Aparte* (1994, a clear homage to Godard) and, of course, *Academia* (founded in 1991), the house journal of Spain's Film Academy. Though a professional and promotional outlet for the industry in Spain, *Academia* frequently contains monographic studies on Spanish, Latin-American and foreign cinemas, though these tend to be informative rather than scholarly. Linked to *Academia* is a monthly news bulletin, or *Boletín*, and a *Foro de la Academia*, or Forum, designed to collect and reflect the views of national and foreign film professionals.

Over the last 20 years or so, we have seen a vast improvement in Spain in general levels of finance, infrastructure and official bodies and institutions whose remit is to support and promote the national industry (via official grants and prizes, European schemes, festivals, film schools and university departments) as well as to raise levels of film literacy among Spanish citizens. There has been a proliferation of film schools, public and private, in response to sustained demand from aspirants to the industry. And as a corollary, we find a huge increase in publications (dictionaries, primers, manuals, etc.) to do with the practice of film making, scripting, editing, set design, sound, special effects, cinematography, digital compositing and so on. Less in evidence have been the kind of books on Film Theory we are used to in the UK, Europe and the USA, though the Cátedra series, *Signo e Imagen*, has provided excellent service in its translations of foreign theoretical works, as well as scholarly studies on Spanish film and media. However, while one looks very hard for the Spanish equivalent of the collectively written, introductory theory manuals of Jill Nelmes or Pam Cook, we are just as likely to see Spanish students toting the latest edition of Bordwell's *Film Art. An Introduction* in translation.

CONCLUSION ☐

In *Tesis* (1996), Alejandro Amenábar's debut feature, Professor Castro announces to a Film Studies class that a colleague, the asthmatic Professor Figueroa (thesis supervisor of female lead, Ángela, played by Ana Torrent), has had a heart attack and has died while watching a film in a downstairs screening room. Chema (Ángela's student admirer, fellow sleuth and suspect serial killer, played by Fele Martínez) responds to the news with a deadly jibe: 'Española, seguro' (Bound to be a Spanish film).

Chema's vicious put-down of the national film industry (one of many metacinematic instances throughout *Tesis*) is symptomatic of a long-standing aversion towards Spanish cinema which, until the 1980s and 1990s, was still prevalent among many Spanish film-goers, especially the 15–25s. Spanish films were generally perceived as poorly scripted and poorly crafted, lacking variety and entertainment value and dominated by didactic historical dramas, stolid literary adaptations and sleazy, comic 'subproductos'. Even in the early 1990s, it looked as if Spaniards had all but abandoned their own cinema. In 1994, for example, audience figures stood at a seriously low 7.1 million for domestic output, and at 44 films (36 national and eight *copros*, measuring 7 per cent of market share), Spanish film production had reached its lowest level for well over a decade (see ICAA: *Evolución del cine español*: 1996–2003 and Gubern, 1995: 402).

Since the early to mid-1990s, however, there has been a remarkable turnaround, the result of deeper and longer term transformations in Spain's film and media industries, changes in government policy and in new patterns of media consumption and use of leisure time. Film production figures, for example, have risen rapidly to stabilize at around 90–100 films per year (generating an average 13–16 per cent market share), though in 2003 there were 110 and in 2002, a colossal 137 films produced (ICAA, *Evolución del cine español*: 1996–2003). In terms of domestic audience numbers, in 1999, thanks largely to the huge success of Almodóvar's *Todo sobre mi madre* and Alex de la Iglesia's *Muertos de risa*, Spanish films attracted over 18 million spectators. By 2003, following the success of *La gran aventura de Mortadelo y Filemón* (Javier Fesser, 2002) and *Días de futbol* (David Serrano, 2003), they stood at 21.7 million. And in 2001, Spain's *annus mirabilis* in terms of box office, reflecting the enormous domestic success of Santiago Segura's *Torrente II. Misión en Marbella* (2001) and Amenábar's co-pro blockbuster *Los otros* (2001), figures rose to 26.2 million, a truly exceptional number by Spanish standards.

Spaniards were clearly going back to the cinema in large numbers, strongly attracted by 'neo-vulgar' trash comedies (Triana Toribio, 2003: 151) but even more so by a haunted house thriller, starring Nicole Kidman, made in English by a young Chilean/Spanish director and then dubbed into Spanish.

This dramatic and sustained recovery in the domestic industry has been accompanied by major artistic, critical and commercial success abroad. Since the late 1980s, Pedro Almodóvar has been the Spanish director who, perhaps more than any other, has been the standard-bearer and icon of Spanish cinema abroad, exporting his comedy-melodrama hybrids and portrayals of gay and bisexual relationships to admiring national and international audiences. His prestige as Spain's leading auteur (which has helped open doors in Europe for Bigas Luna, Gómez Pereira, Aranda, Medem and others) culminated in 1999/2000 with two Goyas and an Oscar for *Todo sobre mi madre* (1999) and a best director award at Cannes (2000). So far, the only young Spanish director to equal if not exceed Almodóvar's commercial and critical standing is Amenábar, mentioned above, whose *Los otros* broke all box-office records in Spain while *Mar Adentro* (2004) won an Oscar for Best Foreign Film. Amenábar's films confirmed that Spanish film makers could achieve major success abroad as well as at home, an example not lost on other recent films shot in English by Spanish directors, e.g. *Food of Love* (Ventura Pons, 2000) and *Darkness* (Jaume Balagueró, 2002).

Spain also has a growing number of exportable film stars. After the Oscar for *Belle Époque* (1992), for example, Fernando Trueba shot *Two Much* (1995) in English, hoping to break into the American market. Though it misfired in the USA, the film allowed its Spanish star Antonio Banderas (soon to marry Melanie Griffiths) to reinvent himself, gradually moving away from Hispanic or 'Latin lover' stereotypes (as seen in *The Mambo Kings, Desperado, Miami Rhapsody,* etc.) to more mainstream English-speaking roles (*Spy Kids* 1, 2 & 3). Like Trueba, Alex de la Iglesia went to the USA/Mexican border to shoot *Perdita Durango* (1997), a curious, violent, bricolage of psycho thriller, road movie and tragedy of ill-fated lovers, which sadly bombed in the USA. Yet, despite a rather camp performance (Perriam, 2003: 104), Javier Bardem was noticed. And for the first time in its history, Spanish cinema soon received its first 'Best Actor' Oscar nomination for Bardem in Julian Schnabel's *Before Night Falls (Antes que anochezca)* (2000). This is not to downplay for a moment the strong international profile of many more acclaimed Spanish actors such as Victoria Abril, Carmen Maura, Marisa Paredes, Sergi Lopez (a matinée idol in France) and of course the inescapable Penélope Cruz, star of *Captain Corelli's Mandolin* (2001) and *Vanilla Sky* (Cameron Crowe, 2002) and recently fêted with a David de Donatello (an Italian Oscar) for *Non ti muovere* (Italo-Spanish co-pro directed by Sergio Castellitto, 2004). Such commercial success and increasing international recognition suggest that Spanish films, film makers and performers have successfully reconnected with their domestic audiences by making popular and entertaining films, which film-goers want to see. At the same time, at the international level, Spanish film making appears to have thrown off for ever its image as a marginal, irrevocably colonized, Third-World, 'cottage' industry, championed abroad by a handful of oppositional auteurs, and has re-established contact with international audiences and tastes, and indeed with global industries and markets.

GLOSSARY OF FILM TERMS
IN ENGLISH AND SPANISH

angle (camera)	ángulo de encuadre/de cámara
aerial shot	toma aérea
assistant (director)	ayudante (de dirección)
auteur	autor
authorship	autoría
background	fondo
background (in the)	en el fondo/en segundo plano
boom microphone	jirafa
box office	taquilla
box office receipts	recaudación
camera operator	el cámara
cast	reparto
casting director	director de casting
clapperboard	claqueta
close-up	primer plano
closed framing	encuadre cerrado
closed shot	toma cerrada
continuity	raccord
costume	vestuario
costume designer	figurinista
crane shot	plano de grúa
crime thriller	thriller policíaco
cross cutting	acciones paralelas
cut (n.)	corte
cut (v.)	cortar
decor	decoración
depth of field	profundidad de campo
depth of focus	profundidad de foco
designers	diseñadores
diegetic	diegético
dissolve	encadenado
dubbing	doblaje
editing	montaje

editor	montador
effects track	banda de efectos
ellipsis	elipsis
extra	figurante
extras	figuración
extreme close-up	primerísimo primer plano/gran primer plano
fade (to black/white)	fundido (a negro/blanco)
feature film	largometraje
filming/shooting	rodaje
film set	plató
final credits	créditos
flashback	flashback/salto atrás
flash forward	salto adelante
foreground	primer plano
frame	cuadro
frame within a frame	doble encuadre
framed	enmarcado
framing	el encuadre
freeze-frame	imagen congelada/un congelado
frontal shot	toma frontal
general shot	toma general
genre	género
graphic design	diseño gráfico
hand-held camera	cámara en mano
height (of camera)	altura de cámara
height (of framing)	altura de encuadre
high angle shot	plano picado
high-speed camera	cámara acelerada
iconography	iconografía
intertitles	intertítulos
lens	lente
lighting	iluminación
locations	exteriores
long-shot	plano largo
long-take	toma larga/plano secuencia
low angle shot	plano contrapicado
low contrast	bajo contraste
make up	maquillaje
make up artist	maquillador
making of	making off/making of
master shot	plano master

media	medios
medium close-up	primer plano medio
medium shot	plano medio
mise-en-scène	puesta en escena
model	maqueta
off-screen (sound)	en-off/fuera de campo
open framing	encuadre abierto
outcome	desenlace
out-of-focus	fuera de foco
out-take	descarte
pan	toma panorámica/paneo
performance	representación/interpretación
plot	argumento
point of view	punto de vista
point-of-view shot	toma de punto de vista
première	estreno
producer	productor
production assistant	ayudante/auxiliar de producción
props	atrezzo
publicity stills	fotogramas
record soundtrack (v.)	sonorizar
re-take	re-toma
reverse angle shot	contraplano
reel	rollo
runner	peón
screen	pantalla
script	guión
sequence	secuencia
sets	escenarios/decorados
sharpness of focus	nitidez de foco
short film	cortometraje/corto
shot from above	toma en picado
silent cinema	cine mudo
slow motion	cámara lenta
sound bridge	puente sonoro
sound cinema	cine sonoro
sound effects	efectos de sonido
sound engineer	ingeniero de sonido
sound mixing	mezclas
sound studio	estudio de grabación
soundtrack	banda de sonido

split screen	pantalla dividida
spotlight	spot
static camera	cámara estática
stuntman	especialista/actor de doblaje
sub-titles	subtítulos
superimposed	sobreimpreso
superimposition	fundido encadenado
take	toma
time-lapse	salto de tiempo
tracking shot	travelling/traveling
voice-over	voz en off
whip pan	barrido
zoom	zoom

BIBLIOGRAPHY

WORKS IN ENGLISH

Abel, Richard (1984) *French Cinema. The First Wave 1915–1929* (Princeton NJ: Princeton University Press).

Abel, Richard (1988) *French Film Theory and Criticism: A History/Anthology 1907–1929* Vol 1, (Princeton NJ: Princeton University Press).

Abrams, Nathan, Ian Bell and Jan Udris (2001) *Studying Film* (London: Arnold).

Alberoni, Francesco (1972) 'The Powerless Elite: Theory and Sociological Research on the Phenomenon of Stars' in Denis McQuail (ed) *Sociology of Mass Communications* (London: Penguin), 75–98.

Allinson, Mark (1997) 'Not Matadors, Not Natural Born Killers. Violence in three films by young Spanish directors' in *Bulletin of Hispanic Studies (Liverpool)*, No. 74, 315–330.

Allinson, Mark (2001) *A Spanish Labyrinth. The Films of Pedro Almodóvar* (London and New York: I. B. Tauris).

Allinson, Mark (2003) 'Is the Auteur Dead? The Case of Juanma Bajo Ulloa', *International Journal of Iberian Studies*, Vol. 15, no. 3, 143–51.

Anderson, Benedict (1991) *Imagined Communities*, 2nd edn. (London: Verso).

Andrew, Dudley (1976) *The Major Film Theories* (New York: OUP).

Andrew, Dudley (1984) *Concepts in Film Theory* (Oxford: OUP).

Arroyo, José (1998) 'Pedro Almodóvar' in *The Oxford Guide to Film Studies*, (Oxford: OUP), 491–4.

Arroyo, José (2000) '*La comunidad*', *Sight and Sound*, 13. 7, 37–8.

Aumont, Jacques, Alain Bergala, Michel Marie and Marc Vernet (eds) (1992) *Aesthetics of Film*, 2nd edn (Austin, Texas: University of Texas Press).

Austin, Guy (1996) *Contemporary French Cinema. An Introduction* (Manchester: MUP).

Barthes, Roland (1972) *Image, Music, Text* (London: Fontana).

Bazin, André (1967) *What is Cinema?* 2 Vols., trans. Hugo Gray (Berkeley: University of California Press).

Besas, Peter (1985) *Behind the Spanish Lens: Spanish Cinema under Fascism and Democracy* (Denver: Arden Press).

Besas, Peter (1997) 'The Financial Structure of Spanish Cinema' in Kinder, M. (ed) *Refiguring Spain. Cinema/Media/Representation* (Durham and London: Duke University Press), 241–59.

Black, Jeremy (2002) 'Realist Horror: From Execution Videos to Snuff Films', in Mendik, X and Schneider, S. J. (eds) *Underground USA: Filmmaking beyond the Hollywood Canon* (London: Wallflower Press), 63–75.

Blandford, Steve, Barry Keith Grant and Jim Hillier (2001) *The Film Studies Dictionary* (London: Arnold).

Bordwell, David (1985) *Narration in the Fiction Film* (London: Routledge).

Bordwell, David (1989) *Making Meaning. Inference and Rhetoric in the Interpretation of Cinema* (Cambridge MA: Harvard University Press).

Bordwell, David and Carroll, Noël (eds) (1996) *Post-Theory: Reconstructing Film Studies* (Madison: University of Wisconsin Press).

Bordwell, David and Kristin Thompson (2001) *Film Art*. 6th edn. (New York: McGraw Hill).

Bordwell, David and Kristin Thompson (2003) *Film History. An Introduction*, 2nd edn. (NewYork: McGraw Hill).

Bordwell, David, Janet Staiger and Kristin Thompson (1985) *The Classical Hollywood Cinema: Film Style and Mode of Production to 1960* (New York: Columbia University Press).

Brown, Cecilie (1999) 'Production and Finance', Rix, R. and Rodríguez-Saona, R., (eds) *Spanish Cinema. Calling the Shots*, Leeds: Leeds Iberian Papers, 145–49.

Bruzzi, Stella (1997) *Undressing Cinema* (London: Routledge).

Buckland, Warren (2003) *Film Studies*, new edn. (London: Teach Yourself).

Buckley, Christine A., (2002) 'Alejandro Amenábar's *Tesis*: Art, Commerce and Renewal in Spanish Cinema', *Post Script*, Winter–Spring, Vol. 21, 2, 1–15.

Buñuel, Luis (1984) *My Last Breath*, trans. Abigail Israel (London: Jonathan Cape).

Buñuel, Luis (2000) *An Unspeakable Betrayal. Selected Writings of Luis Buñuel* (translated from the Spanish and French by Garrett White, *Le christ à cran d'arrêt: oeuvres littéraires*, 1995) (Berkeley: University of California Press).

Butler, Judith (1990) *Gender Trouble* (London: Routledge).

Cabello-Castellet, George, Jaume Martí-Olivella and Guy H. Wood (1995) *Cine-Lit II. Essays on Hispanic Film and Fiction* (Portland State University, Oregon State University and Reed College).

Canudo, Ricciotto (1911/2002) 'The Birth of the Sixth Art' in Fowler, Catherine (ed.), *The European Cinema Reader* (London: Routledge), 19–24.

Carroll, Noël (1988) *Mystifying Movies: Fads and Fallacies in Contemporary Film Theory* (New York: Columbia University Press).

Carter, Cynthia and C. Kay Weaver (2003) *Violence and the Media* (Buckingham: Open University).

Caughie, John (ed) (1981) *Theories of Authorship. A Reader* (London: Routledge).

Clover, Carol J. (1992) *Men, Women and Chainsaws: Gender in the Modern Horror Film* (Princeton: Princeton University Press).

Cohan, Steve and Ina Rae Hark (eds) (1993) *Screening the Male: Exploring Masculinities in Hollywood Cinema* (London: Routledge).

Collins, Jim (1993) 'Genericity in the Nineties: Eclectic Irony and the New Sincerity', in Collins, Jim, Radner, Hilary and Preacher Collins, Ava (eds) *Film Theory Goes to the Movies* (London: Routledge), 242–63.

Cook, Pam (1982) 'Masculinity in Crisis', *Screen*, Vol. 23 (3–4), 39–46.

Cook, Pam (1985/1999) *The Cinema Book* (London: BFI).

Cook, Pam (1998) 'No Fixed Address: the Woman's Picture from *Outrage* to *Blue Steel*' in Steve Neale and Murray Smith (eds) (1999) *Contemporary Hollywood Cinema* (London: Routledge), 229–46.

Corrigan, Timothy (1991) *A Cinema Without Walls. Movies and Culture after Vietnam*, (London: Routledge).

Corrigan, Timothy (1998) *A Short Guide to Writing about Film*, 3rd edn (New York: Longman).

Creed, Barbara (1998) 'Film and Psychoanalysis' in *The Oxford Guide to Film Studies*, John Hill and Pamela Church Gibson (eds). Oxford: OUP), 77–90.

Crumbaugh, Justin (2002) 'Spain is Different: Touring late-Francoist Cinema with Manolo Escobar', *Hispanic Research Journal* 3.3 (October), 261–76.

Darley, Andrew (2002) *Visual Digital Culture: Surface Play and Spectacle in New Media Genres* (London: Routledge).

Davies, Ann (2004) 'The Spanish *Femme Fatale* and the Cinematic Negotiation of Spanishness', *Studies in Hispanic Cinemas*, 1(1), 5–16.

D'Lugo, Marvin (1991) *The Films of Carlos Saura* (Princeton NJ: Princeton University Press).

D'Lugo, Marvin (1994) 'Authorship and the Concept of National Cinema in Spain', in *The Construction of Authorship, Textual Appropriation in Law and Literature*, Martha Woodmansee and Peter Jaszi (eds) (Durham and London: Duke University Press), 327–42.

D'Lugo, Marvin (1997) *Guide to the Cinema of Spain* (Westport, CT: Greenwood Press).

Delegto, Celestino (1999) 'Motherland: Space, Femininity and Spanishness in *Jamón*', in Peter William Evans, *Spanish Cinema. The Auteurist Tradition* (Oxford: OUP), 270–85.

Delgado, María (1999) 'Saura's *Los golfos*' in Peter William Evans, *Spanish Cinema. The Auteurist Tradition* (Oxford: OUP), 38–54.

Deveny, Thomas G. (1993) *Cain on Screen: Contemporary Spanish Cinema* (Metuchen, NJ: Scarecrow Press).

Doane, Mary Ann (1984) 'The "Woman's Film": Possession and Address' in *Re-Vision. Essays in Feminist Film Criticism,* Mary Ann Doane, Patricia Mellencamp and Linda Williams (eds) (Los Angeles: University Publications of America, Inc), 67–82.

Donald, James and Stephanie Hemelryk Donald (2000) 'The Publicness of Cinema', in Christine Gledhill and Linda Williams, *Reinventing Film Studies* (London: Arnold), 114–29.

Dyer, Richard (1998) *Stars* (London: BFI).

Dyer, Richard (2004) *Heavenly Bodies,* 2nd edn. (London: Routledge).

Edwards, Gwynne (1982) *The Discreet Art of Luis Buñuel. A Reading of his Films.* (London: Marion Boyars).

Edwards, Gwynne (2001) *Almodóvar: Labyrinths of Passion* (London: Peter Owen).

Ellis, John (1992) *Visible Fictions: Cinema, Television, Video,* revised edn. (London: Routledge).

Evans, Peter (1995) 'Back to the Future: Cinema and Democracy' in *Spanish Cultural Studies. An Introduction.* Helen Graham and Jo Labanyi (eds). (Oxford: OUP), 326–31.

Evans, Peter William (1996) *Women on the Verge of a Nervous Breakdown* (London: BFI).

Evans, Peter William (1999) *Spanish Cinema. The Auteurist Tradition* (Oxford: OUP).

Fiddian, Robin W. and Peter Evans (1988) *Challenges to Authority: Fiction and Film in Contemporary Spain* (London: Támesis).

Finney, Angus (1996) *The State of European Cinema* (London: Cassell).

Freeland, Cynthia A. (1995) 'Realist Horror', in Freeland, C.A. and Wartenberg, T.E., *Philosophy and Film* (New York: Routledge), 126–42.

Geraghty, Christine (2000) 'Re-examining Stardom: Questions of Texts, Bodies and Performance' in Christine Gledhill and Linda Williams (eds) *Reinventing Film Studies* (London: Arnold), 183–201.

Giannetti, Louis (1990) *Understanding Movies,* 5th ed. (Englewood Cliffs, NJ: Prentice-Hall).

Gibbs, John (2002) *Mise-en-scène. Film Style and Interpretation* (London: Wallflower Press).

Gledhill, Christine (1991) (ed) *Stardom: Industry of Desire* (London: Routledge).

Gledhill, Christine (2000) and Linda Williams (eds) *Reinventing Film Studies* (London: Arnold).

Gómez-Sierra, Esther (2004) 'Palaces of Seeds: from an experience of local cinemas in post-war Madrid to a suggested approach to film audiences' in Antonio Lázaro-Reboll and Andrew Willis (eds) *Popular Spanish Cinema* (Manchester: MUP), 92–112.

Gorbman, Claudia (1998), 'Film Music' in John Hill and Pamela Church Gibson (eds) *The Oxford Guide to Film Studies* (Oxford: OUP), 43–50.

Graham, Helen (1995) 'Gender and the State: Women in the 1940s' in Helen Graham and Jo Labanyi (eds) *Spanish Cultural Studies* (Oxford: OUP), 182–95.

Graham, Helen and Jo Labanyi (eds) (1995) *Spanish Cultural Studies. An Introduction* (Oxford: OUP).

Hayward, Susan (1996) *Key Concepts in Cinema Studies* (London and New York: Routledge).

Hayward, Susan (2000) *Cinema Studies: The Key Concepts*, 2nd edn. (London and New York: Routledge).

Higginbotham, Virginia (1988) *Spanish Film Under Franco* (Austin: University of Texas Press).

Hill, John and Pamela Church Gibson (1998) *The Oxford Guide to Film Studies* (Oxford: OUP).

Hills, Matt (2003) 'Whose Postmodern Horror? Alejandro Amenabár's *Tesis* (1996)' in *Kinoeye*, Vol. 3, Issue 5, May, 1–9.

Hjort, Mette and Scott Mackenzie (2000) (eds) *Cinema and Nation* (London: Routledge).

Hollows, Joanne and Mark Jancovich (1995) *Approaches to Popular Film* (Manchester: MUP).

Hooper, John (1995) *The New Spaniards* (Harmondsworth: Penguin).

Hopewell, John (1986) *Out of the Past. Spanish Cinema after Franco* (London: BFI).

Hutchings, Peter (1995) 'Genre Theory and Criticism' in Hollows, J. and Jancovich, M. (eds) *Approaches to Popular Film* (Manchester: MUP), 59–77.

Jordan, Barry (1991) 'Culture and Opposition in Franco's Spain: The Reception of Italian Neo-realist Cinema in the 1950s', *European History Quarterly*, Vol. 21, No. 2 (April), 209–38.

Jordan, Barry (2000a) 'How Spanish is it? Spanish Cinema and National Identity', in Barry Jordan and Rikki Morgan-Tamosunas (eds) *Contemporary Spanish Cultural Studies* (London: Arnold), 68–78.

Jordan, Barry (2000b) 'The Spanish Film Industry in the 1980s and 1990s', in Barry Jordan and Rikki Morgan-Tamosunas (eds) *Contemporary Spanish Cultural Studies* (London: Arnold), 179–92.

Jordan, Barry (2002) (ed.) *Spanish Culture and Society. The Essential Glossary* (London: Arnold).

Jordan, Barry (2003a) 'Revisiting the *comedia sexy ibérica: No desearás al vecino del quinto* (Ramón Fernández, 1971)' in *International Journal of Iberian Studies*, Vol. 15, No. 3, 167–86.

Jordan, Barry (2003b) 'Spain's New Cinema of the 1990s: Santiago Seguro and the Torrente Phenomenon', *New Cinemas. Journal of Contemporary Film*, Vol. 1, no. 3, 191–207.

Jordan, Barry and Rikki Morgan-Tamosunas (1998) *Contemporary Spanish Cinema* (Manchester: MUP).

Jordan, Barry and Rikki Morgan-Tamosunas (2000) (eds) *Contemporary Spanish Cultural Studies* (London: Arnold).

Kaplan, E. Ann (1983) *Women and Film. Both Sides of the Camera* (London: Routledge).

Katz, Steven (1991) *Film Directing: Shot by Shot* (Los Angeles: Michael Weise).

Kinder, Marsha (1983) 'The Children of Franco in the New Spanish Cinema' *Quarterly Review of Film Studies*, Vol. 8, No. 2, 57–76.

Kinder, Marsha (1993) *Blood Cinema. The Reconstruction of National Identity,* (Berkeley: University of California Press).

Kinder, Marsha (1996) 'Spain after Franco' in Geoffrey Nowell-Smith (ed) *The Oxford History of World Cinema* (Oxford: OUP), 596–603.

Kinder, Marsha (1997) (ed) *Refiguring Spain. Cinema/Media/Representation* (Durham and London: Duke University Press).

King, Barry (1991) 'Articulating Stardom' in Christine Gledhill (ed) *Stardom: Industry of Desire* (London: Routledge), 167–82.

Kolker, Robert (2001) *Film, Form, and Culture*, 2nd edn. (New York: McGraw-Hill).

Labanyi, Jo (1997) 'Race, Gender and Disavowal in Spanish Cinema of the Early Franco Period: the Missionary Film and the Folkloric Musical', *Screen*, 38.3 (Autumn), 215–31.

Labanyi, Jo (2000), 'Feminizing the Nation: Women, Subordination and Subversion in Post-Civil War Spanish Cinema', in Ulrike Sieglohr (ed.), *Heroines without heroes. Reconstructing Female and National Identities in European Cinema 1945–51* (London: Cassell), 163–82.

Lambert, Gavin (1952) 'A Last Look Round', *Sequence*, 14, 4–8.

Lapsley, Robert and Michael Westlake (1988) *Film Theory: an Introduction* (Manchester: MUP).

Lázaro-Reboll, Antonio and Andrew Willis (2004) *Popular Spanish Cinema* (Manchester: MUP).

Lev, Leora (2000) '*Tesis* (Critical Essay)', *Critical Quarterly*, 54.1 (Fall), 34–8.

Lev, Leora (2001) 'Returns of the Repressed: Memory, Oblivion and Abjection in Spanish Cinema', *Revista de Estudios Hispánicos*, 35, 165–78.

Maltby, Richard (2003) *Hollywood Cinema*, 2nd edn. (Oxford: Blackwell).

Mar-Molinero, Clare and Angel Smith (eds) (1996) *Nationalism and the Nation in the Iberian Peninsula* (Oxford: Berg).

Martín Márquez, Susan (1999) *Feminist Discourse and Spanish Cinema* (Oxford: Oxford University Press).

Maxwell, Richard (2000) 'New Media Technologies in Spain: a Healthy Pluralism?' in Barry Jordan and Rikki Morgan-Tamosunas (eds) *Contemporary Spanish Cultural Studies* (London: Arnold), 170–78.

Metz, Christian (1977/1982) *The Imaginary Signifier*, trans. Celia Britton, Annwyl Williams, Ben Brewster and Alfredo Guzzetti (Bloomington: Indiana University Press).

Mitry, Jean (2000) *Semiotics and the Analysis of Film*, trans. Christopher King (London: The Athlone Press).

Monaco, James (1981) *How to Read a Film* (New York: OUP).

Montero, Rosa (1995) 'The Silent Revolution: The Social and Cultural Advances of Women in Democratic Spain' in Helen Graham and Jo Labanyi (eds) *Spanish Cultural Studies. An Introduction* (Oxford: OUP), 381–5.

Moreiras Menor, Cristina (2002), *Cultura Herida: Literatura y Cine en la España Democrática* (Madrid: Ediciones Libertarias).

Morgan, Rikki (1999) 'Female Subjectivity in *Gary Cooper… que estás en los cielos*' in Peter William Evans, *Spanish Cinema. The Auteurist Tradition* (Oxford: OUP), 176–193.

Morgan, Rikki and Barry Jordan (1994) '*Jamón, Jamón*: A Tale of Ham and Pastiche' *Donaire*, 2, 57–64.

Morin, Edgar (1957) *Les Stars* (trans.) Richard Howard (New York: Grove Press).

Mulvey, Laura (1989) *Visual and Other Pleasures* (London: Macmillan).

Munsterberg, Hugo (1970) *Film: a Psychological Study*, 2nd edn. (New York: Dover).

Neale, Steve (1980) *Genre* (London: BFI).

Neale, Steve (2000) *Genre and Hollywood* (London: Routledge).

Neale, Steve and Frank Krutnik (1990) *Popular Film and Television Comedy* (London: Routledge).

Nelmes, Jill (1996) *An Introduction to Film Studies* (London: Routledge).

Overby, David (1978) *Springtime in Italy: a Reader on Neo-realism* (London: Routledge).

Pavlovic, Tatjana (1995) 'Bienvenido Mister Marshall' in Cabello-Castellet, George, Jaume Martí-Olivella and Guy H. Wood (eds) *Cine-Lit II. Essays on Hispanic Film and Fiction* (Portland State University, Oregon State University and Reed College), 169–74.

Perriam, Chris (2003) *Stars and Masculinities in Spanish Cinema* (Oxford: OUP).

Pinedo, Isabel (1996) 'Recreational Terror: Postmodern Elements in the Contemporary Horror Film', *Journal of Film and Video*, 48 (1–2), 17–31.

Powrie, Phil and Keith Reader (2002) *French Cinema: a Student's Guide* (London: Arnold).

Pudovkin, Vsevolod (1960) *Film Technique* (New York: Grove).

Rabalska, Carmen (1996) 'Women in Spanish Cinema in Transition', *International Journal of Iberian Studies*, 9(3), 166–79.

Richards, Michael (1996) 'Constructing the Nationalist State: Self-Sufficiency and Regeneration in the Early Franco Years' in Clare Mar-Molinero and Angel Smith (eds) *Nationalism and the Nation in the Iberian Peninsula* (Oxford: Berg), 149–67.

Rix, Rob and Roberto Rodríguez-Saona (1999) (eds) *Spanish Cinema: Calling the Shots* (Leeds: Leeds Iberian Papers).

Roberts, Graeme and Heather Wallis (2001) *Introducing Film* (London: Arnold).

Rolph, Wendy (1999) '*¡Bienvenido Mr Marshall!*' in Peter William Evans, *Spanish Cinema. The Auteurist Tradition* (Oxford: OUP), 8–18.

Ryall, Tom (1998) 'Genre and Hollywood' in Hill, J. and Church Gibson, P. (eds) *The Oxford Guide to Film Studies* (Oxford: OUP), 327–38.

Santaolalla, Isabel (1999) '*Vacas:* Historicizing the Forest' in Peter William Evans, *Spanish Cinema. The Auteurist Tradition* (Oxford: OUP), 310–324.

Sarris, Andrew (1968) *The American Cinema. Directors and Directions, 1928–1968* (New York: Dutton).

Smith, Anthony D. (1991) *National Identity* (London: Penguin).

Smith, Paul Julian (1999) 'Between Metaphysics and Scientism: Rehistoricizing Víctor Erice's *El espíritu de la colmena* (1973)' in Peter William Evans, *Spanish Cinema. The Auteurist Tradition* (Oxford:OUP), 93–114.

Smith, Paul Julian (2000) *Desire Unlimited. The Cinema of Pedro Almodóvar*, 2nd edn. (London: Verso).

Smith, Paul Julian (2001) 'The Others', *Sight and Sound*, 11:11, 54.

Smith, Paul Julian (2004) 'La pelota vasca/The Basque Ball', *Sight and Sound*, 14:5, 45–6.

Stacey, Jackie (1994) *Star Gazing: Hollywood Cinema and Female Spectatorship* (London: Routledge).

Stam, Robert, Robert Burgoyne and Sandy Flitterman-Lewis (1992) *New Vocabularies in Film Semiotics* (London: Routledge).

Stam, Robert (2000) *Film Theory: an Introduction* (Massachussets: Blackwell).

Stone, Rob (2002) *Spanish Cinema* (Harlow: Longman).

Talens, Jenaro and Santos Zunzunegui (1998) (eds) *Modes of Representation in Spanish Cinema* (Minneapolis: University of Minnesota Press).

Tasker, Yvonne (1993) *Spectacular Bodies: Gender, Genre, and the Action Cinema* (London: Comedia/Routledge).

Taylor, Lisa (1995) 'From Psychoanalaytic Feminism to Popular Feminism' in Joanne Hollows and Mark Jancovich, *Approaches to Popular Film* (Manchester: MUP), 151–71.

Thompson, Kristin (1985*) Exporting Entertainment. America in the World Film Market 1907–1934* (London: BFI).

Thomson, David (2002) *The New Biographical Dictionary of Film*, 4th edn. (London: Time Warner Books).

Triana Torribio, Núria (2000) 'A Punk Called Pedro: *la movida* in the films of Pedro Almodóvar' in *Contemporary Spanish Cultural Studies* (eds Barry Jordan and Rikki Morgan-Tamosunas) (London: Arnold), 274–82.

Triana Toribio, Núria (2003) *Spanish National Cinema* (London: Routledge).

Tudor, Andrew (1974) *Theories of Film* (London: Secker and Warburg for the BFI).

Tudor, Andrew (1997) 'Why Horror? The Peculiar Pleasures of a Popular Genre', *Cultural Studies*, 11 (3), 443–63.

Tudor, Andrew (2002) 'From Paranoia to Postmodernism? The Horror Movie in Late Modern Society', in *Genre and Contemporary Hollywood*, Steve Neale (ed) (London: BFI), 105–15.

Vernon, Kathleen M. and Barbara Morris (1995) *Post-Franco, Postmodern. The films of Pedro Almodóvar* (Westport Conn: Greenwood Press).

Vernon, Kathleen M. (1999) 'Culture and Cinema to 1975' in David T. Gies (ed) *Modern Spanish Culture* (Cambridge: CUP), 248–66.

Vincendeau, Ginette (ed) (1995) *Encyclopedia of European Cinema* (London: Routledge).

Wayne, Mike (2002) *The Politics of Contemporary European Cinema: Histories, Borders, Diaspora* (Bristol: Intellect).

White, Anne (1999) '*Manchas negras, manchas blancas*: Looking Again at Julio Medem's *Vacas*' in Rob Rix and Roberto Rodríguez-Saona (eds) *Spanish Cinema: Calling the Shots* (Leeds: Leeds Iberian Papers), 1–14.

White, Anne M. (2003) 'Seeing Double? The Remaking of Alejandro Amenábar's *Abre los ojos* as Cameron Crowe's *Vanilla Sky*' in *International Journal of Iberian Studies*, Vol. 15. No. 3, 187–96.

White, Patricia (1998) 'Feminism and Film' in John Hill, and Pamela Church Gibson (eds) *The Oxford Guide to Film Studies* (Oxford: OUP), 117–34.

Wollen, Peter (1972/1998) *Signs and Meanings*, 4th edn. (London: BFI).

Woods, Eva (2004) 'From Rags to Riches: the Ideology of Stardom in Folkloric Musical Comedy Films of the Late 1930s and 1940s' in Antonio Lázaro-Reboll and Andrew Willis (eds) (2004) *Popular Spanish Cinema* (Manchester: MUP), 40–59.

WORKS IN SPANISH

Academia. Revista del cine español: el proceso creativo del último cine español, 26 (Summer 1999).

Aguilar, Carlos (1996) *Las estrellas de nuestro cine* (Madrid: Alianza).

Aguilar, Pilar (1998) *Mujer, amor y sexo en el cine español de los 90* (Madrid: Fundamentos).

Allinson, Mark (2003) *Un laberinto español: las películas de Pedro Almodóvar* (Madrid: Ocho y Medio)

Anuario Fotogramas 2003 (2003) (Barcelona: Comunicaciones y Publicaciones).

Arocena, Carmen (1996) *Víctor Erice* (Madrid: Cátedra).

Azevedo Muñoz, Ernesto R. (2003) *Buñuel and Mexico. The Crisis of National Cinema* (Berkeley: University of California Press).

Ballesteros, Isolina (2001) *Cine (Ins)urgente. Textos fílmicos y contextos culturales de la España posfranquista* (Madrid: Fundamentos).

Barroso, Miguel Ángel and Fernando Gil-Delgado (2002) *Cine español en cien películas* (Madrid: Ediciones Jaguar).

Borau, José Luis (ed) (1998) *Diccionario del cine español* (Madrid: Academia de las Artes y las Ciencias Cinematográficas de España, Fundación Autor y Alianza Editorial).

Camí-Vela, María (2001) *Mujeres detrás de la cámara* (Madrid: Ocho y Medio).

Caparrós Lera, J. M. (1992) *El cine español de la democracia* (Barcelona: Anthropos).

Caparrós Lera, J. M. (1999) *Historia crítica del cine español (Desde 1897 hasta hoy)* (Barcelona: Ariel).

Caparrós Lera, J. M. (2000) *Estudios sobre el cine español del franquismo* (Valladolid: Fancy).

Castro, Antonio (1974) *El cine español en el banquillo* (Valencia: Fernando Torres).

Cobos, Juan (2000) *Las generaciones del cine español* (Madrid: Sociedad Estatal España Nuevo Milenio).

Colmenero, Silvia (2001) *Pedro Almodóvar: Todo sobre mi madre* (Barcelona: Paidós).

Díez Puertas, Emeterio (2002) *El montaje del franquismo. La política cinematográfica de las fuerzas sublevadas* (Barcelona: Laertes).

Díez Puertas, Emeterio (2003) *Historia social del cine en España* (Madrid: Fundamentos).

Donapetry, María (1998) *La otra mirada: la mujer y el cine en la cultura española* (New Orleans: University Press of the South).

Evans, Peter (2004) *Bigas Luna: Jamón Jamón* (Barcelona: Paidós).

Fanés, Félix (1982) *CIFESA: La antorcha de los éxitos* (Valencia: Institución Alfonso el Magnámimo).

Fernández Blanco, Víctor (1998) *El cine y su público en España* (Madrid: Fundación autor).

Fernández Colorado, Luis and Pilar Couto Cantero (2001) *La herida de las sombras: el cine español en los años 40* (Madrid: Academia de las Artes y las Ciencias Cinematográficas de España y Asociación Española de Historiadores de Cine).

Font, Domènec (1975) *Del azul al verde. El cine español durante el franquismo* (Barcelona: Avance).

Font, Domènec (2003) 'D'un temps, d'un país y de un cine anfibio. Sobre la escuela de Barcelona', in Heredero, Carlos F. and José Enrique Monterde (eds) *Los 'nuevos cines' en España, ilusiones y desencantos de los años sesenta* (Valencia: Instituto Valenciano de Cinematografía), 175–94.

Fotogramas, No. 1864 (February 1999), 142–4.

García de León, María Antonia and Teresa Maldonado (1989) *Pedro Almodóvar, la otra España cañí* (Ciudad Real: Biblioteca de Autores y temas Manchegos).

García Fernández, Emilio C. (1985) *Historia ilustrada del cine español* (Barcelona: Planeta).

García Fernández, Emilio C. (2002) *El cine español entre 1896 y 1939. Historia, industria, filmografía y documentos* (Barcelona: Ariel Cine).

Gasca, Luis (1998) *Un siglo de cine español* (Barcelona: Planeta).

Gómez Bermúdez de Castro, Ramiro (1987) *La producción cinematográfica española (1976–1986)* (Bilbao: Mensajero).

González, Palmira (1997) 'El golfo' in Pérez Perucha, Julio (ed) *Antología crítica del cine español 1906–1995* (Madrid: Catedra), 37–9.

González Portilla, Manuel (ed.) (2002) *Cine e historia. (Revista de Historia Contemporánea, 22)*. Bilbao.

Guarner, José Luis (1971) *Treinta años de cine en España* (Barcelona: Kairós).

Gubern, Román (1981) *La censura. Función política y ordenamiento jurídico bajo el franquismo 1936–1975* (Barcelona: Península).

Gubern, Román *et al.* (1995) *Historia del cine español* (Madrid: Cátedra).

Heredero, Carlos (1993) *Las huellas del tiempo: cine español, 1951–1961* (Valencia: Filmoteca Española).

Heredero, Carlos (1997) *Espejo de miradas: Entrevistas con nuevos directores del cine español de los años noventa* (Madrid: Festival de Cine de Alcalá de Henares).

Heredero, Carlos F. (1999) *20 Nuevos directores del cine español* (Madrid: Alianza).

Heredero, Carlos F. and Antonio Santamarina (2002) (eds) *Semillas del futuro. Cine español 1990–2001* (Madrid: Sociedad Estatal España Nuevo Milenio).

Heredero, Carlos F. and José Enrique Monterde (eds) (2003) *Los nuevos cines en España. Ilusiones y desencantos de los años sesenta* (Valencia: Instituto Valenciano de Cinematografía).

Hernández, Marta and Revuelta, Manolo (1976) *30 años de cine al alcance de todos los españoles* (Bilbao: Zero S.A.).

Hopewell, John (1989) *El cine español después de Franco* (Madrid: El Arquero).

Hurtado, José A., and Francisco M. Picó (1989) (eds) *Escritos sobre el cine español 1973–1987* (Valencia: Ediciones Textos Filmoteca).

ICAA, (2003) 'Evolución del cine español 1996–2003' www.mcu.es/cine

Losilla, Carlos (1989) 'Legislación, industria y escritura' in José A. Hurtado and Francisco M. Picó, F. (eds) *Escritos sobre el cine espanol 1973–1987* (Valencia: Filmoteca de la Generalitat Valenciana), 39–43.

Mérida de San Román, Pablo (2002) *El cine español Larousse* (Barcelona: Spes Editorial).

Millás, Lola (1997) *Cine y libros en España* (Madrid: Polifemo).

Monterde, José Enrique (1993) *Veinte años de cine español (1973–1992)* (Barcelona: Paidós).

Monterde, José Enrique (1995) 'El cine de la autarquía (1939–1950)' in Gubern, R. *et al*, *Historia del cine español* (Madrid: Cátedra), 181–238.

Monterde, José Enrique (2003) 'La recepción del nuevo cine. El contexto crítico del NCE', in Carlos F. Heredero and José Enrique Monterde, *Los Nuevos Cines en España. Ilusiones y desencantos de los años sesenta* (Valencia: Instituto Valenciano de Cinematografía), 103–20.

Payán, Miguel Juan (2001) *Cine español actual* (Madrid: JC).

Peláez, José Vidal, and Rueda, José Carlos (2002) (eds) *Ver Cine. Los públicos cinematográficos en el siglo XX* (Madrid: Ediciones Rialp).

Pena, Jaime (2004) *Víctor Erice: El espíritu de la colmena* (Barcelona: Paidós).

Pérez Perucha, Julio (1995) 'Narración de un aciago destino (1896–1930)', in Gubern *et al*, *Historia del cine español* (Madrid: Cátedra), 19–121.

Pérez Perucha, Julio (1997) *Antología crítica de cine español 1906–1995* (Madrid: Cátedra).

Ponga, Paula (1993) *Carmen Maura* (Barcelona: Mitografías).

Reig Tapia, Alberto (2002) 'La autoimagen de Franco: la estética de la raza yel imperio', *Archivos de la Filmoteca*, 1 (42–3), 96–121.

Ríos Carratalá, Juan A. (1997) *Lo sainetesco en el cine español* (Alicante: Universidad).

Sánchez Vidal, Agustín (1984) *Luis Buñuel. Obra Cinematográfica* (Madrid: ediciones JC).

Seguin, Jean-Claude (1995) *Historia del cine español* (Madrid: Acento).

Sempere, Antonio (2000), *Alejandro Amenábar. Cine en las venas.* (Madrid: Nuer).

Torreiro, Casimiro (1995) 'Una dictadura liberal (1962–1969)' in Gubern *et al*, *Historia del cine español* (Madrid: Cátedra), 295–340

Torreiro, Casimiro (1995) 'Del tardofranquismo a la democracia (1969–1982)' in Gubern *et al*, *Historia del cine español* (Madrid: Cátedra), 341–97.

Torres, Augusto M. (1994/96) *Diccionario Espasa. Cine español*, 2nd edn. (Madrid: Espasa Calpe).

Torres, Augusto M. (1997) *El cine español en 119 películas* (Madrid: Alianza).

Trenzado Romero, Manuel (1999) *Cultura de masas y cambio político: El cine español de la transición* (Madrid: CIS).

Tubau, Iván (1983) *Crítica Cinematográfica Española, Bazin contra Aristarco: la gran controversia delos años 60* (Barcelona: Universidad de Barcelona).

Tubau, Iván (1984) *Hollywood en Argüelles* (Barcelona: Universidad de Barcelona).

Vanaclocha, José (1974) *Cine Español, Cine de sub-géneros* (Valencia: Equipo Cartelera Turia).

Vallés Copeiro del Villar, Antonio (1992) *Historia de la política de fomento del cine español* (Valencia: Ediciones de la Filmoteca).

Vellido, Juan, Leticia P. Rivillas, Roberto Cuadros and Jesús García (2001) *Cine español: situación y perspectivas* (Granada: Grupo Editorial Universitario).

Vera, Cecilia (2002) *Cómo hacer cine 2:* El día de la bestia *de Alex de la Iglesia* (Madrid: Fundamentos).

Vidal, Nuria (1988) *El cine de Pedro Almodóvar* (Barcelona: Destino).

Villegas López, Manuel (1967/1991) *El nuevo cine espanol. Problemática* 1967, 2nd edn. (San Sebastián, Festival Internacional de Cine).

Zunzunegui, Santos (2002) *Historias de España: ¿De qué hablamos cuando hablamos de cine español?* (Valencia: Instituto Valenciano de Cinematografía).

USEFUL WEBSITES

Below, you will find a set of website references and brief descriptions covering both Spanish (and some Spanish American) cinema sources and a number of useful general web resources on Film Studies. They are hardly exhaustive given the huge number of websites nowadays devoted in one way or another to national cinemas, international film and Film Studies. We have found many of them extremely useful in the preparation of this volume. We have also found that our students are becoming increasingly 'web literate' in relation to such sources and urge readers of this volume to try them out and get back to us if they come across other sites of value and interest. The web addresses we have included were all functioning successfully at the time of writing.

SPANISH
INSTITUTIONS

www.mcu.es/cine
Key site of Spain's Ministry of Culture, containing information on all official activities to do with cinema, including ICAA and the Filmoteca Española.

Instituto de la Cinematografía y de Artes Audiovisuales, access via www.mcu.es/cine
This is the ICAA, Spain's National Film Institute, a key government site for all kinds of official publications and statistics relating to Spanish cinema.

Filmoteca Espanola, access via www.mcu.es/cine
Spain's official film archive, containing holdings of virtually all available Spanish films as well as facilities for research and viewing.

www.sie.es/acacine
Official site of the Academia de las Artes y Ciencias Cinematográficas, Spain's National Film Academy. See also www.sie.es/pgoya or www.geocities.com/premios_goya/ for news of the annual Goya prizes.

www.cervantes.es
Portal for the Cervantes Institute network around the world. The organisation engages in a great deal of activity related to Spanish film (visiting lectures by directors, talks by film scholars) and provides a hire scheme for Spanish films via its libraries.

www.filmotecadeandalucia.com
The Filmoteca de Andalucía site includes details on archives, film programming, timetabling, libraries and a useful listing of book publications sponsored by the Filmoteca.

cultura.gencat.es/filmo
Filmoteca de Cataluña site, with details on film programming, film seasons, archives, libraries, activities, etc.

www.paisvasco.com/filmoteca and www.filmotecavasca.com
Euskadiko Filmategia or Basque Filmoteca, with sections on research and recovery, filing and preservation of film holdings, news on screenings and film seasons, libraries and archives.

www.cgai.org
Galícian Filmoteca or Centro Galego de Artes das Imaxe.

www.ivac-lafilmoteca.es/
The Instituto Valenciano de Cinematografía Ricardo Muñoz Suay. Excellent site, with extensive information on archives, libraries, restoration projects, screenings and film seasons, as well a very useful '*enlaces*' section for search engines, databases, reviews, production companies and specialist bookshops.

Don't forget that smaller regional Filmotecas also exist in Albacete, Oviedo, las Palmas de Gran Canaria, Santander, Castilla y León, Extremadura, Murcia, Salamanca, Cáceres and Zaragoza. A quick web search will show the way, or use the '*enlaces*' at the Andalusian, Catalan or Valencian Filmotecas as a jumping off point.

DATABASES/SEARCH ENGINES

www.buscacine.com
Excellent search engine for all types of Spanish cinema enquiries.

www.cervantesvirtual.com
Very useful site with extensive databases on actors, directors, films, etc.

w3.fiu.edu/ciberia
Ciberia is a very useful portal for information on films, actors and directors, plus interviews, features, reports, reviews and courses.

www.cine.blogspot.com
Useful hub for links to Spanish and other films.

www.cineiberico.com
Extensive web portal with information on new releases, reviews, festivals, awards, prizes, etc.

www.cineytele.com
Useful website for information on media news and legal, commercial and industrial matters, plus film listings and new releases.

membres.lycos.fr/cinecita/
Very useful portal and search engine for Spanish and Latin American cinema, including links to cinema bookshops, film reviews, webzines, databases, historical materials and auteur sites. Also links to a webring, membres.lycos.fr/cinecita/webring.htm, hosting 23 other useful links.

www.terra.es/cine
Film section of the Terra portal, with subsections on news of recent and current Spanish releases, biographies, interviews, reviews, trailers, etc.

www.todocine.com
Another useful database containing recent releases, listings, reviews, news, gossip and useful links.

Also worth checking out are
www.filmomanía.com, www.infocine.com and www.publicine.es.

DIRECTORS
www.egeda.es/eldeseo
The official site of Spain's leading auteur film maker, Pedro Almodóvar. See also a related site www.Almodovarlandia.com.

www.alejandroamenabar.com
Alejandro Amenábar's official web site. See also www.clubcultura.com/prehomes/amenabar/ and movies.groups.yahoo.com/alejandroamenabarclub

www.juliomedem.org
Unofficial site for Julio Medem, run by Alberto Marroquín Ruiz, containing biographical information, up-to-date filmography, notes on actors and specialist film crew, plus news, miscellany and a chatroom on Medem himself. Also check out Ignacio Bravo Villalba's site on Medem: socios.las.es/~bravo/inicio.htm.

www.alexdelaiglesia.com
Official site for Alex de la Iglesia.

MAGAZINES AND JOURNALS

www.cinemania.com.ar/
Site of monthly magazine *Cinemanía*, a useful source of information on films in production as well as classic movies and issues/debates.

www.cinespain.com
Official magazine, supported by ICAA, containing data on releases, shoots, box office and general information.

www.Cineinforme.com
Film magazine containing a wide range of information on Spanish film.

www.fotogramas.es
One of Spain's main monthly, general film magazines. Packed with information, gossip, interviews and lots of photographs.

www.labutaca.net
Helpful webzine providing listings, new releases, reviews, news, etc.

www.nickel-odeon.com
Journal containing useful articles, interviews, reviews and interviews, plus scripts of Spanish and other world cinemas.

www.otrocampo.com
Web film magazine published in Argentina, which often includes substantial Spanish content.

www.pcb.ub.es/filmhistoria/
On-line version of the magazine *Film Historia*, containing editorials, essays, reviews and book reviews, directed by José María Caparrós Lera.

www.rtve.es/tve/program/version
Website of the Friday night television film magazine *Versión Española* (broadcast on La 2), hosted by Cayetana Guillén Cuervo and devoted to promoting and examining Spanish cinema.

www.rtve.es/tve/program/cartele
Cartelera: another television-based show devoted to Spanish film.

Also try: www.ciendecine.com, www.elcine.com, www.porlared.com, www.cinerama.es, www.cinevideo20.es, claqueta.com, filasiete.com and www.estrenosvideo.com.

GENERAL:

afronord.tripod.com/theory.html
Useful site on film theory and basic semiotics, which calls itself 'Drive Through Film Theory'. Provides useful supplementary information to the material contained in this volume.

www.bbc.co.uk/film
A helpful page containing listings on all BBC output on film and film-related programming, including details of BBC Four's World Cinema offerings.

www.bfi.org.uk/sightandsound
One of the UK's leading film magazines, with fairly regular reviews and articles on Spanish and Latin-American cinema releases.

www.boxofficemojo.com
Very helpful site for all manner of reviews and statistical information on film in general and Spanish film in particular.

www.culturevulture.net/Movies/MovieIndex.htm
Useful site for review material on mainstream and art movies, as well as specific sections on auteurs.

www.cult-media.com
Site for the useful web magazine, *Intensities: Journal of Cult Media*.

www.davidbordwell.net
An excellent resource from one of the world's great film scholars, which, apart from biographical information, contains selections from Bordwell's own essays and books, as well as much useful pedagogical material, including excellent glossaries.

www.eyeroom.com
Useful web journal including current and recent film reviews as well as many helpful essays and links.

www.facets.org/asticat
One of a number of very useful film catalogues.

www.filmsite.org
Very useful resource on classic movies, many of which often find their way into Spanish movies via intertextuality. For example, check out the James Bond films or the Dirty Harry series in connection with *Torrente*, or the classic *Frankenstein* (Carl Laemmle, 1931) in relation to Erice's *El espíritu de la colmena*.

www.theory.org.uk/directory.htm
A very useful hub with many links to a broad range of theoretical sources, including cultural studies, gender, identity, sexualities, etc.

www.geocities.com/WorldCinema
A helpful site with overviews of the major Hollywood, European and world cinema directors, plus good links.

film.guardian.co.uk/
Useful site for information, reviews and interviews on world, European and some Spanish directors.

www.imdb.com
The Internet Movie Database, which provides all manner of information, including production data, data on audiences, reviews, trivia and photographs, on virtually any film. A 'must use' site, very good for basic research about Spanish film.

www.imagesjournal.com
A very useful, wide-ranging web magazine, including articles, reviews and reports on classical and modern, mainstream and art cinema, plus interviews and profiles.

www.jahsonic.com/CultMovies.html
Useful site for locating cult, independent, non-mainstream movies. Also serves enquiries on European cinema and offers profiles of individual Spanish directors such as Almodóvar and Jess Franco.

www.kinoeye.org
A web journal devoted to mainly European cinema, both art and popular, with frequent contributions on Spanish cinema.

www.findarticles.com
A useful search engine for locating academic articles, mainly in English, relevant to a particular topic, director or writer.

www.mastersofcinema.org
For the cinephile, a 'must consult' auteurist website, packed with excellent material.

www.mediaknowall.com
A useful starting point for media research on the net, targeted at A level and GCSE students.

www.movie-reviews.colossus.net
James Berardinelli's film review website, with a vast range of review material.

www.mrqe.com
'Movie review query engine'. Very useful search engine for film reviews.

www.rogerebert.com
Roger Ebert's very useful review webpage.

www.sensesofcinema.com
Online film journal for the more serious student. Useful site for theoretical information, monographic numbers, reviews and practical work on film analysis.

INDEX